Letters to the Boatyard

By

Bob and Christine Harper

Copyright © 2009, 2022 Bob Harper and Christine Harper

Second Edition, 2022
Published in the UK by Dare BC Publishing
ISBN: 978-1-7397987-0-3 (Paperback)
ISBN: 978-1-8382373-9-4 (Hardcover)
ISBN: 978-1-8382373-8-7 (eBook)

A CIP catalogue record for this book is available from the British Library.

Cover image by Jamie Harper
Second edition cover based on an original design by Denzil Browne

First Edition (2009) published by Dolman Scott Ltd
ISBN 978-1-905553-40-2

Fair Winds
Bob & Christine x

In 1996 we set off on the journey of a lifetime...

This book is dedicated to all our family and friends for their support. And, of course, the Boatyard.

Bob and Christine

Foreword (2009)

The stories that came back from around the world amused, inspired and entertained many hundreds of us here in Northern Ireland. For the Belfast *News Letter* to publish Bob and Christine's travel tales in the Saturday supplement was inspirational, for they reached far and were looked forward to each week. They were our very own weekly 'soap'.

To be the recipient of the letters and given the responsibility of conveying one per week to the *News Letter* was a privilege. I got to read them before anyone else, and in reading them felt closer to our travelling friends.

Over five years, 260 letters dropped through my letter box, sometimes two or three in a week. Other times I would have to wait for two or three weeks if they were on a long sea passage. For instance, before heading from the Galapagos to the Marquesas Islands (3,000 miles), Bob made sure I had enough articles to keep going, not only until they arrived there, but another week for the post to reach Northern Ireland.

In all those years only one letter went astray, article No 213. I remember it particularly well as I had to write it, in the 'Harper' style of course, and pretend it had come from Bob in Bali! We never missed an edition.

After many pleas of 'come out and see us', Norman and I headed to the Maldives. The handsome young Maldivian Customs Officer looked at my passport, "Northern Ireland?" he questioned.

"Yes," I said, "Have you been there?"

"Londonderry," was his reply.

We had arrived in the Maldives.

Bob and Christine often refer to the yachts they meet up with, how much each depends on the other for weather information, sharing vital supplies, helping one another when in difficulty or just socialising and enjoying life. It is just like any other community, looking out for each other in times of adversity, celebrating the good times, or simply meeting down at the local for a pint and a chat. For five years *Breakaway* enjoyed the security of such a community, contributing to it in the many instances related here in *Letters to the Boatyard*.

Read and enjoy!

Wendy (Moore) Grant

Contents

Foreword (2009) iv

The Plan - 1996 - Carrickfergus 54.32N 5.48W 1

The Journey Begins 5

La Coruna 43.22N 8.23W 6

Northern Spain and Portugal - The First Letters Home 8

On Passage to Porto Santo 11

Porto Santo 33.5N 16.42W 12

Madeira 32.39N 16.42W 13

The Canary Islands 15

Arrecife 28.59N 13.34W 17

On Passage to Tenerife 21

Santa Cruz 28.50N 14.14W 22

The Atlantic Crossing 25

Extracts from *Breakaway*'s Atlantic Log 25

The Caribbean, St Lucia 13.46N 61.04W 32

Friends from Home 36

St Valentine's Day, 14th February 1997 39

Falmouth Harbour 40

A New Toy 42

Pigeon Island, Guadeloupe, Les Saintes, Montserrat 45

29th April 1997 – the Robbery 47

Passage to Trinidad 10.40N 61.37W 51

Trinidad 10.40N 61.37W 52

Hummingbird Marina 53

The Special Olympics 56

A Tale about a Dog 58

Chacachacare Leper Colony 61

Westward Ho 65

South America, Los Testigos, Venezuela 65

On the Move Again 10 59 N 63 47 W 67

Margarita Island 69

Time to Leave Venezuela 71

Bonaire (ABC) Islands 11.05N 63.53W 72

Colombia, Cartagena 12.07N 68.54W 76

Green Island, San Blas, Panama 9 35N 78 35W 79

An Interesting Encounter 80

Christmas in Paradise 82

Lemon Cays 09 32.7N 78 54W 86

Panama Yacht Club Marina, Cristobal 09 20N 78.54W 88

The Pacific, Balboa Yacht Club, Panama 08 56N 79 33.2W 94

Log of *Breakaway* on Passage to Galapagos 97

Galapagos Islands 00 44S 90 18W 99

Galapagos to Marquesas, French Polynesia 100

Hiva Oa, French Polynesia 09.48S 139.01W 105

Marquesas to Tahiti, Society Islands 106

Tahiti 17 23S 149 22W 108

Captain Cook's Bay, Moorea 17 30.16S 149 49.14W 111

The Chance of Employment 115

Autonomy Day in Papeete 116

Rarotonga, Cook Islands 21 12S 159 47W 119

On Passage to Tonga 123

Neiafu, Kingdom of Tonga 18 39.29S 173 58.55W 125

The Garden Party 128

The Arrival of Jamie, Our Youngest 131

Suva, Fiji 18 07S 178 25W 132

Suva to Musket Cove 138

On Passage to Bay of Islands, New Zealand 144

New Zealand 147

Auckland 148

12 November 1998 148

Westhaven Marina, Auckland 149

Settling into Life in New Zealand 150

Westpark Marina, Clearwater Cove 151

A Very Special Delivery 154

News of Daughter Kirstie 156

Ken's Car 159

Rotorua 161

The KISS Method – Keeping it Simple, Stupid 163

Gulf Harbour 165

Whangarei Town Basin   34.43S 174.19E............................... 168

Voyage to New Caledonia 171

Port Moselle, Noumea, New Caledonia 22.24S 166.25E 173

The Coral Sea 176

Australia 179

Boom Court Aquatic Quays, Brisbane S27.29 E153. 13 180

King of the Road 182

Queensland Coast 187

Townsville Motor Club Marina S19.15 E146.49 188

The Creek 192

The Launch of *Chinook II* 194

Rosslyn Bay 197

Burnett Heads 198

Time to Regroup 200

Tin Can Bay, the Great Sandy Strait 25.48S 153.12E............. 201

Aquatic Quays, Brisbane 27.29S 153.13E 204

A Fridge at Last! 207

Son Jamie is Back Amongst Us Again 209

Mooloolaba, Queensland 25.35S 153.39E............................. 211

The Queensland Coast 214

Escape River, Near Cape York 11.00 S 142.40E................... 216

Red Island.. 220

Black Point, Port Essington 11.09S 132.06E........................ 221

Darwin, Northern Territories 222

Indonesia, the Timor Sea 225

Rote, Indonesia 10.35S 123.22E 227

Labuan Bajo, the Island of Flores 231

The Island of Rinca 233

Bali International Marina S 08.44 E 115.12 234

Lovina Beach, Bali... 239

Kumai River, Borneo 242

South China Sea, North of the Equator 01.11N 104.05E.................. 245

South East Asia, Singapore 01.17N 103.45E 247

Malaysia, The Malacca Strait 02.27.219N 101.50.246E..................... 250

Klang River, Port Klang 03.00N 101.23E.. 252

Phuket, Thailand 7.48N 98.22E 255

Christmas Eve, Phuket 258

Island Hopping 259

Indian Ocean, Thailand to Sri Lanka 262

Galle Harbour, Sri Lanka... 268

The Maldives 04.07 N 3.26E.. 276

Male 04.13N 73.32E.. 279

Arabian Sea, Maldives to Oman 282

The Middle East, Salalah Harbour, Oman 16.56N 54.00E................. 283

The Gulf of Aden and the Red Sea, Oman to Eritrea 286

Massawa Harbour, Eritrea, Africa.. 287

The Sudan 290

Egypt.. 292

Time to Set Sail for Suez 296

Suez N29.57 E32.34 297

The Suez Canal.. 299

The Mediterranean 302

Larnaca Marina, Cyprus 34,55N 33.38E 302

Parting of the Ways 304

Running Repairs 305

Ayios Nikolaos, Crete 35.11N 25.43E 307

The Ionian Sea 35.33N 17.58E.. 310

Valletta Harbour, Malta 313

Msida Marina, Malta 35.54N 14.30E 316

Mallorca 317

Fuengirola, Costa del Sol 36.32N 04.36W 319

Gibraltar... 320

Back in the Atlantic, Cascais, Lisbon, Portugal 38.41N 09.25W 322

The Irish Sea 324

Carrickfergus 54.40N 05.40W... 325

Afterword (2022)... 327

Throughout the book references to Latitude and Longitude
are for interest only and not for navigational purposes.

Voyage of *Breakaway*

Five year circumnavigation

1996 to 2001

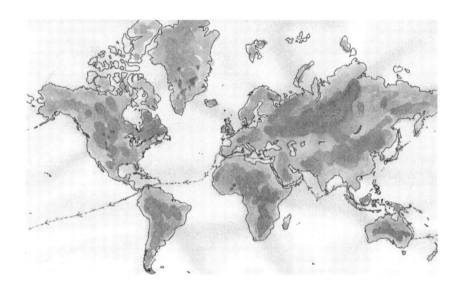

"There is a tide in the affairs of men when taken at the flood, leads on to fortune. Omitted, all the voyage of their life is bound in shallows and miseries. On such a full sea we are now afloat and we must take the current where it serves or lose our ventures."

Shakespeare

"It won't work."

"It will."

"How do you know?"

"I just know."

The wind and rain were hammering the side of the corrugated shed. The 00:33 forecast was for sleet and rain with gales later, but no icing in Iceland.

"When are you leaving?"

"July 8th."

"Why July 8th ?"

"Why not?"

"Do you fancy a drink?"

"All right, if you insist."

My throat was closing over with thirst. Norman and I adjourned to the tea room. He went and washed the mugs. We relaxed as rain was driven under the sliding doors of the boat yard, slowly easing as it turned to snow. The bone of contention was the bowsprit for *Breakaway* – only at the planning stage but neither of us could agree. Norman scratched his beard, got out the pencil and paper and we started again.

"What if -"

"Well maybe -"

"Do you think?"

"No that won't work."

He dropped me home in the early hours and as I approached the old Georgian terraced house on the sea front of Carrickfergus, County Antrim, Northern Ireland, my head was full of sail plans, rigging problems and underwater profiles. The major decision had now been made, the date my wife Christine and I would leave Belfast Lough on a circumnavigation of the globe on board our sailing boat *Breakaway* - July 8th 1996 - the countdown had started.

As I opened the door the warm house closed around me, time for bed but not without a last look at the Lough from the windows of the upstairs drawing room. There were a few embers glowing in the fireplace, the snow fell gently, only momentarily sticking to the windows before sliding down into oblivion. The Lough lay quiet except for a ship moving slowly to allow the Pilot to disembark. White over red lights appeared as the small Pilot vessel, the *PBI*, made her lonely way home and I made my way to bed, wondering where the ship was going. Christine was half-awake.

"What about the bowsprit, pet?"

"We leave on July 8th."

"Goodnight and God Bless."

"Goodnight love."

A foghorn blew out on the Lough, the snow was over and Tahiti was a long way away. Maybe tomorrow Norman and I would agree on the bowsprit. Was a bowsprit essential? Maybe not – but Norman was.

When you start to dream during the day instead of at night, friends are very necessary, otherwise dreams may not come true. My – Christine's – our plan to sail away had been kindled many years earlier. We met as two young immigrants, me bound for New Zealand and Christine off to settle in Perth, Western Australia. Since those early days many things had happened, family reared or nearly, fortunes made – not as yet. That night in the bedroom, the window overlooking the sea, Christine slept and I 'done sums'. I worked out the finances and divided by three score and ten. Christine slept on as I realised that if I lived to 70 we would enjoy each other's company in abject poverty.

Norman knocked the door early. He looked tired, obviously the night had been spent worrying about *Breakaway*'s bowsprit or the lack of it.

"There are two boats to launch today."

"Norman, it's snowing."

"Do you want a bowsprit or not?"

I put a coat over my jumper and helped launch two boats. Why anybody would put boats in the water at that time of year is beyond me. Back up to the yard for more discussions. Wendy was measuring *Breakaway* for new upholstery and Mary, Wendy's sister, was helping Christine look at samples of material.

Norman muttered, "Don't get involved, do you want an inner forestay?"

That evening he asked, "Why are you doing it?"

There really wasn't an answer. Fifty-four years of age, a mortgage on a lovely old house, a reasonably successful business, along with a yacht. I could use the yacht most days if I wished.

"Can we come with you – as far as Spain?"

"Course you can."

He was caught up in the dream along with me. I knew the bowsprit would be finished. We were going to ask Wendy and Norman to join us anyway, but volunteers are great.

The rain was on again and it was bitterly cold. Black ice was forming on the roads as an orange flashing light brightened the darkness. The salt lorry was out laying grit. Now we knew why we were going to La Coruna on the north coast of Spain. It was also nice to have someone along to argue with.

What with one thing and another, word got out that we were leaving. The house was on the market and all the neighbours, along with my mother's friends, came to look at it. Not to buy, just to look. Our eldest son, Neill, realised he had to do something and bought himself a house. His moving out eased the guilt complex we had been building up - well the thought of the homeless family sleeping in the streets and us sailing the South Seas was a bit worrying.

Kirstie, our daughter, was managing a show jumping yard in Greece, Italy, Switzerland, or somewhere - at my age it was hard to keep up. Jamie, the youngest, was studying art and living in contented poverty in a garret in West Belfast. They all seemed quite happy. When I asked Neill for his thoughts on what we planned he said,

"It's all part of growing up."

It had been talked over many times - the family supported us.

Then a Northern Ireland newspaper got into the act. A journalist came down to the boat and the next Saturday the headline in the Belfast *News Letter* read, 'Dream Team take on the World'.

Things were getting out of hand. Word has it that this is the oldest morning newspaper in the world. It had reported on the

Gettysburg address, Napoleon's defeat at Waterloo, the transport ships going to Australia, Custer's Last Stand.

As our deadline got closer, the tension built. The boat was far from ready. Launch day was the day the real work started. As the hoist lowered *Breakaway* into Carrickfergus Marina, Norman ran about giving instructions and I checked down below. Everything seemed dry until I looked at the engine department. The water was flooding in. A copper pipe, which fed the stern gland, had sheared. The hoist driver said he was going home. He was encouraged to stay. Norman denied later reports.

Harry, Liam, Graham, Ray and many others helped Christine and I move *Breakaway* around to her berth. That night the work continued. Wendy was down fitting the new upholstery. Graham was checking the rigging. Harry was running his eye over the engine. Norman admired the brand new bowsprit. Northern Ireland was a happy place that night as we all dreamt together.

The next morning came very early. Gerry had arrived to sort out the toilet; Nigel was wiring the mast. We seemed to have a cast of thousands. I was running out of jobs for the supporters. Christine was making countless cups of tea and then the TV crew arrived. They wanted us on the six o'clock news. It seemed like the whole of Northern Ireland was cheering us on.

I went into the bank a few days before embarkation day. This is the bank that caused me to quote Shakespeare - badly I may add,

"Many a time in the past you have abused me about my money and its usages - still I have borne it with a patient shrug."

I wanted some traveller's cheques as a back-up to modern plastic. The staff rose as one and started to sing,

"Here we go, here we go, here we go."

The customers applauded. We were now committed. Too many people had joined the voyage, if only in their imagination. And at this stage we had only said we were going to Spain.

The house had sold, supplying us with funds for the voyage, but an awful lot of the money was being spent on *Breakaway*. The lists were endless, anchors, chain, warp, winch palls, sheets, halyards, engine filters, fuel filters, gasket sets, pump diaphragms, socket sets,

Pilot books, charts, spare guitar strings, tinned and dried food, trysails, headsails, gas bottles, paraffin, candles, fire extinguishers, sailcloth, sewing kit, oars, electrical wire, and plumbing bits.

We just kept piling on the equipment and spares that would allow us to be self-sufficient on the oceans along with the bits and pieces necessary to make *Breakaway* a comfortable home for the foreseeable future. Kitchen rolls, teapot, spices, quilts, clothes to suit the varied climates of the world – she was slowly sinking under the weight.

When this was all going on there was a constant stream of visitors, all bearing gifts. One woman drank tea as she changed her baby's nappy on the starboard bunk. To this day, neither of us knows who she was. The evenings were taken up with endless 'goodbye to Bob and Christine' parties.

Breakaway leaves the Boatyard

The Journey Begins

The day of departure duly arrived. Wendy and Norman turned up punctually at nine o'clock, only an hour late. A small armada had gathered to escort us down Belfast Lough past the Norman Castle, the pride of our home town Carrickfergus, and out to sea, an emotional morning as we made our tearful farewells to my mother and the three young adults who are our children.

The wind wasn't strong but the tide was fair as *Breakaway* moved down the coast of County Down, bound for La Coruna in Northern Spain.

Things went off reasonably smoothly, apart from a short delay in Howth, just east of central Dublin. There we had to remove the engine to stop an oil leak, so much for a year of preparation. Ireland was not proving that easy to leave.

We had known Norman and Wendy for many years, sharing a few adventures together in the past. Wendy owned a sail loft while Norman ran their Boatyard in our home port of Carrickfergus. They both had offshore sailing experience and two-handed had taken *Breakaway* down to the Azores.

The following year the four of us headed for the high latitudes on a three week trip to Iceland, with foul weather but good company, so we had a great team to tackle the Bay of Biscay. The trip was in the way of a 'thank you' for all the efforts they had both put into *Breakaway* in preparation for our extended cruise.

The idea was one week down to Spain and then two weeks of gentle sailing exploring the Rias of Galicia, Northern Spain.

La Coruna 43.22N 8.23W

The Bay of Biscay treated us kindly and seven days out of Carrickfergus we entered our first foreign port of call.

Yachts were at anchor in the sunshine outside the marina and a young woman in a bikini, taking washing down from the rigging, waved at us as we dropped sail. What with one thing and another it looked like the escape plan had worked so far. The delights of La Coruna were beckoning and that night the four of us made it to the pub at the end of the quay, tired but excited.

We soaked up the atmosphere. Cured hams of various ages were suspended from the ceiling. Norman decided it was bread rolls and ham for dinner. We drank wine as the barman stood on a chair slicing bits from the chosen pig under Norman's instruction.

Slightly tipsy, we wandered the medieval streets eventually finding a cobblestone square. The evening was still warm as the ladies of Spain paraded past in all their finery and the young males preened themselves. A last coffee and brandy before heading back to *Breakaway*. A full moon caressed the boats as rigging played a tune of accompaniment. It was warmer here at night than in Ireland during the day.

Our first introduction to foreign officialdom was quite pleasant. The Customs Officer kissed me on both cheeks and told me to enjoy Spain.

Breakaway did not have to cross the Atlantic until November, giving time to arrive in the Caribbean for Christmas, so the north coast of Spain and the coast of Portugal left us plenty of time to explore. The four of us pottered gently, sometimes anchored off a beach just enjoying the sunshine. The coast around Finisterre is renowned for fog and we had our share of that also. With straining eyes you peer into nothing as the fog envelops, the moisture running off the rigging, ears attuned for any noise. Voices of fishermen drift towards you then they appear out of the afternoon gloom, hauling their crab pots, creating a sense of unreality.

The echo sounder indicates a shelving bottom as fog horns moan out the loneliest sound in the world - time to put the anchor down. Of course it dragged and was re-lifted, dragged again before finally digging in. We could smell the land and the swirling fog gave occasional glimpses. Tomorrow we would explore a new village.

The time together passed too quickly and soon Norman and Wendy were winging their way back to Belfast and the Boatyard. It was an emotional farewell as they were the last physical contact with home.

Christine and I were now on our own, no help, no outside influence, just each other for company. Either one of us could sail the boat, that was not difficult, but no fridge, no washing machine, no television. Would the nights be long, boring or fun? It transpired that they were all three.

Northern Spain and Portugal - The First Letters Home

The following morning I was awakened by someone shouting,

"Gee-oorge."

Sticking my head out of the hatch to see who was causing the racket solved nothing. Shortly afterwards a man sauntered along the pontoon. He was well in excess of six feet in height with the bearing of a guardsman. His long silvery hair was tied back in a ponytail, a white beard stretching to his chest. He looked more like someone from an earlier century. I was later to learn that his name was Tony.

Behind him came George - khaki shorts, white ankle socks and good sensible sandals, poor George looked harassed.

"Top 'o' the mornin' to ya," roared Tony, he had obviously seen Belfast on the stern.

George winced with embarrassment.

"Just got in, have you? I'll catch you later. Come on, hurry up Gee-oorge. We haven't got all day."

He ambled off as far as the next boat, stopping there to pass the time of day. Good to his word Tony joined us for a lunch time beer. After serving in the army he found life on civvy street not to his liking and made a career delivering yachts around various parts of the world. He regaled us with tales of the oceans, days drifting in the Pacific, charters in the Indian Ocean and gave us a few good tips.

When we met up with him he was on his way from the Mediterranean to England with George as crew. George was helping towards expenses. Tony was being paid and had a list of people who were willing to contribute financially for the sailing experience he could give them. This is not unusual in the sailing community, folk doing shore-based exams, but needing sea miles, are glad of the experience. Tony accepted them and their money with no complaints.

Later that day I met George in town, not a happy man. He was finding Tony hard to handle. I tried to smooth things over a little by explaining that some people would not be able to have an adventure unless they became involved with the 'Tonys' of this world who saw life as a challenge.

"I accept that but if only he would stop calling me Gee-oorge!"

The weather was fair for England the following morning. Tony and George were heading north. As they slipped from the dock Tony could still be heard,

"Gee-oorge coil that line, stow the fenders Gee-oorge."

I felt for George – it was going to be a long passage. We never saw them again, but we were to meet many 'Tonys' on our travels.

To plan five years of your life is nearly impossible, certainly when your future is going to be of a transient nature dictated by wind and weather. Mentally we had split the world into four parts - the Atlantic, the Pacific, New Zealand/Australia and the Indian Ocean - deciding to take on the world in small bites, each area being again divided into even smaller pieces, the first being Galicia in Northern Spain. The Atlantic crossing was dependent on arriving in the Caribbean for Christmas but also to coincide with the end of Hurricane season.

'June too soon – remember November,' was the old sailors' aide memoir for the West Indies. So *Breakaway* had a few months to spend quietly exploring the Atlantic coasts of Spain and Portugal. The lifestyle was simple and easy to adjust to, gently drifting from place to place - no real timetable - no real urgency. If the anchorage was good we stayed enjoying the sun.

Breakaway was starting to encounter other yachts and crews in the various anchorages, some heading for the Med, others on the Atlantic circuit, a year out to 'do' the Atlantic with some sunshine cruising in between. Others were young families looking for a paradise to raise their children, with vague notions of New Zealand or Australia as the final destination - a European way of life in the South Pacific escaping the cold Northern winter.

Fledgling was a 34 footer, with mum, dad and the two young ones, Jack and Robert, aged four and two respectively. *Celtic Wave* was owned by Bob and Lyndsay, with Beth and Kathy, aged 11 and nine. Jean-Paul and Susanne on *Diablo*, a French couple on a year's sabbatical with their two young boys. The three boats were to become a major part of our cruising life over the months that followed.

The little fleet continued to move, eventually crossing the border into Portugal, coasting south with the sun. The distances between harbours were further apart on the exposed Atlantic coast but with an early morning start, the south-going current and north wind allowed us to reach safe haven every evening. The gentle, easy sailing was preparing us for the longer passages that lay ahead.

The anchorage at Cascais at the mouth of the entrance to Lisbon was exposed to swell with a constant movement, making life uncomfortable on board. With the shipping forecast not so good, a journey up the River Tejo to the port of Lisbon was the alternative. Along with commercial traffic, varying from cruise liners to oil tankers, we made our way upstream dodging fishing boats and tugs.

The Port Authority had to be informed of our arrival but their reply to my request for entry was 'keep her coming' – so we did. Entry into the old dock of Alcantara was restricted to the opening times of the swing bridge, but inside the marina was far enough inland to prevent us worrying about weather forecasts.

More boats arrived in the harbour. Some were Americans and Canadians on their way home. Others, Australians just up through Suez and the Mediterranean with a couple of blue water cruising years behind them and of course ourselves and the likes, setting out on the grand adventure.

Christine
You can pick up good advice from other sailing folk on how to keep bugs at bay and most of it is using natural products, not chemical sprays. Bay leaves in flour, rice and cereals will deter weevils. Vanilla pods placed round the boat in nooks and crannies give off a pleasant scent and cockroaches hate it. Eat plenty of raw garlic and

mosquitoes won't come near you. Neither will anyone else, so that seems a bit drastic.

On Passage to Porto Santo

With a few days of tourism behind us, it was time to prepare for our voyage to Porto Santo and Madeira on the way to the Canary Islands. *Fledgling* and *Diablo* made their way down the river with us, ready as we were ever going to be to face the Atlantic.

The Portuguese island of Porto Santo was the destination, 450 miles to the west. The first night was spent cautiously crossing the shipping lanes with the masthead lights of the two other yachts a welcome sight. The Atlantic swell was gentle, at least for a while.

Early the next evening lightning could be seen on the horizon. Counting the time in seconds between the flash and the roll of thunder and dividing by five gives the distance in miles between *Breakaway* and the possibility of a strike. We were counting in minutes.

As the night wore on, the time shortened as the danger crept closer. To prevent damage to *Breakaway* from a lightning strike a chain was attached to the foot of the mast and hung over the side. This was supposed to earth the rigging to the sea, acting like a lightning conductor on a tall chimney.

Christine remarked that during thunder storms her granny always closed the curtains and put the cutlery away. Who was I to argue, we adopted the same tactics. The wind shifted and built in strength. As the strikes hit the sea around us the other two boats were not to be seen. Next morning *Fledgling* came up on the radio to make sure we were safe - *Diablo* did not answer.

Five days out of Lisbon found us safely tucked up in the harbour of Porto Santo. *Fledging* and *Diablo* arrived the following day. *Diablo* had suffered a lightning strike quite close to the yacht; close enough to damage the radio antenna. Jean-Paul's wife waved furiously and shouted,

"We were lonely for you."

How's that for French flair.

Porto Santo 33.5N 16.42W

Madeira is the island of flowers with the inhabitants using Porto Santo to the north as a holiday destination with its superb beach and low level tourism. Formalities had to be dealt with. The Capitania and Policia Maritimia share an office with the Guarda Fiscal close at hand. Not too difficult when everyone wishes you welcome.

On an earlier voyage to the Azores, another Northern Atlantic group of islands, we painted a picture of *Breakaway* on the harbour wall at Horta.

This idea was an old sailing ship practice, said to appease the Gods of the sea but more likely used to let others know that you had been there and to carry the word home.

The same custom was observed in Porto Santo. A two mile walk into town to buy some paint was no hardship, with the cactus flowering on one side and the magnificent beach on the other.

Meanwhile the painting competition was hotting up. All the sailing boats were crewed by people hoping to cross the Atlantic and not only was the painting fun, tradition said it brought luck and a bit of that never hurts. The locals would wander down the pier to view our efforts. The happiest man of all on the island owned the paint shop with the small tins of paint on the shelves to keep the old custom alive and his pockets full.

Madeira 32.39N 16.42W

Once again it was time to move on with a short voyage to the harbour of Funchal on the island of Madeira. Madeira was part of the lost kingdom of Atlanta - or so legend has it. Columbus lived here for a while, long enough to marry the governor's daughter. But most of all it is famous for its wine. I had been to Madeira before but this was to be Christine's first visit.

On a previous occasion I had joined a yacht in Funchal to skipper it to Gibraltar. The crew were Joe and Frank, both from the north coast of Ireland - Joe a retired doctor and Frank a 'nearly retired' engineer. You could not have wished for better company. On one long night watch Joe was relating tales of a country practice.

He told of a call to a local farm house, home to three generations of the same family. On arrival he was ushered upstairs to the bedroom where the 90-year-old grandfather was lying in a weakened state suffering from an extreme case of diarrhoea.

"Doctor, Doctor," says he, "I'm finished. I'm so weakened, there's no chance of survival."

Joe started to examine him.

"There's no point Doctor," the old man mumbled, "I'm just done."

Joe finished his checks, wrote a prescription, which he issued to a young one to take to the chemist shop, with orders not to return until the medicine was prepared and in his hand. Taking his leave, Joe said that he would return in a couple of days to check up on the patient. On the good doctor's return he found the old man sitting up in bed drinking a cup of tea.

"Doctor, Doctor," he cried, "You are a miracle worker. I am one hundred per cent better – today I allowed myself a cautious fart."

With shipmates like this I had only good memories of these Portuguese islands.

An easy sail along the archipelago brought us to the anchorage at Funchal. The inner harbour was full of fishing boats with yachts rafted five deep alongside the wall. *Fledgling* and others we recognised, were already there lying to anchor in the outer harbour – not a good place to be if the weather turned nasty. The forecast was reasonable for the next few days and then we would have to leave, but meanwhile we had time to explore.

The local bus was an adventure on its own, with roads more designed for an Alpine climber than a second hand Bedford. Twisting and turning, with the blossoms growing on the hillside on one side and a sheer drop into the sea on the other, we enjoyed breath-taking scenery, the whole experience spoilt by the thought of *Breakaway* lying at anchor in such an exposed place.

The bus stopped for a while – journey's end at the far north of the island. Time for coffee and back on board as the driver honked the horn. Once again the scenery was outstanding as the gears crunched going back up the hills we had only so recently come down. But at the last bend, when the harbour came into view, we both strained our necks and eyes for the first sight of *Breakaway*.

Never again in five years of wandering would we leave her if there was any doubt about the anchorage or weather. This time we had got away with it.

The next day *Breakaway* left in a bad forecast, destination Graciosa, the most northerly of the Canary Islands. It was just safer to go to sea. Part of the passage is the leaving and we were clearing Portugal for the islands of Spain so we paid a visit to the bureaucrats.

The other yachts had told us the paper work was simple and the officer friendly, a five minute job. Not for us. Our inheritance was Northern Ireland. Passports were removed and we waited as the

Swiss, the Swedes, the Finns and the French, along with everyone else, cleared out with ease.

Eventually the officer returned and handed our passports back declaring that the computer had decided we were not terrorists. Well that was good to know. We left. Others left also - all wishing for more time in Madeira but the risk was too high.

The Canary Islands

After two days, or was it three, *Breakaway* managed to make landfall at Graciosa with the conditions worsening all the time as night fell. The entrance to the anchorage was not one to be attempted in the dark, certainly not with the sea conditions as they were.

The Canaries is a popular destination for the package holiday makers of Northern Europe and on our approach to the islands, with charter flights flying over our head, we picked up the local English speaking DJ on the radio giving out a list of entertainments for the evening in Lanzarote – discos, karaoke bars and 'wet T-shirt' competitions all part of the attractions. But Graciosa was not the place for these sorts of festivities. It is said about the island that when you land you must take off your shoes and forget the world.

The main anchorage was full, but the bay to the west was nearly empty giving good protection, so we tucked in there along with *Celtic Wave* who was already securely anchored. This small island, only six and a half kilometres long and three kilometres wide, did seem remote from the rest of the world. Sand covered everything and the only mechanical transport was one elderly Land Rover. The population consisted of two small fishing communities.

Tourists arrived from Lanzarote by ferry across the 300 metre wide strait, El Rio, complete with their own accommodation – tents strapped to their backs along with rucksacks. They pitched camp on the beach. As we approached the small fishing hamlet, I was humming the tune from *The Good, The Bad and the Ugly*. This was Clint Eastwood country with the tumbleweeds rolling past, pushed by the warm North East Trades. The small bank could not exchange any money for us but it did not really matter as there was nowhere to spend it. We had brought a bottle of water along so we started off back across the sand towards the boat, past the village of tents inhabited by the newly arrived. The heat was intense when we returned to the little bay where *Breakaway* waited.

That night we joined *Celtic Wave* for sundowners.

Next morning both boats set off, tacking hard through the narrow strait between the two islands. *Celtic Wave* was ahead, not pushing too hard as it was school time down below. Each morning the boats with children on board were transformed into classrooms as mother and father settled down to teach the youngsters. The British school system at that time did not seem to have anything to replace the more formal education of the school room.

The French had alternatives. They supplied a full curriculum for the parents to follow each month. All the work was sent back to France to be examined by the professionals, the homework marked and assessments made. The Australians had an excellent system in place, well tried and tested on the remote stations in the outback. A lot of the British boats used this syllabus.

So with mum down below tutoring the children and father Bob on his own manning the deck, we soon overtook them - but not for long. Beth and Kathy decided to play truant and go for an education in yacht racing instead. Mum declared a public holiday and battle was joined. Not to be outdone, another boat joined in and the French took a day off also as *Diablo* picked up the gauntlet.

The three boats fought hard with *Breakaway* holding a slight lead as we made our way to windward. But downwind they had the legs on us. Turning the northeast corner of Lanzarote we slowly dropped behind.

Breakaway arrived in the harbour of Arrecife to the jeers of the winners who did not seem to realise we had managed to get them a day off school. When we first set out on our journey, I had assumed it would be a lonely life on the oceans of the world with just the two of us. It was not quite turning out as we expected, each new anchorage brought new friends. The blue water cruisers were just like us, people with a destination, just not quite sure where the next one was.

The social standing of shore life was not carried as excess baggage. Boats that travelled with young families were inclined to group together and the older cruisers socialised with each other in the evening, dressed in shorts and T-shirts, with the conversations easy and varied.

Language or lack of it did not prevent the storytelling from many lands. The common language was English with all the Europeans using it confidently. It was not unusual - if the alcohol was liberal enough - to watch a French man explaining in French to a Dane, who was listening in Danish, the problems of the world, to which the Dane nodded knowingly. Never mind the United Nations, sometimes the cockpit of *Breakaway* could have solved the disagreements of the Universe.

As the sun went down it was hard to imagine a better lifestyle.

Arrecife   28.59N 13.34W

Arriving in Arrecife, the moorings we had planned to use, and which were so nicely illustrated in our Pilot book, were no longer there. The local council had decided the risk of litigation from a visiting yacht was too high if disaster struck.

The harbour was chaotic with yachts in the hands of the Gods whilst husbands dived into the depths looking for the abandoned chain on the seabed, following instructions from the wife on the bow. The plan was to take a rope from the bow and attach it to the sunken chain to secure things topside for the night. So navigating amongst the fleet was a trifle tricky as the underwater heroes would keep breaking the surface like sea-to-air missiles, gasping for breath.

Children would cheer each new arrival to the top. Slowly order was restored. *Breakaway* arrived just as Jean-Paul made *Diablo* secure. I had my turn in the murky depths, eventually giving up and tying to *Diablo* in defeat. We spent the rest of the evening telling each other tales of our acts of bravery.

Christine's birthday was only two days away so it was decided to break ranks with our friends and find a marina berth to enjoy the celebration in comfort. Unfortunately there was no room at the inn, so to speak, with all the berths full of visiting yachts preparing to cross an ocean. A safe haven was at a premium. *Breakaway* continued towards the south coast heading for the village of Playa Blanca.

Playa Blanca was a small holiday resort with a harbour crowded with local boats and only one yacht in sight – *Quadrille* - which we had met briefly in Lisbon. The owner David spotted us and invited *Breakaway* alongside. He in turn was tied up to on old sailing ship being refurbished by an Irishman, whose advice to us was 'learn one Spanish word a day if you want to speak the language'.

He was more or less a permanent fixture in the harbour with the old boat unlikely to sail again but making a seaside villa in the sunshine, also providing passers-by with a great photo opportunity.

David's Atlantic crew had joined him for a short acclimatisation trip along the coast of Lanzarote and had hired a car to tour the island. With a day's car hire left and our neighbours 'toured out', we became the proud owners of a nice wee car for the day. Off Christine and I went to explore with everyone driving on the wrong side of the road except me, or was it me that was out of step?

The first crossroads we negotiated had Christine coping with the early stages of a nervous breakdown, as I moved over to the left instead of the right side of the road. I soon settled down to it, getting the confidence to tackle Montana del Fuego or Fire Mountain.

You can ascend into the national park on a camel if you are seeking an alternative means of transport. I was having enough trouble with a car without attempting a ship of the desert. We eventually parked among hundreds of other cars and wandered off to see the volcanoes and gaze into craters. After exploring on foot we returned tired and weary, only to realise we did not even know the colour of the car let along the make. More by good luck than judgement it eventually turned up after almost everyone else had left.

Back at Playa Blanca life went on as usual, the white Germans arriving on Thursday, the red and pink British flying home each Friday after a winter week in the sun. Hotels and time-share villas were doing a roaring trade, but the little street, a five minutes' walk from the beach, was oblivious to it all. Locals were going about their daily business, while down at the sea the Northern Europeans abandoned their bras for another day of sunshine. We drifted somewhere in between. The water was warm enough to swim in comfort, the day tripper boats came and went and the days passed easily. Each evening there was a sundowner to look forward to in the cockpit with the live aboard Irishman and the crew of *Quadrille*.

Breakaway was becoming a home instead of a boat. Thirty three foot long she was proving sufficient for all our needs, bedroom, bathroom, kitchen, living space all crammed into an area smaller than the drawing room of the house we once owned.

If you start at the front there is a double bed with open lockers on each side and just enough room to stand up to put on your trousers. Just aft is a toilet or in sailors' terms 'the heads' on the port side. This works after a lot of pumping, there is no shortage of sea water for flushing this piece of equipment. When close to the shore or tied up alongside, a holding tank is used, to be emptied later out at sea. More lockers and shelves in the heads, some for tools or spares, some for cleaning materials, with a shower on the bulkhead. The oilskin locker, a necessity in the North Channel back home, is now a wardrobe. Further aft is the living room (saloon) with a table and seating for two on each side. A settee which alternates as a bunk and a sea berth second to none, make the area very comfortable. Lockers or cupboards are located on each side of the hull, full of food, light weight packages such as flour, pasta and rice, along with dried food, stored high to distribute the load evenly.

To keep the centre of gravity low, down below under the seats is where the tins live, peas and peaches all marked with indelible ink. The damp in a boat can remove the labels so another form of identification was very necessary. At sea, food is the highlight of the day, but not if dinner is the contents of tins which cannot be identified. Also down under the seats the heavy tins act as ballast to stabilise the yacht.

Further back behind the saloon is the galley or kitchen, a two ring gas burner with grill and oven. It is here that Christine produces a cuisine to be envied from the stores in the lockers and below the bunks. Up the steps and outside to the cockpit there are more lockers dedicated to the working of the boat - spare sails, fuel, spares, engine oil, filters for fuel and engine. We need food but so does *Breakaway*.

The estate agents of the world talk about the practices of selling a house as the 3 Ls - Location, Location, Location. *Breakaway* seemed to be in one of the great locations.

Just up the road past the Scottish Pub and the Chinese Restaurant was a splendid hotel. Christine used the facilities for doing one particular chore - the washing. Part of the hotel was self-catering so there was a complete laundry room. With the clothes in the machine there was time to relax with a coffee alongside the pool. Life was hard.

Christine
Making my way back to Breakaway carrying a rather large load of washing, a man started following me and shouting. I increased my pace thinking it was hotel security. I was trying to give the impression I hadn't heard him, but he caught up.
"Where did you get that lot done? Is there a laundry round here?"
I was able to help him out explaining the procedure of the coin operated machines. Of course it was all above board, it was just my guilty conscience kicking in at the luxury of it all.

On Passage to Tenerife

Quadrille's crew left to return to the bosom of their families in England and prepare themselves for the Atlantic crossing. Meanwhile, David, the owner had to get the yacht to Gran Canaria for the Atlantic Rally for Cruisers (ARC) in preparation for his chums' next arrival from the UK. So it was time for *Quadrille* and *Breakaway* to move along towards the next islands of the group. Our destination was Santa Cruz on Tenerife. David was bound for Gran Canaria. Things don't always work out as planned. The wind was contrary. David arrived where we meant to go and *Breakaway* made a very successful landfall on the wrong island.

Earlier in our travels someone had told me of a new development in a place called Anfi Del Mar, a marina with a wall extending far enough into the bay to give shelter to visiting cruising yachts. We anchored. Some of the disadvantages were reported to be youngsters on jet skis and catamarans full of tourists, to us only a mild distraction in the course of the day.

Each evening the bay would become ours again. Next morning it would all start once more as, over breakfast in the cockpit, the first batch of new holidaymakers would arrive. We would wave and they would wave back. Not a bad start to the day in a place where everyone was on holiday and happy.

The season continued to move along with the Atlantic crossing looming. We left Anfi in the early hours of the morning, slipping out of the anchorage quietly and navigating the coast by the lights of the hotels and apartments ashore. The holiday makers were asleep as *Breakaway* moved gently through the hours of darkness nobody knowing we were there - one above decks looking after the boat, one down below off watch - waiting for daylight to arrive.

Certain sea areas of the Canaries have what is known as acceleration zones, sections where the katabatic winds hurtle down off the mountains reaching sea level at strengths up to gale force. We had encountered these conditions already but daylight gave you warning with white water ahead telling you to reef the sails.

That morning daylight came and we were past the danger area before the heat of the day set in creating the effect. The wind freshened as the day progressed but the direction was enough to just allow us to ease the sails and enjoy a great thrash to weather.

Santa Cruz   28.50N 14.14W

Santa Cruz on the island of Tenerife was the destination and David of *Quadrille* took our lines as we arrived in the newly built marina tucked in the corner of one of the old commercial harbours. This was the last port of call before setting out on the 2,500 miles trip to the West Indies.

On a daily basis the boats were arriving, *Celtic Wave*, *Fledgling, Notre Dame* - all the nations of Europe preparing for the big push. Each day trolley loads of supplies would be carried down.

Water capacity was another point of discussion, some of the more affluent had water makers capable of turning salt water to fresh and were to be envied. We knew our 120 gallons would have to be used frugally.

My mother joined us for a week and became a bit of a local celebrity being in big demand offering departing boats an 'Irish Mother's blessing'. For this service the payment seemed to be the offer of,

"You'll have a little glass of something?"

Fortunately the yachts set off alone rather than in groups, so she did not have too many blessings to do in any one day.

David of *Quadrille* had to move east to the island of Gran Canaria and the port of Las Palmas for the start of the Atlantic Rally Cruise. This event has around 250 yachts all leaving together to do the crossing, with a touch of competition for good measure. David got his blessing and Noreen was paid the usual fee, leaving everyone happy.

Meanwhile Lyndsay of *Celtic Wave* arrived on the dock every day with a variety of plastic boxes. She was obsessed with storage; filling every nook and cranny of the yacht with containers.

Each day it went on as the rest of us watched with interest. Sometimes the previous day's purchases would be discarded as off she would go in search of the perfect container. Again she would return with her two daughters, Beth and Kathy in tow, fed up and bored with their mother's obsession. She was the talk of the dock. Then one wonderful day Lyndsay arrived back empty handed.

"No plastic boxes today, Lyndsay?"

"No Bob, I think I am cured."

Lyndsay had got her head round the Atlantic crossing, knowing that the preparation was over. It was the same for each of us, with his or her fears of what lay ahead.

Noreen flew home to Northern Ireland and Gerry and Nigel arrived, our Atlantic crew. Nigel had been invited and Gerry, well, Gerry just decided he was coming anyway. If we ever cross the Atlantic again we will be sure to invite him. Nobody could have had better crew. Nigel made no claims to his ability. As for Gerry, he assured us he had done 15 Atlantic crossings. He just failed to mention his trips had been by submarine.

It was now countdown with the time getting short. The last-minute supplies were put on board. Each Friday evening the island was lit up by a laser light display pulsing to the music, and water fountains coloured by the lasers reaching for the night sky.

There was a pop concert with everyone under the age of 21 travelling free on the inter-island ferries. All day they kept piling in; young people ready to party, everyone full of fun, entering into the spirit of the event. Gerry decided we had to get involved. With kids Beth and Kathy of *Celtic Wave* attached to Gerry with a piece of rope, our little party set off into the happy crowds. Disco lights on stage, the pop stars gyrated as the mob moved in time to the music, the sound hammered on your eardrums as thousands of young pop fans danced to the beat. What a great night full of good humour - just people living it up.

Letters home

After a bit of recuperation, the following morning I gathered myself and went ashore to review the situation. In the past, before sailing out of Portpatrick, a harbour over in Scotland, for the return journey home to Northern Ireland, it was mandatory to look over the wall to assess the sea state.

With furrowed brows I would gaze out to sea gauging the conditions, decisions were made for or against. After a lot of soul searching we would set off. Let me assure you crossing the Atlantic with this system did not work. I peered out to sea, decision making for a lengthy time whilst the crew held their breath in anticipation.

After a few days of this, *Breakaway* eventually took to sea and immediately ran into one of the afore-mentioned acceleration zones. To put it mildly, this caught us on the hop. Back on shore *Celtic Wave* had hired a car to go to the supermarket. On the journey back to the harbour, following the coast road, Lyndsay spotted a small yacht at sea – *Breakaway*. Among the white crests she would disappear below the waves to occasionally reappear again. Bob turned the car around at Lyndsay's request, she felt an overpowering need to purchase just a few more plastic boxes.

That night off the south coast of Lanzarote it started to blow a bit. Now there were different theories on sailing on a bad day. The principles went out the window. So with the self-steering wind vane working and very little sail we set the small craft journeyed into the grey Atlantic wastes. We did not see a great deal more for 25 days. I do not think any one of us was bored.

The Atlantic Crossing

Extracts from *Breakaway*'s Atlantic Log

Friday 22nd November 1996 22 25 N 19 41 W

At the moment we are 250 miles north east of the Cape Verde islands. *Breakaway* sailed out of Santa Cruz at 15:00 on Monday 18th November 1996. The morning was spent bringing last minute supplies on board and making sure we spent all our Pesetas before departure for the West Indies.

Moving out of our berth there was an eruption of noise as the other sailors bid us farewell. Fog horns, bells, whistles and cheers of "Good luck" and "Safe passage" followed *Breakaway* out to sea. We expected strong winds off the south coast of Tenerife and had shortened sail in preparation. Shortly after darkness fell, *Breakaway* was fighting a full Atlantic gale.

This was not how I had anticipated Gerry and Nigel's first night at sea. It was a black night; more reminiscent of the North Channel at home. The only difference was we had 2,500 miles of sea room. One of our cockpit dodgers was ripped off when a wave broke over the yacht. Dodgers are canvas panels tied along the side rails to protect us from the weather. It was time to stop fighting and run. The seas were breaking on top of a 20 foot swell so we turned and went with it. That night passed slowly with everyone taking it in turn to hand steer *Breakaway*. But all nights pass.

This evening *Breakaway* is drifting slowly west after sailing south down the African coast for the last four days. We are finally able to lay our course for the Caribbean, but it's too far away to plan anything. Let's hope these are the trade winds.

The Atlantic radio net comes on in the mornings, all the yachts doing the crossing looking after each other. They report positions and then give weather conditions for their area. In the evenings the net is entertained by the famous 'Herb' from Bermuda. He is a retired weather forecaster and radio enthusiast. The yachts report to him with their name, position, sea state, wind strength and direction.

The Atlantic crew

From the information, Herb predicts the weather in that particular area of the Atlantic, telling them to move south for a 100 miles for wind, or advising to shorten sail, warning of incoming gales. The man is superb and obviously loves his hobby, what's more, the yachts love him.

Monday 25th November 16 20 N 24 33 W 0400
At dusk yesterday the dolphins joined us. This morning we found flying fish on our deck. We are running in front of a gentle swell with head sails only and nobody is complaining. Our routine is now well established, Nigel, Gerry and Christine do two hours on and four hours off and I am on call 24 hours.

I also take an early morning watch from 04:00 which breaks the routine and ensures that the same person isn't always coming on at midnight. The four of us are usually up and about during daylight hours and the duties are shared equally.

Breakaway is rolling a lot as we are sailing downwind constantly. From every locker there is noise as objects move about. As soon as you trace the source of aggravation and stop the rattle by blocking the gap with a tea towel or something similar, another one starts up. It's a quiet boat now but we'll have to tidy the lockers before Customs comes on board at the other side.

Thursday 28th November 19 08N 31 20 W 0400
Listening to one of the round-the-world single handers today, he had made a call to a computer expert in England to ask for help with his navigation system, which had failed. Gone are the days of the sextant for these guys. Single Side Band Radio (SSB) has been a great help to us. With it we get weather forecasts, world news and a bit of a chat with other yachts. The other good use for the SSB is the ability to make phone calls home. The call is put through Portishead, a BT coastal station and the operators are very helpful as they realise the problems we face. At the moment we are having no luck with evening calls as the signal is not so good.

Sunday 1st December 18 02 N 36 34 W
We have had to use the engine for the past 24 hours. This crossing won't make the record books as a fast one. Christine has started to bake bread, pancakes, potato bread, soda and ordinary white loaves.

Yesterday we stopped *Breakaway* and went for a swim, catching Gerry just in time before he dived in with his specs on. It would have been a long swim to the bottom to retrieve them. The ocean at this spot is about 17,000 feet deep. None of us went too far from the yacht, a quick splash and back on board.

Monday 2nd December 17 13 N 39 56 W 0400
Breakaway has been experiencing a lot of wind today and is pulling back on lost time, but the crew is suffering from lack of comfort. Just before the evening meal Gerry, who was helping Christine by making breadcrumbs, was tossed across the cockpit badly gashing his hand on the cheese grater.

The First Aid kit was brought into use. The worry was he might have cut a tendon as the wound was very deep. Nigel did a grand job patching the hand, Gerry got the night off and the macaroni cheese was saved. Twelve hundred miles from the nearest land and the only help we have is each other. Still, a simple accident turned *Breakaway* into a casualty department for a short while.

Today the Pilot whales surfaced alongside us like old gentlemen of the sea. They came and introduced themselves and when you catch their eye they nod and go about their business, quietly and with determination. The dolphins are like teenagers. They want to play and challenge you to a race, do backward flips and show off in general. They are both a delight in their own way.

Every mealtime is a battle but we are eating well. Today started with fruit juice, porridge and honey. Lunch was homemade soda bread toasted, with sardines. Dinner was boiled spuds, cabbage, ham and mushy peas with parsley sauce. The inner man is not suffering.

On my early morning watch I enjoy *Breakaway* lifting to the seas and putting the miles behind her. On the night watches the stars are bright, there is no pollution out here and the Plough and Orion shine down upon us. I brought no cigarettes on the passage, I would like one now.

Thursday 5th December 6 06 N 45 15 W

We had a school of Pilot whales with us again today. They were great company at the time. We didn't realise it until afterwards, but one of them had "eaten" the propeller of our trailing generator. This propeller spins as it trails behind us on a long rope, for all the world looking like a giant fishing lure, but generating electricity as it spins, keeping our batteries charged up. We will now have to be very careful with our battery power.

Sunday 8th December 15 443 N   50 05 W   04:00 GMT

A French yacht has been dismasted 700 miles astern of us. The Atlantic radio net is co-ordinating the rescue. There are two people on board, a wife and her disabled husband. Through a series of relay calls from yacht to yacht, three yachts are heading to the position of the casualty. Both the British and American Coastguard have been informed. Even though the yachts going to the rescue are at least 24 hours away, there is no-one else closer.

As I write this, the situation is changing and the Coastguard has asked the stricken yacht do they want an International Distress Call put out. At this stage it has been agreed to leave the rescue to the yachts in the vicinity as this means the victim doesn't get involved in a legal wrangle over salvage. The sailboats are making slow progress towards the damaged vessel. I'll continue to listen today and hopefully report better news in the morning.

Monday 9th December 15 11 N 52 17 W 12:00 GMT

Good news, *Gillaroo*, an Australian catamaran has just made visual contact with the French yacht *Nous Deux* after fighting wind and current for 36 hours. Conditions are bad where they are and it's going to mean a 1,500 mile tow to Barbados. Yachts plan to meet them and share some of their diesel. There will be quite a convoy arriving. I can imagine the party that night. All's well that ends well. We have had to do some motoring ourselves today. When there is no wind it is very hot. Today must have been in the nineties.

Christine
We have settled into a routine which coincides with conditions experienced. There is an ever present swell, sometimes more dramatic than others and we learn to work round it. The cooking duties are equally shared, although at the beginning the galley was only inhabited by Bob who can cook in any conditions, no matter how adverse. The meals vary according to the state of the weather. When the motion is bad everything gets thrown into the one pot. When the swell gentles down, more imaginative meals are served. It's Nigel's turn tonight - meatballs in a homemade sauce with spaghetti and freshly baked French bread.
Each day the vegetables and fruit are checked and dubious bits trimmed off. The veggie and fruit locker is lasting us well along with cheese, eggs and butter. But the day will come when everything will be out of a tin or in dried form. Although we can still bake bread.
The crew has been through emergency procedures and life raft drills. In the case of abandoning ship each person is in charge of a piece of equipment.
I'm looking after the Emergency Positioning Beacon and extra water. Gerry is Grab Bag (emergency rations in waterproof container) and Flares. Nigel looks after the Life Raft and Bob will be on the radio and in charge of portable navigation equipment.
Man Overboard Drill has been practised on a cushion that was successfully retrieved I'm glad to say, as I was particularly fond of it. On the stern of Breakaway there is a Dan Buoy - a pole with a florescent orange float to keep it upright and a light and flag on the top for increased visibility. It is attached to a life belt and the whole lot can be thrown over in seconds.
We also have a 'throwing line' handy and extra life belts.

Harnesses are always worn at night for deck work or if you are in the cockpit alone. We're like the Boy Scouts, 'Be Prepared'.

Our one medical emergency - Gerry and his very deep nasty cut - turned out OK but we did have alternative treatment. If it had turned gangrenous the plan was to put his finger on a bread board without unduly alarming Gerry - Bob would then slap Gerry's face to distract him and Nigel would chop the finger off with a sharp knife. Apart from sailing and navigation, which is what we all enjoy and why we are here, there's plenty of leisure time. Ship entertainment consists of music, reading, scrabble, photography and hand crafted Christmas cards.

Whale watching has produced two schools of Pilot whales but no leviathans of the deep unfortunately, well not yet. Plenty to do and reading up on the next port of call is exciting. Then there is always the evening meal to look forward to. Tomorrow night it's Gerry's special - beef curry with rice and homemade naan bread.

Thursday 12th December 14 29 N   50 16 W

The distance is now down to 150 miles to landfall. We have run out of wind again and are now motoring. I think/hope there is enough fuel to make it. We flew our spinnaker all day yesterday, a large coloured sail that is used when the wind is directly behind us, a sail normally used for racing with a full crew and being lightweight doesn't have a long life span. Our chum Wendy, who does sail repairs back at the Boatyard, sewed two old scrap sails together to make us one. It looks like Joseph's coat of many colours. What a shame there is no one out here to see us.

Friday 13th December 14 10 N 60 46 W

Sailors would say Friday 13th is not a good day to go sailing but it was certainly different from our first day out of Tenerife. A quiet, easy night, all the stars in the heavens putting on a show - I have never seen so many shooting stars - I have run out of wishes. We smelt land before we saw it and in the early hours of Saturday morning 14th December 1996 *Breakaway* entered Rodney Bay, St Lucia, the Windward Islands. Twenty five days at sea. Everything from gales to whales, it was great fun. We wish you all a Merry Christmas and a peaceful New Year. Maybe shooting stars work.

The Caribbean, St Lucia 13.46N 61.04W

The Atlantic had been crossed and *Breakaway* was sailing into St Lucia, one of the windward islands of the Caribbean. Unfortunately our arrival was during the hours of darkness which caused a degree of difficulty in finding the island. But the black land could be seen in silhouette against the slightly lighter tropical night sky and we knew that over there in the blackness was security and a drink, after 25 days at sea and abstinence. The marina was finally found, at last a place to tie up. In the process we sailed through an anchorage but the *Breakaway* team had no interest in finding somewhere that kept us away from the land.

The Windward Islands

The scent from the tropical plants was like perfume in the air as Nigel, Gerry, Christine and I walked through the darkened marina complex towards the sound of people enjoying themselves. Past the palm trees and up a set of stairs on the side of a building just beyond the darkened offices of Customs and Immigration, there was a party going on. Everything was totally foreign to our ears, eyes and noses.

The hostelry was without walls. In their place were large shutters which could be lowered on pulleys during the rainy season.

The African barmaid bid us welcome, her dress was provocative, decorated with Christmas tree lights placed in strategic positions. I dread to think where she concealed the batteries. Someone handed me a rum punch and said, "Well done!" From there on in, the night went downhill, slowly at first but with increased momentum as the intake of punch continued. We all deserved a little celebration, after all it is not every day you cross the Atlantic on a 33 foot boat.

The sailors who had arrived earlier were killing us with kindness, the information coming thick and fast. How to clear into the island state - where to get much needed supplies - where to find transport - how to get into Castries, the capital city. The rum kept pace with the flow of knowledge, sadly decreasing the ability of the memory cells as each of our benefactors competed with the others in generosity. If every landfall was going to be like this I was starting to wonder at our chances of survival.

Back on *Breakaway* it was hard to believe that we had achieved our first major goal and crossed our first ocean. Sleep came eventually with no interruptions by a change of watch during the night - no sails to reef - no courses to lay.

The following morning we awakened to the sunlight streaming though the hatches, accompanied by the sound of a reggae beat. There was a knock on the side of the hull.

"Hello missus, Blossom Laundry, you need ice, fruit fish, T-shirts, ironing?"

The first of a steady stream of local traders had turned up whose only aim in life was to deprive us of our wealth, but all done with a happy smile, recognising us as the greenhorns who would not reject them out of hand – the learning curve had started.

Off we went to clear Customs and Immigration, all made easier by the arrival of the ARC yachts, officials being very aware of the effect the influx of new crews had on the economy, we were treated with kid gloves, papers stamped and forms signed without difficulty.

St Lucia is an ex-British island, now independent, and *Breakaway* was here to explore, so after all the formalities were completed we made our way out of the marina complex in Rodney Bay. Once more the local entrepreneurs were out in force trying to part us from our money in exchange for hummingbirds, grasshoppers and other forms of tropical wildlife.

On the main road to Castries we awaited the Castries bus, nearly too grand a name for the local form of transport. A beat-up mini bus eventually screeched to a halt with the sound of metal on metal substituting for brake pads. In we got as the local inhabitants squeezed up to make us welcome. The driver was surrounded by religious artefacts which I supposed compensated for the lack of stopping power. The sacred heart of Jesus and a plastic Mary adorned the dash board. From the rear view mirror hung the rosary beads swaying in time to the reggae beat and indicating the angle of lean as the driver hurled his passengers into the next bend in the road.

Shacks flashed past, along with the banana plantations; the whole experience one big adrenalin rush as the field workers would stop to wave us on our way. The bus station in the capital city seemed to work on large doses of chaos with crowds milling around.

The market was only a few minutes' walk away from where our coach deposited us, the streets throbbed with activity. Alongside the dock Cruise Liners were disgorging passengers to go on the various organised tours, the tourists looking apprehensive as they gazed at the alien scene. The covered-in market was alive with colour and the aroma of herbs and spices, fruit and vegetables laid out in abundance on tables, as local farmers competed to sell their produce. We were the obvious target for their attention as all the other white faces had by now disappeared on the tourist buses, along with Nigel and Gerry who had lost interest.

The press of people was starting to tell after the quiet of the ocean. Traffic pollution, along with the heat was also taking its toll, so we retraced our steps to try and find a bus. Christine and I joined the orderly queue and as each small bus moved forward it would sit until it was full of fare paying passengers carrying their purchases and then depart with the conductor hanging out of the side door waving a handful of dog-eared notes to anyone who wished to be impressed by him.

The Caribbean was going to take a bit of getting used to but the first day had been fun. Still it was nice to get back to *Breakaway*. Gerry and Nigel were ensconced by the swimming pool, Gerry catching the last of the UVs before his flight home to Ireland. Nigel, well he was just enjoying the ambience of the trade winds with the now essential Planters Punch. We joined them. I retired to the bunk with a head full of steel bands and a bit of Bob Marley,

"One love - one heart - let's get together and be alright."

Gerry had another couple of days left to enjoy the islands whereas Nigel still had a week and a half to go. On his last evening Gerry emptied the contents of his kitbag into the lockers of *Breakaway* saying,

"There's not much there I need back in Ireland."

That night he slept in the cockpit under the stars and the next morning he was gone, winging his way back to the dark wet streets of Belfast – the Atlantic crossing only a memory.

Nigel's time on *Breakaway* passed quickly and soon we had left Rodney Bay to sail round to Vieux Fort on the South East corner of the island to drop him off near the airport. We beat our way along the south coast against the prevailing easterly winds, or rather Nigel did. Christine and I retired for a siesta. There was plenty of passage making ahead for us.

Vieux Fort was not a holiday centre, but a sizeable town next to the airport and all the tourists and their money passed it by. *Breakaway* arrived during an electricity failure with the town in darkness. A boat builder on the beach, working by the light of a hurricane lamp, said he would look after our dinghy for a small fee – custom and practice in this area of the Caribbean.

Off we went following a track along the edge of bushes, heading for the main street. Finding the local police station, Nigel explained he was a brother in arms in need of direction, and they suggested a meal at Sophia's, the recommended centre of eating elegance in the area.

It was a vast breeze block building with a concrete floor and a rusty corrugated iron roof and appeared to cater for two different groups. The back end of the hall was inhabited by the drinkers - there the rum was weakened with water, a spoonful of sugar and a squeeze of lime. To get to that area you had to make your way past the rest of the locals on their night out, watching American evangelists on a big screen TV, who every so often gave out a 'Praise the Lord' or 'Hallelujah'. Huge ceiling fans revolved slowly, moving the warm air about.

Nigel and Christine had chicken, a Caribbean favourite. I had soup or 'goat water' as it is so called in the local patois. Served in an aluminium basin the size you could bath a child in, with globules of fat congealing on the surface, my meal was a mistake. It consisted of goat meat and tripe I found out later. The chicken was better and had obviously died from natural causes.

Nigel's day of departure arrived along with the local constabulary in the guise of taxi drivers, there to look after their brother. With great formality we were chauffeured to the airport where our crew member was treated with deference.

After the goodbyes were said, Christine and I were then abandoned to our own devices. Deciding to hitch a lift back to town, we abandoned the idea after our former taxi, now a police car again, passed us without a nod. There was a woman at the side of the road, standing in the dust waiting for the bus. She had a wooden crate, a small goat and two hens as what you might term 'hand luggage'. So after helping her onto the bus, we found out it was going our way. Next day *Breakaway* and the crew of two sailed back to Rodney Bay.

Friends from Home

Saturday 18th January 1997
We have a couple of friends from home with us at the moment, Jim and Deborah. They joined us just after the New Year and are staying for three weeks for a gentle cruise around St Vincent and the Grenadines.

It's a change of flag for another new country, once again the flag was hand crafted by Christine. It's blue, yellow and green stripes with three green diamond shapes in the middle.

When Captain Bligh set off on the *Bounty*, his orders from the King were to return to the West Indies with breadfruit from the Pacific, the idea being cheap food for the slaves and a great saving for the plantation owners. It didn't work out so cheaply as Bligh and Christian disagreed. What with one thing and another, like a lot of good ideas, this one didn't work first time round. Bligh eventually returned to England, only to be sent out for another go. This time he was successful, except for one thing, the slaves didn't like the taste of breadfruit and wouldn't eat it. The three diamond shapes on the flag are to commemorate Bligh's voyages and the introduction of breadfruit to the West Indies.

We have finally tied *Breakaway* to a palm tree. There is an unofficial system operating in the islands known as boat boys - local villagers who sit in little rowing boats off an anchorage waiting on an unsuspecting yacht, and then after a small charge, claim to help by taking a line ashore to the nearest tree. Off Wallilabou Bay on St Vincent two of the boat boys started to argue over who had come across us first. One word led to another and, if not exactly threatened, I felt slightly intimidated.

Breakaway beat a hasty retreat. As we left the bay I met what can only be described as an unsuccessful boat boy, if the appearance of his craft was anything to go by, called Winston. He hailed us and I went to see if he needed help. The locals here talk patois, a language made up of various tongues. I explained to him I couldn't take any more aggravation that day. He assured me he would guarantee all the aggravation I required in a bay further along the coast. I told him to lead on and he asked for a tow. I did this assuming, like many great men in the past, he led from behind. Winston led us to paradise, the name of which I won't reveal as exposure would spoil it.

The crew dropped the anchor and tied countless ropes together to reach our tree, then sat back and enjoyed the Caribbean experience. The beach became alive with people, and youngsters swam out to *Breakaway*, clambering aboard, calling,

"Captain, give me a sweetie, give me a biscuit."

My heart went out to them. Apart from anything else, nobody had ever called me Captain before. Christine got out some biscuits and Deborah made jam sandwiches. We couldn't make them fast enough. I joined the motley mob for a swim and great fun ensued. After our swim our new young friends nearly sank *Breakaway* under their combined weight. More jam sandwiches.

Next morning it all happened again. We awoke to the babble of voices. The children had come to repay us for our biscuits. We had fresh fruit and fish in abundance that day. Something given, something received.

Prior to this anchorage, *Breakaway* called at the Pitons in St Lucia, one of the famous stop-overs. An estate there has now been bought by Colin Tennant, who is a Lord I believe. This was the man who made the Island of Mustique popular as the playground of the rich and famous. He has now sold the island which houses Mick Jagger, Jerry Hall, Raquel Welch, Michael Caine, Phil Collins and David Bowie, to name but a few, and of course Princess Margaret visited regularly.

He suggested we call there, so we decided to make Mustique our next stop over. It certainly is an island paradise, but exclusively for a limited few. I preferred our first paradise. I suspect the above mentioned celebs might also, as nobody would have turned to look at them in the street. Mustique means the island of mosquitoes, so much for paradise. The next time you see one of the superstars strutting his stuff on stage, it could be he's just back from holiday and going mad with itch.

Christine

Most folk hire a taxi or go with a bus tour to explore, but not so with Breakaway's crew. The boat boy Winston, who tied our line to our own personal palm tree, offered to take us on a walking tour. We set off through the little fishing village of Bottle and Glass where he pointed out the local boat builder, the water supply, his local bar, and then on to the road which ran alongside the nearby bays and anchorages.

Our goal was the local waterfall and on the way Winston gave us excellent information on the flora and fauna. We stopped every so often to be shown and pick delicious green beans growing wild along the route, nutmegs ready for picking, mango trees, bananas, plantains, ginger and sorrel, the latter two used for making beer.

I was specifically looking for peppercorns but it was not the season for them unfortunately.

At last the waterfall came into sight and we all took the opportunity of a dip in the pool and a swim right under the water where it cascaded from above - a magical moment and very cool and refreshing to boot.

On our way back to the village we met the local women who had been doing their laundry further down the river from the falls. They were intrigued with Bob's T-shirt which has all the flags of the world on it, with their own flag of St Vincent bang in the middle. Now when I grate my hand-picked, St Vincent nutmeg onto my rice pudding, I'll remember its exotic location, and Winston, with affection, as we say goodbye to Jim and Deborah returning home with a little bag of nutmegs to add to their memories.

St Valentine's Day, 14th February 1997

Three days ago *Breakaway* sailed into Dominica from Martinique. Dominica was one time British. Every 30 sea miles or so we change countries and have to face Customs and Immigration, both on arrival and departure. Trying to clear Customs in Dominica proved impossible as the Harbour Master and Customs Officer had taken the day off to go to the Carnival. *Breakaway* anchored without official clearance. Late that night I heard a ship call the harbour Pilots on radio with no success. He continued to call and received no response. I called him and explained the situation,

"It's Carnival time and work starts tomorrow – maybe."

We lifted anchor at daybreak. The only one up was the local cock that crowed and the sky to the east was red. As *Breakaway* moved from the palm-lined bay into the fairway, two cruise liners, a low pressure gas tanker and a cargo ship were queued up waiting for clearance. It can be a bit aggravating when in a hurry - we're not.

Falmouth Harbour

The anchor watch was over and I had seen enough of English Harbour, Antigua. Dragging all over it, I could write a survey on the state of the sea bed. There was a hint of sun on the horizon as we left to move *Breakaway* to Falmouth Harbour two miles down the shore - home to Antigua Sailing Week, one of the great events in the yachting calendar. Boats congregate from all over the world to attend. It is on a par with rowing at Henley, motor sport in the Principality of Monaco or tennis at Wimbledon.

Working our way into this most famous of anchorages, we ran aground. In sailing terms this means *Breakaway* ran out of water of a depth required to float. In our language it meant our home was on the beach. Everything we own is on *Breakaway*, but unlike a house, to us she is a living thing and she was hurting, or would be if we didn't respond to the situation. How to make her more shallow? Every weight was put on the starboard or right hand side to make her lie over. She started to move through the sand slowly, then stopped again. Sails were put up as a last resort as this could have driven her harder on to the reef.

The pressure of wind on the sails made her keel over at a greater angle, thus diminishing her draught. The boat began to strain. We didn't speak as the tension built. Would she or wouldn't she? She did. *Breakaway* was up and running again. As we moved into deep water Christine said,

"Will I put the kettle on love?"

I nodded. We're a long way from home. I did not start the engine again as *Breakaway* sailed into the anchorage in case the cooling system had been polluted with sand and eventually we dropped anchor and came to rest among the super yachts of the world. *Breakaway* may be small, but she's among them.

The day was now over. Our third party insurance is £2 million. The yacht behind us is worth at least £10 million. I hope his anchor holds, I couldn't take a court case. Some of the yachts out here are so big their masts have red lights on top as a navigation warning to aircraft.

The local mini-buses are our transport when ashore, about 50p is the usual charge - good fun and a touch of excitement thrown in. A big lady forced her way onto the bus today. She said,

"Ah's fat but ah's cuddly, give me room."

She wore a lovely straw hat and a T-shirt that said, 'Be Wise, Exercise'. The folk out here are great with a good sense of humour. We went to the local museum this afternoon and viewed a most dramatic exhibition on the Slave Trade; a people with their roots pulled out and then abandoned. Now they have independence.

Christine
The food locker needs to be restocked today so a trip into town is on the agenda. Breakaway is totally out of flour, sugar, rice and our tinned stores are low too. St Johns was a mixture of market stalls, local shops, the usual Caribbean street with open storm drains down each side and a brand new, ultra-modern shopping mall full of duty free shops for the cruise liners that call daily, bringing great

prosperity to the town. I found a large supermarket and bought
what we needed. There was even tinned butter which was a great
bonus. As we trudged back, loaded down with bags, a young man
looking the worse for wear stopped us to see if we wanted to buy a
local newspaper. An old lady looked over his shoulder and said,
"Don't buy that, it's last weeks."
She was not amused at him trying to hoodwink us.
Further down the road I bought half a pound of root ginger for
20p, a bargain at last.
PS Handy tip storing fresh ginger Caribbean style: peel root, cut
into strips. Place in screw-topped glass jar and cover in cheap rum.
Rum is less than £2 a large bottle here.

A New Toy

I took possession of our new outboard engine today. I must say it's
very efficient, starts immediately, runs quietly, and is economical on
fuel. It is also devoid of character, mass produced in Japan and used
all over the world.

Now, our British Seagull outboard was different, designed a
long time ago and never changed. The Japanese engine handbook
gives you instructions,

'Turn on the petrol, pull the starter cord' - that's it.

Today proved that works very satisfactorily.

The Seagull handbook advises –

'Lastly, remember that in any motor boat, however quiet, your
voice can be heard much more clearly by surrounding craft than by
your own companions. A supposedly confidential and innocent
comment about people and their boats may well become unknowingly
a public broadcast. There's probably enough trouble awaiting ashore
without adding to it'.

Now, isn't that a nicer and more human approach.

Yesterday we went up to Shirley Heights, named after one of
the British Admirals. It overlooks English and Falmouth Harbour and
British soldiers were stationed on the heights. They could see any ship
approaching Antigua and, with a system of flags, indicate to the fleet
in the harbour below if they were friend or foe.

Times change and it's now a pub. Each Sunday the best steel band in the Caribbean plays here. Christine and I, for reasons of economy, walked up and it took us two hours. The cold beer was good, money spent, the walk home had to be faced. Making our way down the hill a taxi stopped.

"Do you want a ride?"

I explained we had no money so he reduced the price. I explained again we had no money and he said,

"Jump in, I'm going your way."

Super Al was his name. We owe him one.

A supermarket here is closing down after 20 years. I spoke to the cashier who at the end of this week is out of work. She's not sure what will happen now after all these years of steady employment. Work is not easily found in the islands.

Everything in the store is at half price so we bought some varnish. Down below, *Breakaway* is looking a touch weary. Today we went to town on her, another coat tomorrow and she'll be like brand new.

Breakaway is anchored outside the marina of Antigua Yacht Club. It's not a big marina even by Northern Ireland standards but they have big boats - some old, some new, all gathering for Antigua Week. One came in yesterday, originally driven by steam, she was built in 1927. One hundred and fifty feet long, her two funnels disguise the electronic navigation and communication systems as she is now powered by diesel engines. You can smell the Brasso as you walk past.

The crew of 10 spend every day cleaning, varnish work is washed down every day with chamois leathers, the slightest pick of dirt is removed, and the slightest crevice is attacked with tooth brushes and polish. Each day it starts again. I wonder when at sea, do the elements know they are not allowed to harm this boat.

At the entrance to the marina there is a Rastafarian called Byron who lost his leg in a motor bike accident, "turning right before he looked", as he put it. What would have been a minor injury at home was serious here. Infection set in and the onset of gangrene was the result. Within 100 yards you change worlds, from rich and affluent, to the poor and needy. Byron is an intelligent man who is now condemned to poverty by the loss of a limb.

Our son Neill joins us on Sunday week. Apart from looking forward to seeing him, it means he'll be doing all the anchoring and sail work.

Christine
We are at Antigua for the next couple of weeks and it gives us a chance to do some work on Breakaway. It was the bilges for me today, not the most pleasant of jobs but they have to be done.
Every island we visit we make new friends and bump into them again as we all move about. An invitation to dinner on someone's boat is a special treat and we have been fortunate to be invited to some very special evenings.
What goes round comes round and it's our turn to entertain. There are some single-handers anchored close by so we're having a bachelor night on Monday. Mind you, it's a daunting task because these lads really know how to cook. The pressure's on but I've got my book on 'Real Irish Cookery'.
I wonder would I get away with that simplest of meals, mashed potato/scallions/milk served with a blob of butter affectionately known as Champ?
Bob had said to invite them for Sunday lunch, but out here it's not feasible. The heat at mid-day is intense. The boat is covered with awnings or biminis (a sailing term) to keep her cool.
Above some of the hatches are wind scoops to direct the breeze below.
Our main meal is in the evening when the sun has dipped below the horizon.
We have a solar shower. It's a plastic bag with a hose. The sun heats it during the day and you can shower in the evening. What a lovely feeling knowing that the sun has heated the water naturally.
Also, if you put your feet in a bucket with the laundry, as you shower you can do the washing with some added soap powder and clean your feet as well. There's economy for you.

Eldest son Neill has joined us and this afternoon *Breakaway* is anchored off Pigeon Island in Guadeloupe, one of the French islands.

Anchorage is restricted to certain areas to protect the coral and there are a few buoys laid for yachts to tie to. Dropping anchor in the designated area about a mile away, close to a little beach, the dinghy was launched and son went off to explore. The area is a national park. The visibility of the sea is awesome, you can look over the bow and see the anchor on the bottom and the day ended with a wonderful sunset going down somewhere off Mexico.

Next day was the old routine with a slight difference. Neill lifted the anchor and hoisted the sails while I read a book. The energy of youth can be overcome with the cunning of age, still he seemed to be enjoying it.

Breakaway slipped quietly down the coast heading for the capital, Basse-Terre. There's a marina there and we decided to treat ourselves to a night tied up and a meal ashore. As *Breakaway* entered the marina it was like driving an articulated lorry on ice, with no brakes, up a tight entry. We managed to extricate ourselves and anchor outside. The money saved bought us pizzas ashore.

22nd March 1997
An early start and down to Les Saintes, the small group of islands to the south of Guadeloupe. Christine and I were keen for Neill to see them as they have a very French flavour and a walk round the small town of Berg Des Saintes in the evening is a pleasure. The main

population is white, one of the few places in the West Indies where slaves were not imported.

As we worked our way back north next morning towards Guadeloupe, time was getting short. Neill has only a week left and then it's back to Ireland. On our way past Pigeon Island I thought I recognised a yacht at anchor. A handbrake turn and then back for a closer look. It was *Fledgling*, last seen in Santa Cruz, Tenerife. This was the yacht with the two young boys on board, Jack and Robert. Mum and dad, Pauline and Bran, agreed to lift anchor and follow us up the coast to spend the night. When the two boats anchored for the evening Jack and Robert jumped in the water and swam over to *Breakaway*. As Robert, only two and a half, swam up to us he shouted,

"We live in a swimming pool."

He's near enough right.

On the Atlantic crossing Bran cut his foot very badly and Pauline was left to sail the boat on her own. She managed to contact another yacht on their SSB radio. The other yacht *Papango*, crewed by a Canadian couple, had also been in Santa Cruz and were known to have two friends crossing with them who were doctors. Clever old Pauline managed to rendezvous with the Canadians in mid-Atlantic and one of the doctors boarded *Fledgling*, sewed Bran back together while Pauline held a torch in the darkness. Both boats carried on their separate ways meeting up again in Barbados.

A lot of yachts are out for one year only and doing the Atlantic circuit. The Canaries to the Caribbean, up to Bermuda, across to the Azores and back home to the UK. The clockwise circuit follows the natural direction of winds and currents.

On the SSB radio in the morning we all listen to each other's gossip. Boats like *Breakaway* heading for Venezuela are starting to exchange information, while vessels heading north listen with envy, knowing they still have the Atlantic ahead of them. I suspect those heading home will only stay there long enough to regroup and will be back again in a couple of years.

Today *Breakaway* sailed past Montserrat. The south of the island is evacuated every night because of the danger of volcanic eruption. The ash was floating on the water. Yachts can still go but are not really welcome as they only add to the population and create more problems for the authorities.

Today was the first day in weeks we carried full sail. Visibility is back to 20 miles, the winds are free - passage making is easy. We continue to enjoy the boat. Our son Neill leaves us on Sunday and tonight we are making lists of what he has to organise from home. The lists are endless. I'll not even start to describe them. Daughter Kirstie joins us next week. I think we need a bigger boat. We ran away from home and they keep following us.

Christine
Folk use the VHF radio out here instead of making phone calls or going to the bother of calling round. From a fresh bread delivery to the boat, to installing a new engine or a taxi to the airport, it's all available on channel 68. People have invented some unusual names for their shore party who would have a hand held radio. When you contact another boat you use their boat's name and then yours, to signal a desire to talk. It's only legal to raise another radio licensed vessel. To get round this, the shore party uses fictitious boat names, saying things like, "Soup Dragon, Clanger, over," or "Parker, My Lady, over." Our dinghy is called Biscuit.
There used to be an advert on television, 'Don't take away my Breakaway', referring to a biscuit bar, hence the link. We do get the mickey taken out of us by those who remember the slogan. Another reason is security. When ashore there is a good chance that your boat is unattended so it's best not to advertise that fact.
We're anchored again in Antigua harbour. As luck would have it, daughter Kirstie arrives on the same day Neill has to return home. He will be catching her plane back. We have missed the family over the last months and it's wonderful to see them. Neill has had to go for a swim every day off a golden sandy beach into a warm clear turquoise blue sea. It's a hard life but someone has to do it.

29th April 1997 – the Robbery

Our plan was to leave St Lucia on 29th April. We are still here.

Kirstie had arrived and the three of us were having our last night ashore on an island we would probably never see again. Christine and Kirstie went for a shower and I headed to the yacht club for a beer. Then it was back to *Breakaway* for a few hours' sleep in preparation for an early start. We chugged back in the dinghy, full of happiness and good fellowship to find *Breakaway* violated.

Obviously the ruse of a different name on the dinghy hadn't worked. There had been a robbery on board, our clothes strewn all over the boat, locker doors opened, food lying on bunk cushions. The boat was completely vandalised. After the initial shock, Kirstie and I went ashore to phone the police. Christine regrouped to try to make an inventory of our losses.

The police eventually arrived. The detectives assured me it was too dark to get in the dinghy and go out to the yacht and the next morning would be a much better time to investigate the crime. He said with great sincerity,

"Don't disturb anything."

I'm not sure, with the small place we live in, where he wanted us to sleep and still leave the crime scene untouched. That night no one slept well. A quick inventory of our losses came to about £5,000. We only carry third party insurance and are aware of the risks but this night safety equipment had been lost and some of our navigational systems. *Breakaway* was not going anywhere.

There's humour in every situation. Our Visa and Master Cards had gone also. Now Christine panicked at this stage as she has always seen them as the means to eternal wealth. We were now in St Lucia, on a ransacked boat and no means of getting money.

Her precious BT phone card had also been stolen. Into the dinghy again to cancel the cards. Before doing this, the hole in the wall was visited to clear our account in order to survive until things were sorted. This was done with a card left in my pocket. After all was organised we phoned BT to cancel that card also. This was handled with the usual efficiency. Still with the BT operator, we asked to make a phone call home. She said,

"Sorry Madam, your card has been cancelled."

Christine had shot herself in the foot.

I went ashore the next morning to collect our detective friend and bring him out to the boat. He enquired would I give him a statement. I assured him this was not a problem. This caused more trauma. He had no pencil and no paper to write on. Searching through the debris I managed to get him both.

The paper I found wasn't acceptable as it had to be lined. I searched again. Statement taken, I asked for a copy. He said this wasn't possible as there were no facilities for photocopying in the Police Station, but if I wrote it out again he would sign it. At this stage I gave up. He did however spot a rather snazzy sunglasses case in a shiny silver metal finish that the thieves had missed.

"I'll take that," he said, "It might have a fingerprint."

It seemed what happened was not uncommon and our mistake was anchoring too close to the mangrove swamp. *Breakaway* had been spied upon until we left the boat and the thieves swam out to board us. Our video camera, cameras, clothes, binoculars, water colours and painting pads were taken, add to this money stolen, one GPS and Christine's handbag with our plastic cards. Our video tapes held a lot of memories which we wanted to share with others.

One problem leads to another. We had cleared Customs to leave St Lucia and we had no money to come in again. As *Breakaway* hadn't actually left, this was a bit of a problem. I am not quite sure how bureaucracy handled this. I think they made us citizens of the commonwealth state and said,

"Stay as long as you like," which was most decent of them.

As a Celt I made it known that the perpetrators of this crime are cursed. It has been explained to all the locals that I am in touch with a famous Irish witch at home, the Queen of all witches. Some night when it rains and the wind howls the banshee will arrive in the Caribbean. I wish I had thought of this before, 'Breakaway' is now given a wide berth. Last thing at night I now give a rattle on the bodhran drum just to let them know I am still in touch with the 'auld country'.

To every down side there is an upside. The offers of financial help from other yachts have been overwhelming and not small amounts, I can assure you. Complete strangers were approaching me offering loans of up to $1,000, until our finances are sorted out. All nationalities have put out the hand of friendship. One of the things we lost was some bacon for the next day's breakfast. I was really looking forward to it, until an American boat came across with a mandarin and fresh cream cheesecake. It was great, who needs bacon!

Putting the robbery to the one side, the great thing has been family joining us. Kirstie, our daughter, son Neill, and looming ahead is youngest son Jamie, the Irish Rastafarian. The lifestyle is certainly not boring. There are things you miss, like bacon, but all in all the climate and palm lined beaches help compensate. Our first landfall in these islands was St Lucia and we spent some time here after crossing the Atlantic.

I am sure the happy memories are the ones that will last. We will always be vulnerable to robbery and lots of boats out here carry firearms to protect themselves. To me this all seems a bit extreme. To lead a gentle lifestyle like ours while armed to the teeth doesn't fit in with the general philosophy. In saying all that, I would kill for a bit of bacon now.

Christine
Today we ran out of water, so it was up anchor to take Breakaway alongside to fill up. Also a good opportunity to off load rubbish gathered so, as Kirstie took the bags ashore, I put some Milton in the tanks to purify the water and off we went to anchor again. Being a Monday it was a good day to do the laundry but misfortune hadn't finished with us yet and the dirty washing had been taken ashore, mistaken for a bag of rubbish. Bob and Kirstie went off to the rescue in our trusty dinghy but in St Lucia Monday is also the day the bins are lifted, so they returned empty handed. Mind you, there's always a bright side to everything, so the washing is one chore I won't have to do today. To cheer us up, Kirstie's face paints were produced, taken ashore and it did not take long for the local children to appear to see what was happening. We had water colour paints with us as well so a full session was soon underway. Everyone had such a good time they asked us back the next day.

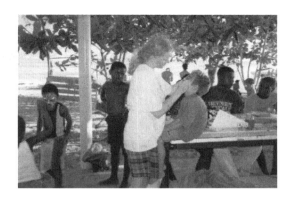

Passage to Trinidad 10.40N 61.37W

Before reaching Trinidad we sailed through the Grenadines, a group of islands owned by St Vincent and Grenada, two different countries which were once under British rule but both have got their independence. What a great cruising ground they make. With Bequia to the north, Palm Island to the south, and lots of islands in between, each different but beautiful in their own way, we made our way south.

Every one of them is inhabited by the most colourful of characters. Tobago Cays is spectacular, a few small islands protected from the Atlantic by a coral reef. You lie at anchor in calm water as the surge of the ocean breaks a 100 yards away. To sail out here you negotiate coral reefs, each of which could be the death of a yacht. It is eyeball navigation the whole way, altering course when the water changes colour and keeping to the dark blue.

The nervous breakdown is worth it. As you enter the narrow channel between two small islands and turn right, it opens up to you. The finest desert island you are ever likely to see.

Next stop for us was Grenada, with anchor down in Secret Harbour, one of the best places we have stayed. In 10 feet of water with a 100 feet of chain out *Breakaway* was going nowhere. We spent a pleasant couple of days there.

A few years ago the Americans decided to invade Grenada to crush the Communist Government. The locals were quite surprised as they didn't know they were a major threat to old Uncle Sam. In fact they didn't know they were communists. After a week or two the

Americans went home and everything settled back to its slow normality.

With an 80 mile, overnight passage to Trinidad ahead of us we left in company with *Quadrille*. The wind held for most of the passage and the only trauma was caused by me trying to avoid the Japanese whaling fleet in the early hours. With no insurance we couldn't handle an international incident. As daylight broke it transpired that I had spent the last few hours sailing round an oil rig and the Japanese were at home making transistor radios. The Atlantic current was setting us to the west but we managed to hold our course and make a good landfall at nine in the morning. The dolphins met us in the narrow channel called the Dragons Teeth, and against the strong tide *Breakaway* forced her way in to the anchorage. A long night was over.

Trinidad 10.40N 61.37W

6th June 1997

Happily Kirstie is still with us to enjoy the delights of Trinidad as we are finally ready to stop sailing for the moment.

The first year of our trip is nearly gone and *Breakaway* is tied up in the Hummingbird Marina, Chaguaramas Bay, Trinidad. The large anchorage is one of the few in Trinidad and up until a few years ago was purely a commercial harbour with very few yachts. The havoc caused by hurricanes in the north of the Caribbean over the last few years has made Trinidad attractive as a place to get out of the danger zone. You can no longer get insurance north of latitude 12 from June to November. As Trinidad lies in latitude 10 they took advantage of their position.

Now there are some of the best yacht yards in the West Indies, if not the world, to be found here.

Today we helped our old friend David of *Quadrille* lift his boat out. The operation was by boat hoist and it was no trouble at all, everything happened with great ease and efficiency and before we knew it *Quadrille* was out of her element, sitting on the hard, propped up and receiving a well-earned rest.

Trinidad has a live-aboard yachting community who have organised themselves. In the morning at eight am it kicks into action, over the VHF radio - weather forecasts, followed by announcements of local events and the swap shop. A boat with something to sell advertises over the radio. Now rules prohibit the sale of goods between foreign yachts. Today I 'swapped' £25 for a wind generator, the best bargain I have ever had. To buy one here is in excess of £700.

Kirstie, leaves us shortly to fly home. This last 11 months has slipped by. There has been the odd bad moment, like the robbery in St Lucia, but all in all the whole adventure has been a lot of fun. The boat is now safe and so are we, apart from the fire on board yesterday, everything is all right, but that's another story.

Christine
It's the rainy season here in Trinidad. Hot and humid and when the rain comes down, which it does every afternoon, it's torrential. But the up side is, the air is much fresher after the downpour and the evenings are usually dry so you can sit in the cockpit and enjoy the cooler air. Trouble is with the humid weather the mosquitoes and no-see-ums are out in abundance at night. I was complaining the other evening about getting bitten and there is always someone with helpful advice. Tip from Karen on the sailboat Walkabout - SKIN SO SOFT by Avon. Karen assures me this keeps her free from insects. Now I'd like to try that. I wonder where in the Caribbean I could find the Avon lady to come calling and ring our bell.

Hummingbird Marina

20th June 1997
It's a year to the day since *Breakaway* splashed in Carrickfergus (launch day). Things haven't changed much, it's still raining. When they talk about the rainy season here, they mean something that Noah, another old seaman, understood.

In the little Marina where *Breakaway* is berthed our security man is called Philip. I had to find replacement parts and Philip would not let me go off on my own. Now you must understand that Port of Spain is one of the most dangerous towns in the Caribbean. At one stage our bus was stopped by Police dressed in black with bullet proof vests and carrying machine guns. A little tear rolled down my cheek. Philip put his arm round me and said,

"Don't worry, I'll look after you."

"I'm not worried, just a bit homesick for Belfast," I told him.

He has a little shed which he shares with his guard dog Blackie and they are here to look after us 24 hours a day. When we make our evening meal Christine usually makes enough for us to share with Philip. When I go and wake him for his dinner I feel quite secure as Blackie lies on her back for a scratch. I know how she feels, if someone comes up to me unexpectedly in the dark, I'd be inclined to lie down and surrender also. Still, joking aside, Philip and Blackie are doing a great job looking after us.

I mentioned a few weeks ago a fire on *Breakaway*. This was a bit of an exaggeration, but given another half an hour it may not have been. Sailing down from Secret Harbour in Grenada, our trailing generator was in action. The device is wired through an electric plug on the aft deck. There's a little cupboard at the stern known as the lazarette where we keep our spare sails and vegetables.

Christine stuck her head in to get out that evening's dinner and was driven back by black smoke from an electrical fire. The only thing that saved us was the lack of oxygen in the area and the fire couldn't take hold. Things never got out of hand and we managed to control the situation.

Fire is probably the worst hazard that boats face, apart from the sea. There have been a few incidents we have encountered. One French catamaran caught fire. He was putting a refrigeration system on board and this entailed working with foam. Being a wise man, all precautions had been taken. The gas was turned off to avoid any danger as the cooker was close to the refrigeration area. He was working with no clothes on because of the heat and humidity out here. Anyhow, his wife decided to make a meal, a glass of wine, a light lunch and a cup of coffee.

Our French friend went back to work. He sprayed a bit of expanding foam, the Pilot light on the cooker caused it to catch fire and a hairless French yachtsman disappeared over the side leaving a section of the boat in flames. Madame stayed on and saved the yacht with the help of other sailors who rallied round with fire extinguishers. That day was eventually over, the boat was back in action and a few lessons have been learnt.

The tang, a bit of stainless steel that holds the forestay, which in turn holds our mast up, was cracked half way through. Gear failure is another big fear of any yachtsman and because of this I do rigorous checks. There are no repair shops in the ocean. We are lucky to have discovered this problem. It would have held together for a while but wasn't quite up to the challenge of the Pacific Ocean.

Our bowsprit has been taken off and the repairs are in hand. In one year *Breakaway* has done, in sailing terms, about eight sailing seasons, so some damage must be expected along the way. So far we have gotten away with it.

Trinidad is a multiracial community. The man who welded our bowsprit was what they call out here East Indian. His great grandparents were brought out to Trinidad from India as indentured apprentices to work on the sugar plantations. They had to work for five years with no wages and at the end of the period were handed £50 and thrown out. They had no choice but to go back to the Master to look for work, joining the rest of the slaves.

Bequia, one of the Grenadine Islands, was known as 'the place of the red knees' as that island's indentured slaves were Scots who wore kilts. The expression becomes obvious in this climate.

Montserrat was populated by the indentured Irish fleeing from the potato famine. The clan names have been handed down through the years.

The local population still carry their heritage of slavery very close to their hearts. When I explain that the patron Saint of Ireland was also a slave, they are quite shocked.

8th July 1997

The beautiful island of Montserrat is in chaos tonight. The volcano has erupted. We sailed past it a few months ago when it was on Orange Alert. It's now red with a vengeance. There are nine dead on the island, people missing and many injured. The experts of the world had been there monitoring the situation and had generally agreed there was no immediate danger. Somewhere along the way nobody informed the volcano. This was nature at her worst.

The Special Olympics

Today I was off to the horse riding for children with disabilities whilst Christine went to the races. Kirstie had kindly offered my services to a charitable group, as she is prone to do. I thought my role was to drive a mini bus, wrong again. It seems I am now recognised as an equestrian expert, me, the man who hates horses.

The event was the Special Olympics. The children train all year for the event with medals to be won and a chance to represent their country. I helped out by washing a horse down and lunging it round a field. At one stage the animal was standing and I was running round it. The television crews then arrived along with the Mayor of Port of Spain, accompanied by the Olympic Chairman of Trinidad and Tobago. I turned out to be the first event. Horses, apart from race horses, are scarce on the island. So the beasts used by the young Olympians are retired from the race track. They are gentle enough animals normally but, like all the retired, can get quite excited when they remember their past experiences.

The parents of the competitors were positioned at the bottom of the Olympic Stadium (a field) in a makeshift grandstand of old scaffolding, dressed in their Sunday best. I was asked to advise them that any form of applause or cheering as their children trotted past could evoke old memories, causing the animals to think they were entered in the four furlongs on the flat. My advice fell upon deaf ears. As the first child trotted gently past led by myself the excitement was too much. To thunderous applause, utter mayhem ensued.

Still, the rest of the day worked out all right, prizes won and medals handed out. The last competition involved the competitors riding their horses alongside a 40 gallon oil drum with a tennis ball on top. They picked the ball up and dropped it in a bucket. My job was to return the ball from the bucket to the drum. The real horse experts had finally seen through me, but no doubt my role was important. The day finished with a group of Irish Nuns presenting me with a T-shirt commemorating the event. I felt quite humble as they gave me their blessing. Sometimes I stretch the truth a bit. This time I've got the T-shirt.

Meanwhile, back at the races Christine was treating the horses as they are meant to be treated, from a distance in the grandstand with a cool drink. She laid the odd bet and assures me she came out ahead winning £1.60.

Last night was the 4th of July, Independence Day in the States. There was a big party to celebrate, jazz bands and fireworks with a Bar-B-Q thrown in. It was a great night and everyone seemed to enjoy themselves with much dancing and carousing into the wee small hours. The radio net came on the next morning. I've told you about this before. It's where the Yachties use the radio to pass information to each other and swap what is known as treasures of the bilge. There is also a weather forecast and anything else you need.

The 4th of July in Trinidad will be famous for the number of dinghies stolen, or at least misplaced the previous evening. The net was tied up with reports of losses. All the dinghies eventually turned up safely and the only thing hurt was the odd ego when it was realised the owners weren't as good at tying knots as they thought they were.

We look forward now to exploring more of the island and have already been to the Great Pitch Lake. The first European to discover it was Sir Walter Raleigh and he put the tar to good use caulking his ships. The giant Leatherback turtles also land here to lay their eggs and next week we are off on a turtle watch. It seems there are certain beaches in the world where these creatures come to lay their eggs and we now have the opportunity to watch this amazing event. Everything is done under very controlled conditions so as not to frighten the turtles. The modern world is very dangerous for them as part of their diet is jelly fish and they think a plastic bag is a jelly. It's not - it sticks in their digestive system. The outcome is death. The seas have to be cleaned up.

Christine
Before leaving us, Kirstie organised me to help her with a beach party. The Special Olympics horse riding group was having a day out at the beach, minus the horses, and my presence was needed. The happy group were helped out of the buses and it took off from there. Other yachts had provided sweets, drinks, cakes and sandwiches for the day and activities got underway.
My lasting memory is of sitting at the edge of the sea with a young boy building a sand castle and creating a moat for the sea to curl round. Of course the castle kept collapsing into the water. My young friend had no lower limbs but worked away ceaselessly.
A passer-by said, "You are wasting your time, it won't work."
The young lad looked at me, "We've got to keep trying missus," and so we did. Other children came along to help – a boy with no joints in his limbs, and a little girl with her feet turned under. The tide that day was kind to us and we ended up with a castle and a filled moat. I ended up in floods of tears when no one was looking.

A Tale about a Dog

16th July 1997
There was a stray dog over at one of the boatyards and she had a couple of pups. Christine and I nearly succumbed but came to our senses before we made a grave mistake. As you travel the world, an animal on board creates all sorts of problems, particularly in those countries that have strong ties with Britain.

The quarantine laws in New Zealand are such that a yacht is not allowed alongside if there is an animal on board. You have to deposit a bond of 1,000 New Zealand dollars to ensure the custody of any pets on board, and on top of this, pay a fee of 40 NZ dollars per week for a compulsory visit from a man from the Ministry of Agriculture. If he has to travel to an out-of-the-way anchorage, his expenses are added to the fee.

In Australia the dog or cat has to be kept in a cage, or failing that, it is not allowed above deck. After reading all this you can realise not only were we lucky, so was the pup.

Another couple in the anchorage adopted one of the pups a few days ago. They called her Chaka after Chaguaramus Bay where we are now moored. Tom and Dee are a great couple, totally aware of the problems involved. Dee was the first on the net this morning. They had gone ashore last night and on their return Chaka was missing. I went across to their boat to help them organise a search party, but it seemed hopeless as they are anchored half a mile off shore in a strong current. I followed a long shot and found the pup with its mother and returned it to Dee who was very distressed by the whole escapade. Later in the afternoon the family of Tom, Dee and Chaka came to visit *Breakaway* and thank us.

On top of everything I think the dog is dyslexic, Tom told it to SIT and I had to hose the foredeck. Still, no doubt the disadvantages will be outweighed by the pleasure the little animal will bring their boat.

The humidity down here is unbearable at the moment but there is nowhere else to go. The third 'named' storm of the season is out to the east of us and tracking about 60 miles north. We should feel the effects in the early hours of Saturday morning. In principle these storms move to the northwest and then curve round to head out across the Atlantic to give you a bad day in Ireland.

The first rain of the day has started to fall and Christine has just gone on deck to close the hatches. The next hour will be like a tropical greenhouse. Tomorrow brings the thunder and lightning, followed by a stiff breeze. I'm not complaining, nobody asked me to come. I knew before we left home our lives were going to be controlled somewhat by world weather, I just never realised to what extent.

There is a large Asian community in Trinidad who still follow the traditions of India. Most of them have never been to that great sub-continent but all hope someday to make the pilgrimage. In the evening they come out for a bathe in the bay, mothers, fathers and children. As they swim, the Prayer Flags flutter in the breeze on shore and bowls of food are left out as offerings to the gods. The Chinese leave bowls of rice beside the graves. In Malaya one time I was young and foolish enough to ask when did the dead eat the rice. I was told,

"When yours come up and smell the flowers."

I have since learnt to enjoy other peoples' ways and not to question their beliefs. This is an island of many cultures and everyone seems to live in close harmony.

The quarantine laws of Australia and New Zealand don't allow importation of animal skins, let alone animals. Does this mean I'll have to put the bodhran drum in a cage or keep it below deck, I hope not. If it is the case, I think Christine is inclined to agree with those 'down under'.

Christine
We are surrounded by a transient people and this can be very useful to us. A couple of weeks ago a friend left his boat in Trinidad to return to England, thus avoiding the hurricane season, and took our mail. Our neighbour recently flew back in from Italy after a

fortnight's break and brought us back some salami. Another is having a fortnight's holiday in Wales to see her family and will return with stock cubes (chilli, curry, Italian, Chinese) and tea bags for us. The most mundane items become very desirable when you can't get hold of them, but the fact that people, who have their own needs to attend to, take time to bring you back a wee treat or do you a good turn, is just lovely. The last of the salami is now past its sell-by date but I know a three month old pup that will do it justice.

Chacachacare Leper Colony

6th August 1997

Well, here we are, still in Trinidad. Yesterday a funnel cloud passed over the anchorage and caused havoc. This is something I have never encountered before and it looked like a whirlwind or small tornado as it spiralled upwards, carrying leaves and other debris with it. Yachts lost their awnings and sheets of tin were ripped off the roofs of the surrounding boatyards. It passed *Breakaway* a little too close for comfort and for a short period the yachts around us were at sixes and sevens, but managed to regroup with no damage sustained, although thousands of leaves were dumped on us from a great height.

However, there is always something to do when you are waiting for a weather window. Our friends on *Celtic Wave* kindly invited us to go with them a short sail to the next bay, Chacachacare. So, leaving *Breakaway* safely at her berth in Philip's charge, off we went. This island was a Leper Colony until the late 1970s when a cure was found for the disease.

We arrived in the evening where a few yachts were already anchored in Hospital Bay. It was agreed we would have pot luck - every boat brings whatever they had made for dinner to one boat and it's all shared out. As was the norm on such occasions guitars were produced, songs were sung by the different nationalities present and a good night was enjoyed by all.

Being an early riser, the next morning I borrowed the dinghy and went ashore alone to land on this isolated island, a place where the Lepers called home. Pulling the dinghy up the beach beside the disused landing stage, I went into the first building which had been the receiving centre. The safe was still on the wall and the filing cabinets full of patients' records were still there to be seen. The whole situation was frightening, if not a bit spooky.

Picking up my courage, I adventured on into the surrounding forest where I next encountered the Leper's Church Hall. The floor was still laid out for badminton, with the chairs sitting round as if waiting for the people coming. Experiencing the hair rising on my neck, I explored no further and went back to the boat for breakfast.

Later that day Christine, Lyndsay from *Celtic Wave* and I went ashore for another look. With company I felt much more courageous. Fighting our way through the dense undergrowth we entered the hospital and walked through the wards. The beds are still there and in these silent halls you could feel the pain of the past.

The rain forest is fast encroaching on these buildings and in the gloom, to stand looking into the operating theatre with its rusting table, was quite eerie. The X-ray machine and the pharmacy are as they were left, the benches laid out with the pills and potions that didn't cure, but maybe eased the suffering.

On through the vines and bushes, aware of the jungle creatures around us, we came upon the church. The altar and pews are still in place but nature is taking over. In the hospital the records tell you when people died and when children were born. Babies considered 'normal' were taken from the mother and off the island.

As I read the notes it seemed like an invasion of their privacy. This place is not a museum but an abandoned settlement left to go back to nature. We all felt like intruders on other people's suffering and the anchorage that night was full of ghosts.

It seems that when a cure for Leprosy was found everybody left. It was a case of last one out turn off the lights. Leprosy was seen as divine retribution from God and the French and Irish Nuns, because of their religious beliefs, were felt to be immune. They gave their lives to those who suffered. The Nuns lived on the far side of the bay from the main Leper village and rowed across every morning to help these unfortunate people. They did this in fair winds and foul and in the sixties two of them were lost when their little boat capsized.

For all our fears about Leprosy, it was not the contagious disease we imagine and was worse in myth than reality. The cause wasn't divine retribution but still today one in five Lepers is not treated.

All the yachts out here suffer from their own forms of disease. Wood rots, steel rusts and fibre glass gets osmosis. Wood suffers from the teredo worm which in tropical waters burrows into the hull and eats it away. Fibre glass is porous and can soak up water, eventually delaminating causing structural damage. Our friends Tom and Dee lifted out their vessel *Axe Calibre* three days ago to anti-foul their bottom. Tom built this steel yacht himself over a period of three years. We discovered all the paint was coming off like wallpaper. I have spent the last few days helping him strip the boat down and repaint.

Breakaway comes out next week. Hopefully there won't be too many problems, but Tom is going to help. The barter system is alive and well in Trinidad.

Christine

It was market day last Saturday and a bus had been organised from the marina to take shoppers there and back, with a stop at the Mall supermarket on the return trip, all for £1.20.

The market was amazing, cool, clean and colourful. The covered part was taken up with fish and meat and then an open area for fruit and vegetables, spices and hand-crafted items. Bypassing the meat and fish, including huge baskets full of baby sharks, perfect miniature replicas of their frightening parents, I made my way out the back. Everything was artistically displayed and it made shopping a pleasure. Pausing for a drink from a green coconut, prepared by chopping away at one end with a machete, which was great entertainment value in itself, I then spent some time among the spice stalls being advised on the best ingredients for that evening's curry sauce.

On the way home the driver picked up a colourfully dressed chap who sang calypso music to us and then jumped off the bus with a friendly wave. We hadn't pulled away when I noticed he'd left his machete on the seat. I chased after him waving this very large, fearsome knife in the air, much to the consternation of bystanders. It must have looked rather peculiar to say the least.

The curry that night was unusually good, thanks to the fresh, aromatic spices.

Westward Ho

3rd September 1997

Breakaway is rigged and ready, it's Westward Ho tomorrow, new lands and new adventures. Nelson said that harbours rot boats and men, and he wasn't far wrong. We had fallen into the trap of a safe haven in Trinidad. The living was relatively cheap and easy and it was becoming a habit to talk about sailing rather than go out and do it.

There's a hint of a storm building to the east of us out in the Atlantic, but there's also a weather window of about three days to get to Los Testigos, the first of the Venezuelan islands. It's a downwind run of 95 miles but there should be a good current pushing us and hopefully a fast passage. We will move to Scotland Bay tomorrow, then re-lift the anchor and set sail at dusk. The plan is to sail through the night and arrive at the island in day light rather than darkness, hopefully navigating our way in safety.

We are told the islands are inhabited by a handful of fishermen and the clearing in procedures are relatively easy but will know the truth tomorrow. Christine and I are now taking malaria tablets as there was an outbreak of the disease recently in Venezuela and Columbia.

South America, Los Testigos, Venezuela

5th September 1997 11 25 N   63 02 W

It's now the day after tomorrow and *Breakaway* is anchored in the island group of Los Testigos, our first stopover in Venezuela. As we hoisted sail and moved out in El Bocas del Dragon, I noticed a caution on the Admiralty chart. It warned,

'Combined with north going tidal streams, races of up to five knots can be experienced between the islands of the west coast of Trinidad. A violent race, dangerous to boats, occurs in Bocas del Dragon'.

We negotiated it safely, the tide with us, accompanied by dolphins and sailed offshore to clear the north east coast of Venezuela before heading for the islands. Christine stood the first watch and at midnight I took over. I settled down with a cup of coffee to enjoy a quiet night. The sky started to glow with lightning flashes every few seconds and we were hit with a violent squall followed by a shift of wind.

Breakaway was being affected by the fringes of storm 'Erica'; so much for the weather window. At dawn we sighted the small group of islands. The crew of a small fishing boat gave us a wave as *Breakaway* approached the anchorage and the long night was over.

Today was spent swimming off the side of the boat in crystal clear water (the first in three months). We are on the move again and it feels good. There is another boat in the anchorage. He caught and supplied the fresh fish, Christine cooked it and both boats had a good evening meal. Last night the fishing boats were all lit up. They are pirogues with a small cabin and a sun awning. This morning there were none to be seen so they must be off to the mainland to sell their fish.

Christine
The islands of Los Testigos are beautiful. There are only about 150 inhabitants, made up of fishermen and their families.
Not a car to be seen. The islanders can build a house wherever they like. The land is covered in cactus and bushes so it doesn't look as if much food could grow but as we took a dinghy ride along the shore, thousands of newly hatched butterflies fluttered over the flowering cactus plants. I didn't have a clue what the fish was we were eating for dinner and neither did our guest, though he said it was a hunter. Baked in tin foil with butter, a little lime juice, some parsley and

black pepper, it tasted fine (if a bit bony). I served it with curried vegetables including channa (we call them chick peas) and rice. Not bad for a boat without a fridge and 37 miles by sea from the nearest shop. The Caribbean curry spices are lovely – not too hot but full of flavour. It's a refreshing change to anchor off and not have boat boys coming over to sell you something you don't really want.

The youngsters on the beach just smile, wave and walk on and do not come over begging for money. These islands are so isolated we can't leave rubbish here and the yachting guide books are very responsible in the advice they give. Yachts are at present the only visitors so let's hope we all leave the place as we found it.

On the Move Again 10 59 N 63 47 W

Tonight we went aboard *Walkabout*. They leave for mainland Venezuela tomorrow morning and were giving the last farewell party. *Breakaway* will catch them up in a week or two but as the small boats leave to adventure everyone becomes quite emotional. It's a strange world we live in and as someone goes out to explore new areas a small part of us goes also.

Ian of *Walkabout* is from Blackpool but he has spent a lot of time in America and has fallen into the American ways. He had to sail his boat down from the Florida Keys past Cuba, Porta Rica, fighting wind, currents and communists. Before he left he asked the American Coastguard for advice on the navigational hazards that he was going to encounter. He was told, "Buy a gun", and they gave him the name of an ex-police officer who was a recognised expert in this field.

He found himself in the situation of not knowing what he was doing, but with the capabilities of starting World War III. The ex-cop sold him an M16 machine gun and a 1,000 rounds of ammunition which he was allowed to take on board immediately. The magnum revolver he couldn't pick up till the next day. Anyhow, down island and running short of funds he sold the magnum to a Customs Officer who desired it because it was nice and shiny. I'm not sure about the M16 but I think someone stole it when he wasn't looking. I got the impression that Ian was quite happy to be disarmed again.

Breakaway is armless and harmless. Security is a constant problem in these waters. The most common theft is dinghies and outboard motors. The small runabouts we use are no use to a fisherman but the outboards are and they are sold to the Indians on the Orinoco River. They use them on their canoes to do tourist trips.

I read the exploits of a couple who had just experienced one of these trips. Travelling up river in a canoe 1,600 miles from the coast, constantly at war with mosquitoes and at great risk from the killer form of malaria, they found one of the last great unexplored regions of the world. On arrival at a village of this remote tribe, they produced goods for barter, offering the head man a packet of cigars. He told them he wouldn't smoke that rubbish and if this was all they had to offer they wouldn't get far. Asking could they take some photographs to impress folks back home, they were assured they could, at $1 per shot. He went on to say not to worry if they only had large bills as they could change them, also Deutschmarks and Sterling. So much for the lonely planet.

Anyhow, back to the security problem. How we approach this particular aspect is by lifting the dinghy on board every night. Up to a week ago this meant Christine and me hauling the punt on board after removing the engine. At our age this was not easy. We have now evolved a system of using one of the halyards - ropes whose purpose is to haul the sails up.

The dinghy is now laced with ropes like a bondage victim and, by attaching a halyard to the meeting point and using a mast winch, it can be hauled up level with the deck out of harm's way rather than brought on board. The dinghy then lies alongside, but out of the water.

The other morning I crawled out of the bunk and threw myself off *Breakaway* for the usual early swim. I came to a sudden halt as I landed in the dinghy. I looked around very embarrassed, hoping no one had seen this performance and adjusted the ropes, furiously pretending I was meant to be there. It didn't work.

When I eventually went ashore lots of people said,

"I saw you diving into the dinghy Bob."

You can't win. Still, I keep trying.

Margarita Island

As I have said before, the bureaucracy here has to be seen to be believed. In most countries we clear in and out with the minimum of paperwork. Not here, in each port you have to check in with Port Captains, Marine Police, Customs, Immigration and Doctor.

When you want to leave, it all starts again, with a fee each time. The various offices can be miles apart and the whole escapade can take eight hours in the tropical heat. The trick is to use an agent and for a small fee he looks after everything for you and that evening he returns your papers, signed, sealed and delivered.

A couple we met, Nancy and David, who have been sailing for the past seven years, tried to do it themselves and hit a serious problem. David thought he had it all sorted and left Cumana on mainland Venezuela for Margarita.

On his arrival they wouldn't clear him in as his papers were wrong. Anywhere in the world if you are stamped in on your passport, you must be stamped out when you leave. They are now considered illegal immigrants and the only islands that treat all this with a pinch of salt are the French controlled ones. They now have a 300 mile long slog to windward against current to Martinique where, hopefully, they will get clearance, but Venezuela is definitely off their cruising agenda, until they acquire new passports.

Christine
A beastie has arrived in the anchorage. To save embarrassment and to protect the guilty I won't mention names, but as Bob and I dinghied across to a friend's yacht, the youngest child gleefully shouted out,

"We've got nits and so have Mum and Dad."
No qualms, reticence or reservations there. Breakaway's crew were heading into town so we offered to obtain some specialised shampoo to solve the problem. But how do you ask for treatment for head lice in Spanish? We asked our local agent, who organises everything from yacht clearance to supplying water and handling mail and he gave us the lowdown on this particular pest.

Very prevalent in Margarita, the locals cope with it by removing the eggs carefully by hand and in some cases he assures me, eating them as a source of protein.

We eventually arrived back with the necessary treatment plus one for ourselves as the youngsters had slept on Breakaway, but all seems OK at our end. Bob asked for a clinic hair cut just in case.

18th October 1997

Christine and I have both suffered from an outbreak of something similar to heat rash and we don't seem to be able to clear it up.

Christine was the first to show signs and I wasn't long after her. At first we put it down to mosquito bites which I don't normally suffer from. After a few enquires it turns out that other Yachties are suffering also. One explanation is that the problem might stem from eating fish in Margarita. Ocean fish are not thought to be the guilty party but reef fish carry cicatera, whatever that is, which causes illness or rashes.

What seems to cure the complaint is known locally as 'agua oxigenada', we call it hydrogen peroxide at home. We have now included this item in our medical kit on board as the overall antiseptic cure for any cuts and gashes we get, and to prevent infection. I'm not sure it would be something recommended by mainstream medicine, but it works for us. Please consult your doctor. You could end up with bleached blond hair in the strangest places.

Phillipe and Florence, two French friends, were heading down from the off-shore islands on board their boat *Marie Lee*. Phillipe had just finished the night shift and had gone to put his head down when Florence called him back on deck. There was a small open fishing boat adrift with three men on board. Phillipe threw a line and began towing the boat back to safety. Florence made them a meal of Melba toast, chicken liver pate and red wine.

If I ever break down I want to be rescued by a French yacht. By the time the little convoy arrived back in harbour, the Venezuelans didn't want to leave the comfort of *Marie Lee*.

When Phillipe and Florence were relating this story to us we were all aboard *Walkabout*, the English boat from Blackpool. After a drink to toast the brave French sailors, I walked up the deck to find the outside toilet. Whilst thus occupied, I realised *Walkabout* was living up to her name and was moving without the skipper's permission. All the experts on board ran about shouting orders to each other in different languages, me included. The owner, Ian, re-laid his anchor and no damage was done. It made us aware how vulnerable we all are out here.

The anchor had been down for two weeks with no hint of a problem which was fortunate as Karen was on board on her own. Ian had returned to America in order to retain his 'green card', (permission to reside in America) and had left Karen $2,000 for emergencies. During his absence Karen had bought emergency dresses and emergency jewellery.

Time to Leave Venezuela

It had to happen at some stage, our timing is wrong.

The western Caribbean, on the Central American side, experiences strong winds from October to November. One saving grace is that these winds are forecast from the right direction but we will now have to move through Bonaire, Curacao and Aruba quickly looking for shelter in Cartagena on the Colombian coast.

The above mentioned islands, known as the ABCs are worth a visit. Unfortunately we can now only stop briefly as *Breakaway* continues to push west.

It seems to be a sensible idea to buy an alarm system for the boat, but we might re-consider the decision. It's a small device about the size of a packet of cigarettes, once switched on it can detect heat and movement and omits a shrill noise when an intruder passes in front of the beam. The alarm comes supplied with a personal mace spray designed for your handbag or pocket as an extra precaution against robbery or assault.

An American boat called *Easy Ways* had bought this product. That evening the *Easy Ways* skipper had gone ashore for a few beers with a friend and returned a bit worse for wear to a darkened ship. On climbing on board quietly, the alarm went off and he was hit in the face with the mace spray. He grappled with his assailant – wife - who by this time was up to a hundred screaming for help.

The whole anchorage was awakened by the noise and went to the rescue with dinghies closing in from all parts of the compass. Anyhow, the whole fiasco was eventually sorted out. But when I watched the wife helping her half blinded and crippled husband up the beach the following morning I said to Christine,

"What price security."

Christine
Breakaway is now underway and it's a night sail from Tortuga to Los Roches and I'm on watch. If it's settled conditions at night like we are having at the moment, there isn't much to do other than keep a look out and mark the boat's position on the chart at regular intervals. Mind you, over to the west there are lightning flashes and I hope the storm doesn't head this way. It can also be lonely at night and I have found a personal stereo just the job to help the hours pass. The best thing is a talking book tape and this is popular with other sailors too. We swap them when we all meet up, the same as with ordinary books. Tonight I was listening to a music tape, "The Blood is Strong", Irish music with some Scottish thrown in, or is it the other way round. It made me feel homesick and missing the family, and then dolphins came along and lifted my mood.
By the way, we did finally buy the anti-theft device but it hasn't been fitted yet, however it will be in place before Columbia which hasn't got the best of reputations. Although folks gave Venezuela a bad press, we have found it delightful.

Bonaire (ABC) Islands 11.05N 63.53W

Christine and I were sitting having a sundowner. Now it has to be admitted that the sun was long gone and we were dragging things out a bit. There was some traffic moving in the bay as we watched with interest, wondering what destinations they were heading to and the type of cargoes they were carrying.

Suddenly there was a catamaran almost on top of us before turning around heading out to sea again to regroup. I jumped into our dinghy and with the aid of tired batteries in a torch, helped a man tie his boat to a mooring next to ours. When all was settled, he invited us over the following evening to share a bottle of wine.

Suddenly there was a catamaran almost on top of us before turning around heading out to sea again to regroup. I jumped into our dinghy and with the aid of tired batteries in a torch, helped a man tie his boat to a mooring next to ours. When all was settled, he invited us over the following evening to share a bottle of wine.

Our new friend turned out to be a French single-hander who had sailed with Jacques Cousteau. Cousteau had come out of the French Navy after the war. Whilst in military service, he had been involved in underwater work but at all times had felt restricted because he was always attached to the surface. With the shortage of petrol during World War II, French cars were running on gas carried in flexible tanks on their roofs.

Cousteau realised that if a car can carry fuel on its back, so can a man. What with one thing and another, the aqualung was invented. The French adventurer eventually went over to Scotland to work with a marine physicist to try and evolve de-compression tables which would eliminate the disease known to divers as the 'bends'. He was a man whose whole life revolved around diving and he managed to sell his ideas to somebody in Ireland by the name of Guinness.

He wanted to share the wonders of the underwater world by filming the reefs all round the world but for this he would need a boat. It was agreed that if he found the boat, Guinness would fund it. So a legend was made. The boat was lying in Malta, an ex-British mine sweeper. She was refitted and with a crew of ex-service men from France, set off to make a film. They had no money but a good supply of wine. From these humble beginnings *Calypso* and Cousteau were to become famous.

Dominic, the single handed French sailor on the catamaran called *Blue Manta*, told us he was a youngster when he heard of Cousteau. He liked to paint. One day he met the great man and told him of his idea of children's illustrated books about the adventures of *Calypso* and Jacques. It wasn't to be, Cousteau had no interest.

Fifteen years later Dominic was making a living painting pictures on the island of Martinique when *Calypso* sailed into the bay of Fort de France. The wee boy, who was now a man, went down to say hello. Cousteau remembered him and asked had he written any books yet. Well, by this time in the yarn, he had. Cousteau enjoyed the book and told Dominic to go ahead, with his blessing, and gave him the full rights to use the Cousteau name. Dominic's illustrated books are now published in 15 languages.

Calypso sank in Singapore Harbour and Jacques Cousteau died in June this year, but as an old diver myself, I was fascinated to talk to a man who eventually went on to sail around the world and dive from *Calypso*. His stories enthralled me.

Dominic took me and my imagination into the great depths where the whale and sharks rule. It was worthwhile helping him to tie up his boat. My assistance was repaid tenfold by his stories. I wouldn't have missed Cousteau on television. To meet one of his team was a pleasure. I asked Dominic about the dangers of sharks. His reply was,

"You are not on their menu except..."

"Except what?"

He told me that in the middle of the Pacific where there is very little to eat, you might be the only food available, but in inshore waters there is enough fish for them to eat without starting to peel the wet suit off a human, as the rubber sticks in their teeth. No doubt he's right, but as I have no wet suit and can't outswim a shark, Christine is checking the anchor from now on – only kidding.

Tonight Dominic joined us for a meal on board *Breakaway*. Tomorrow he is diving on a wreck of a Scottish wind jammer sunk in the last century at a depth of 250 feet. The safe limit for sports divers using air is recognised as 150 feet. We are leaving Bonaire in the teeth of a gale in case he asks me to go with him. Does he think I'm mad?

Tomorrow we will fill *Breakaway*'s tanks with fuel and water. At first light the next day we head for Curacao. Christine has been there before. For me it's a first. It's not a long sail, only a journey of 35 miles, but the winds are blowing strongly at the moment. It's a case of two reefs in the main sail and sort it out as we go.

Christine was in Curacao on a cruise liner on her way home from Australia in the early sixties. It will be interesting to see the changes that time has wrought. Then only one person from each family was allowed to hold a job. When this was achieved then someone else in the family could apply for work. It created a strong economy but I believe things have changed and like the rest of the world, unemployment is now no stranger to folk in Curacao.

Bonaire, where we are now anchored, moved in a different direction. They opted for conservation and the sea around the island is a national park. Someone showed great foresight which has paid off. Divers from around the world now travel here to dive the coral reefs in water so clear you can't imagine it.

Christine
As soon as Breakaway anchors or ties up, and if there are no other duties, I paint a wee picture. For me it is a record of the sights we have seen to look back on. Also if the sea state is calm when off watch I paint cards for Christmas, birthdays etc. as an interest. Among the travelling yachts there are others with the same interest and so we would all meet up ashore somewhere and create our masterpieces. It is a lovely way to spend some time in good company, amateurs one and all. What a difference when you come across a professional. Dominic had invited Bob and I on board for a look around and down below his boat was amazing. He had painted an underwater

scene throughout. Coated in a hard wearing varnish, the images flowed over his chart table around the walls over the floor area. It sounds over the top but he could get away with it.

He even offered to give us one of his paintings but unfortunately Breakaway sailed without it. We said our goodbyes and I just hadn't the nerve to remind him in case he thought I was pushy. I could kick myself now - what a wonderful keepsake that would have been.

Colombia, Cartagena 12.07N 68.54W

The boats gathering for the Pacific seem to be smaller. Not quite as small as *Breakaway*, but there are no mega-yachts, with chefs and permanent crew. We are now in a part of the Caribbean Sea not visited by boats except by those that are leaving it.

The fleet is now heading for Panama. Once the Canal is transited it is the point of no return. As we move into the Pacific the winds and currents won't allow us to retreat. *Breakaway* is now positioned in the wonderful harbour of Cartagena of the Indies, 280 miles east of Panama. Between here and there lie the San Blas Islands, a necklace of coral reefs giving shelter from the trade winds. There is a contrary current with a big ocean swell to overcome, but our plan is to spend Christmas down in this cruising area.

Christine is suffering from a cold. In 100 degrees of heat and high humidity it is no fun. Anyhow, today I set off into the old town to do a bit of shopping and restock the supplies, leaving Christine in her bunk to recover. As I made my way through the crowded walkways, the street vendors shouted,

"Bob, amigo, where's Christine?"

In my less than fluent Spanish I explained she wasn't too well and it would be a day or two before she was up and about again. I proved I could manage without her, coming back with 200 cigarettes and a bottle of rum from the contraband area. Looking after yourself is no problem. We are eating out tonight.

At the moment I am coughing from too many cigarettes and feeling slightly tipsy. I tried to stop smoking a few times. I hate them, the taste, the smell, the addiction. Our Pacific crossing will give me the opportunity to go cold turkey. There will be no cigarettes on

Breakaway while we spend a month at sea. I hope Christine is over the cold by then, she is suffering enough already.

There were a few gunshots last night. Where *Breakaway* is anchored its about 100 yards from the beach, close to some very up-market apartments. We are just outside a small marina run by Norm, an Australian. He set up his little complex 20 years ago and at that time employed a security man with a shotgun. At the slightest disturbance the guard would let fire with his gun, all the neighbours would run out with theirs and the whole complex was like World War III, as the residents would then shoot their guns out to sea.

Understandably yachtsmen stopped coming, as fibreglass is not bulletproof. Norm seems to have the whole thing under control now and last night was just a South American marital problem. I'm told the husband is out of intensive care and the wife has been released from police custody to look after him. In the midst of all the excitement Norm was running about shouting,

"You're ruining my business."

There were three outboard engines and dinghies stolen from boats in the anchorage last night. Norm wasn't too concerned as it did not happen in his marina. His main worry is the theft of shoes. When people board their yachts they are inclined to leave their shoes on the dock and four pairs went missing. Norm is distraught.

Colombia is not a country visited by the average yachtsmen because of the reputation for violence. Bogata, the capital, is rated as the most dangerous city in the world. They tell me if you go as a tourist you have to be escorted by armed guards. To leave your hotel you are hustled through the doors and into a waiting cab, which is in gear waiting to burn rubber, ready to make a quick exit. They kidnap tourists and hold them to ransom. Sure, who would pay for us?

Chaka, the little stray pup picked up in Trinidad by Tom and Dee of *Axe Calibre* has just come into season. The howls of the local dogs on the beach are pitiful to listen to. There have just been a few more shots. The residents are either firing at the dogs or sorting out custody of the children. We have parked *Breakaway* in quieter places.

Christine

Bob was not joking when he said the locals were greeting him in Cartagena's old town.

There is a street mainly devoted to emerald shops and we were successfully enticed over the door of one of them by the offer of a look around the jewellery making process, a cup of coffee, a free emerald and no pressure would be put on us to buy.

An interesting afternoon was spent in air-conditioned comfort being shown what to look for in a good emerald and information about the mines in the interior of Colombia. It was a family concern and they showed us photographs of visits to the mine. They have a concession from the government to operate and hand over a percentage of earnings.

A good emerald is recognised by its strong clear colour and all are flawed. The flaw is called an inclusion and if it doesn't have one, it's not an emerald. I foolishly asked could they set one into my own ring as I had lost the original stone and now every time we show our faces in town they ask us about it.

The locals are on commission so it's in their interest to encourage us to buy. I must admit it would be a lovely reminder of a beautiful city to have an emerald from Cartagena of the Indies, as long as the price is right.

Here's hoping.

Green Island, San Blas, Panama 9 35N 78 35W

Two days ago we left Colombia, a country not recommended to the tourist but a place only offering us friendship and hospitality. Our plan was the San Blas islands about 200 miles to the west.

We arrived at daybreak after some of the best sailing either of us has ever enjoyed. As the sun climbed high, *Breakaway* made her approach towards the reefs. This isolated area is still mainly uncharted and the whole exercise was undertaken by eyeball navigation, with me on the bow pointing out the hazards to Christine on the helm and between us we arrived in an anchorage of outstanding beauty.

San Blas is part of Panama and the Kuna Indians, the inhabitants, are thought to be the last of the Caribs descended from the Incas. A lot of years back a Canadian adventurer arrived and started them thinking of independence. Panama was annoyed and preparations were made to sort out the problem. The solution was to rid themselves of the Kuna Indians. The good old U. S. of A. sent a couple of gunboats down to protect them. The Canadian hasn't been seen since and peace reigns.

Green Island Art Club

The Kunas are allowed an autonomy under the umbrella of Panama and a lifestyle as old as time hasn't changed. The local people now live under what has been recognised as the best democracy in the world today. Each island has its own Chief and Council, and in order to move from one island to another, permission has to be granted.

The anchorage is hard to describe without seeming to exaggerate, a small island of palm trees and golden beaches with no inhabitants in sight. At night the moon and stars are the only light to be seen. In the mornings we row over to the beach for a swim, the bleached sand stretching 10 feet until you enter the forest of palms. Other people have been here of course but at the moment we have it totally to ourselves.

The whole experience seems like a dream. We awake to the sound of the surf on the other side of the island. The surrounding reefs protect *Breakaway* from the swell and the ever-present sea breeze cools us down.

There are no mosquitoes as Green Island has no fresh water source. Our own private island to snorkel off and watch the underwater life - sometimes sailing is tiring but the rewards are good.

An Interesting Encounter

This morning I went ashore to walk around our new estate and check that everything was as it should be. The island is not big and the isolated palm lined beach was a joy with not another soul in sight.

As I came round the small group of mangroves there was a dug-out canoe pulling up on the sand with a husband and wife team out looking for the day's catch, which I realised later was me and Christine.

The females are a much-respected part of the community here. The traditional dress is a wraparound skirt and a brightly coloured blouse with an embroidered panel known as a mola, beautifully hand stitched work in a reverse appliqué telling stories of the past. The women's lower legs and upper arms are bound with layers of beads to keep them slim, a bit like the Chinese old tradition of binding their girl children's feet to keep them small, a sign of beauty.

Anyhow, I told them to call out and see us on the way past. Half an hour later they were on board for coffee and biscuits. Not wanting to eat the biscuits, they asked could they save them for their children. As you can imagine this was not allowed to happen. They got to eat the biscuits with more wrapped up for the family. Christine bought five molas from the diminutive Norris. After the sale they continued to talk and we have been invited to their village on the island of El Tigre to meet the family, grandparents included. This is indeed an honour, to even land at a village permission has to be granted from the Chief.

What a good day it has been. Christine has made up a parcel of gifts for our run ashore in Tigre, some flour, sugar, notebooks and pencils for the children. I can't wait. We'll tell you how we get on.

Christine

I realise Christmas is long gone in the high latitudes as you read this, but it's just about to happen for us. We are miles away from the nearest shop and if we haven't got it on board, we'll have to do without. The SSB radio burst into life this morning and friends on other yachts are joining us for Christmas. Their main interest was what we wanted them to bring from the mainland in the form of supplies. Fresh vegetables and vacuum packed turkey and ham was the reply.

There will be quite a few boats gathered at Green Island for the festivities. Each boat will make a dish, either starter, main course or dessert and we will share the feast around a driftwood fire on the sandy point of land on Green Island.

A generator will be onshore and coloured lights will be strung in the palm trees. Upturned dinghies will make dining tables.

The rule for Christmas presents is that you must make them yourself so that no great expense is incurred. I'm doing either shortbread or a poor man's imitation of a whiskey and cream liquor.

> *RECIPE*
> *1 cup hot, strong, black coffee*
> *1 can condensed milk*
> *1 cup whiskey (preferably Irish)*
> *1 teaspoon vanilla essence*

Mix all ingredients together and pour into a sterilised, screw top bottle. We decorate the label with shamrocks and call it Harper's Irish Cream. I don't know how long it keeps, it always goes too quickly for us to find out.

Remember to give it a good shake before you pour over ice.

Christmas in Paradise

27th December 1997

Today's modern world is a place of computers and internet. Communication takes less than a minute, no matter where you are all over the globe. By the time you read this, Christmas will be long gone and I will have sharpened my pencil twice.

Christmas this year was spent in the islands of San Blas, in the most perfect of anchorages. Fourteen boats arranged a get-together in this tropical paradise and formed various committees. There were Germans, Americans, English, Australians and of course Irish. Christine was chairman of the music committee.

In the midst of it all was a single hander. Marie Louise is 69 years of age and speaks eight languages, one of which is Chinese. Herself and I were the chairpersons of the diplomatic section. We were dutied off to go and meet the chief of the next island to seek permission for a Christmas party on the deserted beaches of Green Island.

The Kuna culture is slightly different from the rest of the world. The females are in charge. Now I know this isn't that different but at least here it is official. Anyhow, Marie Louise and I met the local chief and she gave us permission to enjoy the island. We invited her and the rest of the family to join us. In fact we told the whole village to come along. They charged us $5 to rent this bit of paradise for a week. That's about £3. It seemed reasonable.

The palm trees were strung with Christmas lights worked by a small generator. Most of the yachts were dressed overall as everyone got into the spirit of the occasion. Even Paul of *Cat O Fun* told me this was the one time of the year he didn't like being a Jew. In saying that, for a man from Los Angeles, he knew all the words of 'O come all ye faithful'.

The Germans sang 'Silent Night' as it should be sung as we all sat round a driftwood fire on the beach. The trade winds blew from the east, the fronds of the coconut palms swayed above us. Maybe it wasn't traditional but we gave it our best shot. The Kuna Indians arrived in their dugout canoes. They made Christmas very special.

28th December 1997

It was up anchor this morning in company with Tom and Dee of *Axe Calibre*. Our destination was the island of El Tigre about eight miles away. Not a big passage but a difficult one as we worked our way along the edges of the coral reefs.

The idea was to meet up with Norris and Fernandez who sold us the molas at Green Island. We had an invitation to their home. I can't explain the hospitality we received on the island of El Tigre. Brother Morris, a Kuna, now doing missionary work among his own people, was waiting ashore as we pulled our dinghies up the beach. I'm not sure which religion is winning, the old ways or the new.

They traditionally worshipped one God whose son comes down on a regular basis to check up on how things are getting along. That's the only thing different from our own beliefs, so its hard work converting them as their God seems to keep a closer eye on things. Anyhow, Morris is out here doing his best.

We had a grand tour of the island, starting off in the Council House. Here we met the traditional Chief. There is another, a political Chief, who is elected. The village meets three or four times a week to sort out problems. These sessions are chaired by the political Chief, but the old Chief swings in a hammock overlooking the proceedings. It seems at first glance a fairly primitive assembly, but then I thought of the House of Lords. Does much change around the world?

Morris told me an American arrived on El Tigre and was concerned about health problems. Full of generosity, he promised to go home and see what he could rustle up. He came back with the offer of a $1 million for a hospital, which was turned down by the old Chief at the assembly saying that the medicine man didn't feel it was necessary. The old Chief died. Immediately after the funeral the tribe tried to re-group. Too late, their American friend had just died also.

There is now a modern pharmacy on the island, not well stocked but adequate. There are no locked doors on El Tigre, and this is probably the only place in the world where the chemist shop is left open.

Axe Calibre and ourselves are going through our medical chests to see what we can spare. Tomorrow morning there will be a presentation of bandages. There were only two other countries where I experienced this kind of welcome and hospitality. One was Nepal and the other was Cambodia. I always thought Panama was a canal system. When you move beyond that there's another world out there.

The other place we were allowed to enter was the hut where they put the girls who reach puberty. This action removes them from the threat of men until a marriage is sorted out. Once again, not our way, but what parent didn't worry when his or her daughter went on her first date. We have both enjoyed the Kuna people and their culture immensely. It has been a wonderful experience.

Christine
Our visit to Norris and Fernandez came about and it was a
delightful reunion. Trying to find their home among the neat
ordered village of identical palm roofed houses with bamboo sides
was like looking for a needle among a lot of haystacks, but at last
there they were, smiling and obviously glad to see us.
Grandmother was relaxing in a hammock and her fan was snatched
off her and handed over as a gift, while her daughter dashed over to
a neighbour's house to bring a similar one for Dee of Axe Calibre.
They have very few possessions and the only furniture was low stools
carved out of a block of wood. At night they sling hammocks for the

rest of the family. There was an open fire for cooking and clothing was tied up in plastic bags and hung from the rafters to keep it out of the way. A few handmade pots on a raised bench for storage and that was it, but everything was spotlessly clean.

At the opening where the light was good, Norris and her daughter, both traditionally dressed, were working on molas*, as was every woman in the village. The molas are collected when a cruise liner comes into the vicinity and it seems to be the only way they can earn American dollars, the currency of Panama.

The men fish and canoe over to the mainland for fruit, edible roots and whatever game they can catch in the tropical forest.

Domestic pigs are kept on the leeward side of the island for communal use. They too are very well looked after.

It is an extremely ordered society with the youngsters calling, "Hola", from the doorways and waving. If an island was flying a red flag, the Medicine Man was doing his thing and it was taboo to go ashore.

Tom of Axe Calibre had a parting gift to offer, an old spinnaker for Fernandez to make over as a sail for his canoe, with plenty left for other uses. He was delighted.

*Molas. Squares of layered material worked in a reverse appliqué, depicting the Kuna way of life. Traditionally worn on the bodice of dresses, a back and front panel, but bought by tourists because of the intricate quality of the work. Framed or used to decorate cushions etc. they can fetch a good price.

Fernandez handing over a gift of fresh fruit

Lemon Cays 09 32.7N 78 54W

As we entered Lemon Cays, Eastern San Blas, the square rigged sailing vessel *Picton Castle* was lying to anchor surrounded by Kuna Indians in their dug-out canoes. Instead of paying with dollars they trade goods for the Indian handicrafts. It was just like a shot from the film *Mutiny on the Bounty* but the scenery was better than anything Hollywood could have invented.

As we dropped our own anchor we came under heavy attack from the Indians. *Breakaway* is completely out of trading goods. Christine, thinking on her feet, gave the first canoe one of my shirts in exchange for a wraparound skirt that a girl had on her head – don't ask - which caused a small diversion until we could re-group. Meanwhile more dugouts were heading for us and I realised I was on deck alone. For a while I felt deserted but I had misjudged my better half who was in the galley making popcorn at a furious rate.

The sound of the corn popping threw the canoes into retreat for a while, giving us enough time to parcel it up in small portions using cling film. By the time the locals had gathered themselves and come alongside the gifts were ready for them. The hour was saved only by quick thinking on our part. It's a pity about the shirt. I was quite fond of it. Still, in all battles there are casualties.

In the next 24 hours, *Breakaway* starts moving towards Colon, the harbour on the Atlantic side of the Panama Canal. From here the canal transit and the Pacific awaits. It will take a couple of weeks to make *Breakaway* ready for her next ocean passage. The mast and rigging will have to be checked. Sails examined for wear. The engine needs a service, oil filters changed. Colon will be the last service station before New Zealand, about 8,000 miles away. To get there we cross the biggest ocean in the world.

Last night it rained heavily and I had to go on deck in the early hours to close the hatches and put our cockpit cushions down below. Christine was first up in the morning as it was an early start to enable us to arrive in the Isla Linton before darkness fell.

I was still in my bunk when I heard a thump and Christine called out that she was hurt. I found her covered in blood with her eye socket badly gashed. One of the things the Kuna's lack is medical help. We were on our own. I got her to hold a pad over the wound to stem the flow of blood while I emptied our medical kit on the saloon table. Laying her down below on a bunk, I assessed the damage. Clearing away the blood so I could see the wound took a while. It was a very deep gash on the right hand eye socket. The cheekbone didn't appear to be broken but at this stage I couldn't be sure. A lot of antiseptic solution was used, first on my hands and then on Christine's cheek. After that I managed to close the gash with sutures and stop the bleeding.

It was time to call Dee of *Axe Calibre* anchored close by for a second opinion. She came across in their dinghy and gave my repairs the OK giving the patient a 'tablet for shock' and taking two for herself. Christine had slipped and fallen onto one of the winches. These are stainless steel and about twice the size of Frank Bruno's fist.

Either one of us can sail *Breakaway* on our own but on this occasion Dee's son Paul joined us to help out so that I could keep an eye on my patient. His assistance was much appreciated as it helped relieve the pressure on both of us. By late afternoon the invalid was sitting out on the 'veranda' checking the course, giving instructions on the evening meal and looking generally beat about. The medical attentions seemed to have worked out fairly well, no doubt there will be a scar left to remind us how exposed we both are to accidents.

When *Breakaway* arrives in Colon I feel Christine should go and have her wounds sorted out professionally. That's a few days away yet and meanwhile she looks like the result of a violent marriage.

We carry a very extensive medical kit. One of the things we hope we never have to use. Today it proved its worth.

Christine
Before we left home, extensive work was done on Breakaway so that she would be as good as we could make her for the journey ahead. Our own skills had to be worked on to try and make us worthy of the task. Bob took things a stage further with a Ship Captain's medical course and am I glad he did. He patched up my battered face and averted what could have been quite a problem with no

medical help for miles. My accident highlighted one of the hazards of our lifestyle and had all the other yachts in the vicinity (news travels fast) pulling out their First Aid kits to review contents.

Panama Yacht Club Marina, Cristobal 09 20N 78.54W

21st January 1998

Breakaway is now betwixt and between two oceans, moored at the Panama Canal Yacht Club, a small, safe haven for yachts that are now preparing to transit the Canal and move into the Pacific.

On the Atlantic side the tides are negligible. When we reach the Pacific the rise and fall is about 15 feet. *Breakaway* hasn't been in tidal waters for a year now. The old skills are going to be used again. Let's hope I remember how.

With a large rise and fall, marina pontoons are buoyant and they move up and down with the natural forces. In the Mediterranean and Caribbean Seas this is not necessary. In these waters the trick to marinas is to back up to the quay. On the approach you drop your anchor and wait until it takes the strain, then, moving slowly ahead, tie to the dock. When this is accomplished you step onto the quay and off you go to clear Customs and enjoy the facilities ashore. That's the theory. It doesn't always work. In every harbour all over the world at any hour, day or night, there is someone watching. If you do it right no one appears. Get it wrong and the world is there. I always seem to park the yacht with an audience. Anyhow, we are now tied up at the Yacht Club.

Tomorrow *Breakaway* is measured for the Canal, which only happens once in the lifetime of a boat and after measurement the boat is put on file with its own number. Yachts are treated the same way as oil tankers. Four line handlers are required, a skipper in command (me), with a Pilot on board to show us the way. The Authorities also demand a $100 deposit in case we damage one of the locks. The chance of *Breakaway* doing harm to anything is unlikely. She's far too small. The whole concept is very traumatic. We'll let you know how we get on.

Well, we are now measured for the Canal and in future will be known as 376442. Our daughter Kirstie has joined *Breakaway* for the pacific leg and is registered as a line handler. The crew of *Celtic Wave* is coming along to assist.

Today started early when a man appeared with a tape measure along with countless forms to be filled in and signed. He issued the above number and told me on no account was he to blame for anything that could, would or might occur whilst we were in the Panama Canal. The last form I signed made me responsible for feeding the Pilot, supplying him with cold drinks and making sure he didn't fall overboard. The next stage in the operation involved me taking a taxi up to the Chief Cashier's Office where he relieved me of $475 US. While these negotiations were going on, the cashier kept closing his little window. I wasn't going to steal any of his forms. I had seen enough to do me. Only cash is accepted.

With all the formalities accomplished, Christine had to phone the man in charge of transits for a time to pick up our Pilot. Rumour has it that from May 1998 all yacht transits will cost $1500, so we are lucky to have arrived in time to save ourselves a lot of money.

The Canal system employs up to 9,000 people and until now was in the control of the USA. The Canal Zone is not part of the country of Panama. On the 31st December 1999 it all changes. This is the date the Canal is handed over to the Panamanians. There were a few provisos, one being that the Canal has to be run by the Government and not given out to private enterprise.

The Canal is divided up into three parts, three locks up, three locks down with two lakes in the middle (sorry, four parts). The first set of locks lift you about 90 feet above sea level, crossing the lakes you then drop 90 feet, depending on the state of the tide at the Pacific side. We hope to go through the system with Tom and Dee of *Axe Calibre*.

It's unusual for small yachts like ours to manage the transit in one day so we will probably have to anchor up in one of the lakes overnight. However the Pilot goes home, which eases the load slightly. Our additional line handlers from *Celtic Wave* consist of mum and dad and the two girls, Beth and Kathy. Now bearing in mind that

Breakaway has three berths, four at a push, I can see a party coming on in the lake. Let's hope it doesn't rain too much, Kirstie and the kids have opted for sleeping on deck in hammocks.

Colon, on the Atlantic side, has to be the most dangerous place we have visited so far. You can't walk the streets in daytime never mind the dark hours. The security guards wear crossed gun belts with pistols ready for a quick draw. From *Breakaway* we can hear the gun shots at night. Not a place to wander freely.

At present we are living in an enclave and the marina gate is guarded by security men with sawn-off shot guns. To go out for any reason you use a taxi. Yet Panama City on the Pacific side is a wonderful place, malls, shops and stores where anything can be bought at bargain prices. The modern high rise skyline is magnificent, while on the outskirts the Old Spanish City lies in ruins but laid out as parkland, a place used by the locals in the evenings to watch the sun set over the Pacific Ocean.

Panama is a land of contrasts from the Kuna Indians of San Blas to the poverty of Colon - we've experienced it all. In saying all that, it's a pity there is so much paperwork.

Kirstie checking the medical supplies

Christine
With our daughter Kirstie joining us we have finally received our Christmas cards and presents. It has been terrific reading through

all the letters from family and friends and catching up with the news. We even had photos sent out showing how our hometown of Carrickfergus is developing and shots of the family to show our sailing friends. A much needed bimini (sun awning) has arrived for Breakaway from our good friend Wendy, along with new cockpit cushions of high density foam, replacing those stolen in St Lucia. We are looking like 'brand new' again for a wee while. You can buy many's a thing out here but tinned meat pies and bacon grill are not to be found. Once again we are fortunate that our supply has now been replenished. It will be a treat to look forward to. Mashed potatoes, meat pie and peas, we are easy pleased.

23rd January 1998

Today the anchorage emptied and everyone went to Costco, an American Cash and Carry Store. The trip was organised by Paul of *Cat O Fun*, bulk buying to stock the boat up for the next 11 months in the Pacific to New Zealand. A bus arrived and the Yachties piled on board. Costco provided the transport free of charge. When we arrived at the store, an hour and a half bus journey later, there was a scramble for trolleys. As usual I got the one that would only go sideways. There was a sign over the door *NO SMOKING * NO DOGS * NO BARE FEET * NO GUNS*.

Firearms have to be deposited with the security man before you are allowed to enter, a bit like Dodge City in the days of Wyatt Earp. The security guard who was on the door checking in the guns was not to be missed. His pearl handled pistol had notches in it. Anyhow, we managed to buy all that was required at good prices. The store provided free coffee and cookies (wee buns) during the whole adventure. As we left, the security man twirled his pistol and nodded casually at us.

Arriving back at the marina, the bus was unloaded after a whip-round for the driver, a tip for looking after us so well. So much stuff was bought that Costco had to lay on another van. A couple of hours later *Breakaway* was re-stocked and slowly sinking under the weight. Kirstie asked was it not dangerous when a yacht's waterline went under the water. I explained this wasn't really a problem, we just keep painting it up higher.

Anyhow, after all the excitement of shopping I joined Bob of *Celtic Wave* for a quiet beer. His daughter Beth came rushing in.

"Dad, you know First Aid, don't you?"

The problem was on a boat called *Colleen* owned by Mike who we had previously met in Cartagena. At that time a lovely lady called Jane was on board with him, but things weren't working out and on arrival at Colon she left to go home to England. Mike had advertised for crew in the yachting press. The crew had subsequently arrived and Mike had left her on board to familiarise herself with the boat while he went ashore for supplies. When Mike eventually went back to the boat he found his new crewmember comatose in the front cabin. She could not be wakened and he called for help.

This is when *Celtic Wave*, Bob and I came in, leaving Tom of *Axe Calibre* to phone for an ambulance. Off we went in a dinghy, out into the anchorage. On our arrival at *Colleen* we found the lady in question in her bunk unconscious, Bob took her pulse and I was checking her breathing. Now the forepeak of a yacht is not very spacious. We had placed her in the recovery position. Shining a torch in her pupils brought no response. Nipping and pinching was not provoking any reaction. We had a severe problem on our hands.

Meanwhile Tom had organised a boat to transport the paramedics to the scene. While Bob administered First Aid, I started to search her luggage for signs of drugs, insulin or something along those lines. At this stage we had a patient near death. I found a glass of straight gin on a shelf and told Mike to check his drinks locker. Meanwhile Bob was still working and praying hard that we didn't have a fatality on our hands.

Help eventually arrived and we were glad to see expert medical personnel on board. The patient was then taken by stretcher on the workboat to shore where an ambulance was waiting. Bob and I made our way ashore to finish our beer. Later that night Mike came to *Breakaway* to tell us the medical prognosis, that his new crewmember had suffered a stroke and was on her way to Panama City to see a neurosurgeon. On her way she woke up with a hangover.

Who am I to say, but Mike has a serious problem on his hands and the only way to solve it is a one-way ticket to England. Out here, when at anchor, most boats have a sundowner. That's the term for a couple of drinks in the evening and the chance to get together with friends and relax over the day's adventures. With rum at £2 per bottle you have to exercise some control, not always easy, and you certainly do not hit the bottle when passage making.

On to brighter things, Christine is quite worried about the menu for the transit of the Canal as the rules are that a Panamanian Pilot must be on board for the duration. She keeps asking me,

"What if the Pilot doesn't like chicken, maybe he's a vegetarian."

Let me tell you he can stretch or starve. I'm just worried about the Canal and losing our $100 deposit. Though why should I worry, if the lock operators get it wrong, they will crush *Breakaway* like an eggshell and there's nothing I can do about it.

In the next few days a new ocean will mean new places to explore. The peaceful sea lies ahead of us. After a year of gentle cruising we go to work again. The next trip is 4,000 miles. At our speed it could mean 40 days. Let's hope it will only take 39.

Off we go again.

Christine

There is a lot of work preparing Breakaway for the Pacific and another pair of hands has been a great help. Add to that a much-needed extra crewmember on board for the crossing. Every inch of available space has been used and any gaps left are filled with fresh water containers in the hope that us girls will get a chance to wash our hair at least once.

There will be eight people to feed during the transit of the Canal for two days and the food and drinks consumed will have to be replenished at Panama City, our last stocking up place before the Pacific. It has been quite stressful, but tonight finds us back at anchor, waiting for the transit of the Canal. We have done our best to prepare Breakaway and ourselves and are now relaxed, looking forward to the arrival of the Pilot at 06:00 in the morning.

PS We weren't too relaxed an hour ago. When leaving the marina and attempting to pull up the stern anchor, it was caught on another chain. Bob, as quick thinking as ever, donned his Jacques Cousteau Junior Adventurers underwater mask and snorkel kit, recently purchased at Costco, and jumped over and freed us from our bondage to the cheers of the ever present onlookers.

Breakaway tied alongside another yacht, waiting for the last lock gate to open. The Pacific lies beyond.

The Pacific, Balboa Yacht Club, Panama 08 56N 79 33.2W

Breakaway now sits bobbing her bows on a mooring in the Pacific. We have made our transit of the Canal and managed to achieve it in one day. This is rare. Our Pilot arrived at 05:00. He wasn't due until 06:00. As he came alongside he shouted,

"Have you no VHF radio? I've been looking for you since 04:30."

I thought at the time, if I was the Captain of an oil tanker, he might have shown more respect. I shouted across to the Pilot boat,

"If there's been a mistake, it's not on my part."

Two angry men in the early hours of the morning. A few minutes later when he came on board, Christine went slow ahead as Kirstie and I lifted the anchor. *Breakaway* then went alongside *Celtic Wave* to collect the line-handling team who had also had a rough awakening. As we moved out into the Canal in the darkness you could cut the atmosphere with a knife. Not a good start. Approaching the first lock I shook our Pilot's hand and said,

"Good morning, my name is Bob, the day starts now."

He laughed and asked was the coffee ready yet,

"Call me Abdell."

Before the day was over we were all the best of friends as we offered him the hospitality of *Breakaway* and he looked after us with his expertise and knowledge of the Panama Canal. At 17:00 the Pilot boat picked him up at the bridge of the Americas where two great continents are joined, the transit was completed.

While we made our weary way to a mooring at Balboa Yacht Club, *Axe Calibre* arrived also, just an hour after us. It seemed a good idea for both boat parties to go ashore and treat our line handlers to a drink. Now at home yacht clubs concern themselves about the social status of their members and guests. I have spent many hours in committee rooms while the Commodore and Officers vetted people for membership. Here life is much simpler. The rules are posted on the notice board as you enter.

'Wear shoes at all times - Ladies there can be no soliciting in the Yacht Club, this includes the car park'.

I broke the rules again, I'd forgotten my shoes. As I looked round there seemed to be some interesting female sailors. Maybe our own clubs have got it right.

Anyhow, we managed to make our way home to *Breakaway* slightly merry from celebrating a marvellous experience, but otherwise intact. What do we do now? People on other yachts keep asking the question, "Which way are you going to cross?" We are not really sure. There's a new ocean to explore that covers one third of the world. Do we turn right and move up Central America, Costa Rica, Nicaragua, and Guatemala, Mexico?

On the other hand the winds blow fair for the West Coast of Colombia and Peru, maybe Pitcairn and Easter Island, Pitcairn, where the mutineers of HMS *Bounty* landed and set up home, Easter Island famous for its statues that were impossible to build. The other option is the islands of Galapagos, lying 800 miles to the west and well placed to allow us to rest up for the big haul to French Polynesia and the islands of the Marquesas. The trade winds pick up next month, the cyclone season ends in March but it will take a month of good sailing if we leave now. We can then reach the Marquesas when the winds have settled down in that area.

I spent this morning checking our sails. There was no sign of damage except for a small cigarette hole burnt into the staysail. As the only smoker on board I had to fix it. Life must be wonderful if you travel through it with no faults and guilt free. Kirstie and her mother tut-tutted as I sewed. Maybe sails should have a government health warning.

The ocean that now lies ahead of us is the biggest in the world but Pacific means 'peaceful'. It was named by the old navigators. Let's hope they were right. We are a small boat on a big sea. In a couple of days we will be living together for a month or more in a confined space. The big bonus is having Kirstie with us. Her job back home at the moment is delivering mail in Carrickfergus but out here her role is to stand watch.

A month at sea can mean flat calms or ocean gales. Still, the mail has to go through. We will all have to push *Breakaway* hard to make sure Kirstie is back to deliver it. She certainly delivered a lot of letters to us. This is one of the things we miss, news from home, nobody's fault but ours. We give postal addresses to ports, and then don't arrive there. For *Breakaway* and her crew there is no turning back. The winds and currents of the world now decide our destiny.

Breakaway's Pacific crew at the Bridge of the Americas

Christine
It seemed sensible to visit the dentist before the big push across the Pacific to make sure there are no tooth-achy nights ahead of me.

We are at present anchored off what used to be an American Military Base. The Panama Canal Authority has taken over but it's a great place, with all the facilities expected by Americans and left behind for the enjoyment of the rest of us.

I was impressed with the dental surgery and the young Panamanian dentist who took great care and did a super job on my teeth. Even after praising him to the heavens, Bob still wouldn't chance it. I hope he doesn't suffer out there on the ocean. Because if he does, so will the rest of us on board.

Log of *Breakaway* on Passage to Galapagos

22nd February 1998

We are now 450 miles into the Pacific heading towards the Equator, struggling every inch of the way in the light winds as *Breakaway* tries to cross the doldrums, looking for the trade wind belt.

Axe Calibre is about 20 miles astern of us, *Celtic Wave* and *Marie Lee* haven't been seen for three days. They disappeared over the horizon with light weather sails set. Tom and Dee on *Axe Calibre* have SSB radio so we can keep in touch over a long distance. The other two yachts are only equipped with VHF which works over 20 miles or so. We are out of contact with them.

On the radio net yesterday an American called up in a very distressed state. Their refrigeration system had broken down and their whole world was collapsing. An expert came on to explain that they had allowed the system to become iced up and the only cure was to bring the temperature up again using their hair dryer. There's another world out there we are not part of.

Kirstie has made us a rain catcher to supplement our fresh water supply. Tonight was its first trial. She managed to fill two, one-gallon containers in the five-minute downpour. It looks like a canvas bath and hangs under the boom. The rain runs off the mainsail into the catcher and from there it is caught in a container. The system works well. The first fill we use for washing as there is usually some salt contamination from the mainsail. After that we are in business with fine drinking water.

25th February 1998

Progress is painfully slow. We have used up most of our diesel, there are now only a few gallons left in the tank to help us enter Academy Bay, Isla Santa Cruz on the Galapagos Archipelago. Yesterday *Axe Calibre* drifted into sight. They are also short of fuel. We decided to use the fuel capacity of both boats. Tom took us in tow and we suffered the indignity of being trailed across the ocean. This evening it is our turn to do the honours as we tow *Axe Calibre* through the dark hours.

26th February1998

The wind picked up this morning, still light but enough to make the boat move, and with the help of current we are doing two knots. Land seems a long way off. Around noon today the moon covered the sun and we experienced a total eclipse. As *Breakaway* moves along the path of Totality, the temperature has started to drop as the sky darkens. It didn't last long but it was a first for us. Meanwhile we still have *Axe Calibre* tied behind us on our own path of tow-tality. The sun appeared again as we continue to slowly cross the Pacific, sheltering under canvas covers, trying to find some shade.

28th February 1998

The Equator was crossed at 01:00 hours. The sails were just filling as *Breakaway* ghosted along with Christine on watch. She called Kirstie and me on deck where there were four glasses of Bushmills Whiskey ready for the occasion. As soon as we felt the bump we poured one into the sea for the pleasure of King Neptune. We sipped ours slowly and quietly enjoyed the moment. *Axe Calibre* crossed one hour later. We called on the radio to congratulate them. It seemed right to have another one. King Neptune wasn't left out.

We spotted the islands of the Galapagos at 15:00 hours, it's still another day before *Breakaway* would reach the anchorage but the worst was behind us.

End of Log

Galapagos Islands 00 44S 90 18W
(Half way down and a quarter of the way around the world)

1 March 1998
We laid two anchors at mid-day. There were three other cruising yachts already in Academy Bay. All the other boats were local tourist crafts plying their trade, taking visitors from all over the world out to see the wildlife that the islands are famous for.

Without the necessary visa, bureaucracy had to be faced. With 900 miles behind us it was time to go ashore and pay our respects to the Port Captain. The most we could hope for was a 72-hour stopover. I explained in Spanish, which was about equal to his English, that we needed to fill up with fuel. He arranged this for us and we were told *Breakaway* was welcome to stay for 10 days.

Next it was off to the Naval Base to see Immigration, however, it was bad timing as the Navy was playing the Police at a very competitive game of football and the Immigration Officer was the referee. The game was halted while he explained to us he was far too busy and would we mind coming back in two days. So much for bureaucracy. We never did find out the result of the match but it's the only game I have seen where the referee was carrying a gun. There didn't seem to be too many disputes about his decisions.

The wildlife on Galapagos is unique as there were no natural predators to fear, until the arrival of man. It ranges from white tipped reef sharks, four foot long iguanas, pelicans, sea lions, penguins and boobies, to the giant turtles and tortoises which gave the islands their name Galapagos.

After the drama of the football match, we stopped for something to eat and a cold beer. The cafe was at the waterside and the tide was in, covering the floor of the dining room in a foot of water. No one seemed to mind. There was a large heron standing on one leg a couple of feet away, watching us with interest.

A lava gull, of which there are only 400 breeding pairs in the world, was helping Kirstie to eat her chips. If they all have this guy's attitude, it's not surprising there are so few of them. He certainly didn't take surviving seriously or maybe he had done all the begging he could for the day.

I had to take a visit to the hospital the next day, my elbow had been troubling me for a few weeks and was progressively becoming more painful. I was told I had tennis elbow.

I wonder does Martina Navratilova ever get salt-water boils?

Fresh food ready to be stowed for *Breakaway*'s passage

Galapagos to Marquesas, French Polynesia

14th March 1998   Day 1

Just as we were about to leave Puerto Ayora in the Galapagos to start our 3,000 mile crossing of the Pacific to French Polynesia, an American yacht dragged it's anchor and fell down on *Breakaway*, fouling our stern anchor. No damage was done, but our anchor warp was fouling his chain. After half an hour we disentangled the mess and set off in a light breeze. We managed to sail for the rest of the day and with the help of the current were clear of the islands in the early hours of the morning.

15th March   Day 2
Flat calm conditions with a mirror sea reflecting the few clouds in the sky. The engine is running at low revs with the only ripple on the water caused by *Breakaway*. The trade winds are reported to be filling in at Longitude 100W, that's a long way ahead of us. Still, early days yet. When half of our fuel is used, and if there is still no wind, we will drift with the current, leaving enough fuel for our landfall at the Marquesas. The Pacific is the largest ocean in the world, we can't motor the distance. This one could take a long time.

17th March   Day 4 - St. Patrick's Day
Nothing has been sighted since leaving Galapagos, except for the occasional sea bird. There is still very little wind but the sea is calm and the sails are pulling us along slowly.

On the radio this morning our friends on *Axe Calibre* reported battery problems, their alternator having failed. Tom had another one on board but can't find it. We are all a bit like that. We carry so much on our boats the stuff at the bottom of the pile takes forever to turn up. I will be talking to him again shortly. It may mean a retreat to the Galapagos for them as they are only 100 miles out. To continue is a distance of 2,900 miles. *Axe Calibre* has now turned back for repairs. The temperature is in the high 90s. A school of Pilot whales surrounded us. Not a bad day to turn the stone over, start the potato planting and what have you.

18th March   Day 5

Still no wind. We continue to motor towards the southwest in the hope of better things to come. Near disaster was averted today, only by quick thinking on my part. Having my lunchtime beer (rationed to one per day) and a cigarette (haven't kicked the habit yet), the boat lurched causing me to drop the ciggy down my shorts which were hanging loose because of the heat. Only lightning reflexes saved me as I poured the beer down the front of my shorts, averting any long-term damage. Kirstie and Christine appeared on deck to find me with my hand groping about trying to retrieve the soggy butt.

Christine said, "Your Dad must be out in that heat rash again."

22nd March   Day 9

The trade winds have finally filled in. *Breakaway* is on her way with 2,200 miles to go to landfall. This is what sailing is all about, a fair wind sending you in the right direction. It seemed to take us forever to clear the doldrums. Before the advent of engines this area must have been a nightmare. The *El Nino effect hasn't helped things this season. Let's hope the sleigh ride continues.

26th March   Day 13

We are still carrying good wind. Our best day so far has been 140 miles, but we are averaging 120 on a 24-hour run, a good reputable speed for a boat the size of *Breakaway*. Changing watch at midnight, a ship crossed our bow about two miles ahead of us. I called him on the radio but there was no reply. We work a three-hour on and six off watch system, giving us plenty of rest. Kirstie on board makes all the difference, allowing us to have a better sleep pattern.

30th March   Day 17

The distance to go is now down to less than 1,300 miles and the winds continue to be steady. Routine on board is now firmly established as *Breakaway* moves westwards. *Boreal*, a French catamaran, reported problems on the radio net this morning. Their hydraulic steering had burst a pipe and they were drifting out of control. Other yachts in the vicinity were heading to help but the closest is two days away. Let's hope the problems are solved.

31st March   Day 18
Boreal has effected a jury rig rudder using a spinnaker pole over the stern, lashed to a piece of wood. The wind is fading away on us but we have enough to keep moving westwards slowly. Because of El Nino, there doesn't seem to be any of the one to two knot favourable currents we were expecting. A cyclone is moving southeast from the Tuamotu Islands. It is 1,000 miles away from us but maybe *Breakaway* will feel the effects, with a change of wind direction to our advantage. Every morning now the deck is strewn with flying fish that have landed during the night.

3rd April   Day 21
A foul, black, evil night with torrential rain and no visibility at all, we continue to move west slowly. Two birds, we think storm petrels, took refuge on the main boom and roosted for the night. They showed no intention of leaving the next morning. I have found a use for the flying fish - we fed them to our two hitchhikers. These birds of the ocean have no fear of man. I don't suppose they have encountered humans before. We were hand feeding them. *Breakaway*'s decks now look like the bottom of a parrot's cage. They are going to have to go.

5th April   Day 23
Into our third week at sea. The night watch was wonderful, with the stars in all their glory - the Plough to the north and the Southern Cross to the south. *Breakaway* drifted quietly along the path of the moon. Come daylight, the gentle breeze dies. We had enough diesel left for 300 miles with a distance of 750 to go. The birds have flown the roost. We don't have that option. No doubt the wind will come back.

A whale has just surfaced 30 feet from us, much larger than *Breakaway*. Let's hope he's friendly. He was, followed us for a few minutes, then just gave us a nod and carried on his way.

6th April   Day 24
Breakaway rendezvoused with a Danish yacht in mid ocean today. *Ci*

Ju, pronounced C U, as in, "See you Jimmy". They came alongside and we gave them freshly baked bread straight out of the oven. In return they passed over three cold beers and a bottle of whiskey. Both parties were well pleased. When darkness came contact was lost. Still, it was nice to have company, even for a short while.

10th April   Day 28

For the last few days, *Walkabout* has been on the radio with engine problems. It has been overheating. Ian would call up explaining the symptoms and various yachts would offer their opinions as to the probable cause. I spent quite a few hours telling him how to change a head gasket by remote control. It worked for a while, the engine running sweet. Alas, no more, the gearbox has now seized. From all the experts there is only silence. There is a limit to even the Yachties' skill. Ian is emotionally disturbed and drifting, about 80 miles from us, with no wind. He is also suffering a sense of humour loss. We are on our way to help. The least we can do is give him a tow. By the way, he has plenty of fuel and we are very low.

12th April   Day 30

The wind has been fair for the last couple of days. *Walkabout* has managed to sail, making good progress. We are now about 90 miles from the anchorage. If the breeze holds, the anchor should go down tomorrow. Fingers crossed, so far so good.

   Distance 3,300 miles – 32 days at sea.

Christine
* The El Nino effect happens usually in four year cycles, generally about Christmas time, hence the name 'boy child' current, and runs south from the Gulf of Panama. At the equator it meets the Humbolt Current running north from Cape Horn. During an El Nino year the warm current from Panama forces the cold water further south than usual causing a change in the weather patterns of the world. But it also creates the diversity of wildlife that makes the Galapagos Islands famous. It was here of course that Darwin got his ideas for the 'Theory of Evolution'.

Hiva Oa, French Polynesia 09.48S 139.01W

The anchor is down in Hiva Oa. *Walkabout* is also safely in and is lying about 60 feet from us. *Breakaway*'s crew is going ashore shortly. I wonder will our legs still work. We have sailed 3,300 miles since leaving Galapagos. It was all fairly uneventful and so it should be.

Swimming is not advised at Hiva Oa due to the large population in this particular harbour. The dinghy ride to the dock in our small, wobbly inflatable should be interesting.

A strange thing happened on our first walk ashore after a month at sea. The yacht crews gathered together and headed off to see the Authorities. Karen of *Walkabout* was first to go, she fainted as we stopped for some water along the way.

Welcome to French Polynesia

Christine then collapsed in the bank – passed out on the floor in front of the other customers and not one alcoholic drink taken. Kirstie was found sitting outside with her head in her hands feeling dizzy. What was it with all these females? I spoke too soon. While heading back to the anchorage, I succumbed and was physically sick by the side of the road accompanied by a blinding headache. It must have been the lack of physical activity and unaccustomed walking in the heat. I took to my bed. The ladies all recovered and went out to enjoy local food and company at a 'Pension' up in the hills. That first night of undisturbed sleep was absolute heaven.

Marquesas to Tahiti, Society Islands

Breakaway was on the road again. Our stop over at Hiva Oa, Marquesas was a short one and *Breakaway* was bound for Tahiti. Kirstie had to go home and the only place we could organise flights from was Papeete, capital of the French Polynesia Society Islands.

After 32 days at sea, a couple of weeks swinging to the anchor wouldn't have hurt at all. Still, there would be plenty of time ahead of us for that. Tahiti was a 750 mile run that will take us through the Tuamotu Archipelago, known as the Low or Dangerous Islands, the final resting place of many ships. Most of the areas we were sailing were surveyed early in the last century and the modern hydrographic experts haven't caught up yet.

The Polynesians themselves know these waters well. Long before the Europeans had managed to cross the Atlantic, these sailors had explored all of the Pacific, as far north as Hawaii, the Marquesas to the east, Pitcairn and Easter Island, with New Zealand in the south.

It is now recognised that the Polynesians ranked among the best sailors in the world, travelling in canoes sometimes as big as 100 feet long, carrying all they needed to survive and propelled by anything up to 80 paddlers. With palm fronds for shelter and stocked with coconuts to supply them with food and drink, they covered thousands of miles between the islands.

The normal winds and currents move from east to west. Waiting for a break in this weather pattern they would set off certain in the knowledge that the currents would bring them home again.

Before leaving Hiva Oa we encountered French bureaucracy in the form of the local Gendarmerie. When we paid him a visit to sign in and out of the island, we were informed of a monetary bond that had to be placed, amounting to the price of an air fare home for the three of us, something in the region of 3,000 US dollars. You can claim this back when leaving French Polynesia, but lose about £450 on the transaction. Not a good idea. He waved his arms about in true Gallic fashion. We nodded our heads, tut tutted in sympathy and then left. The problem would have to be faced in Tahiti. The French administrators also do their nuclear testing in the Tuamotus, which of course makes world headlines. No wonder they are known as the Dangerous Isles.

The Point of Venus, named by Captain Cook, is on the North West corner of Tahiti and the area behind the reef is still known as Cook's anchorage, where he first observed the transit of the planet Venus. About 500 miles to the west, a tropical depression has been trying to make its mind up for the last few weeks. When a low-pressure system of this nature encounters water of a certain temperature, it then develops into a tropical revolving storm.

As luck would have it, when we were about 100 miles off Tahiti, the sea started to heat up. We were encountering the fringe effects of cyclone 'Alan'. Not the ideal conditions for making a landfall on a strange island.

The winds freshened throughout the hours of darkness. Eventually we picked up the lights of Tahiti on the horizon. At sea *Breakaway* was safe and in severe conditions we had learnt to put up with discomfort and get on with it. As we closed the Point of Venus with its strong light, decisions had to be made. Should we close with the land or keep out at sea? Land is dangerous as it can bring you to a sudden stop. The island started to give us some shelter from the wind as the lights of Papeete appeared. The three of us were riding out a gale while two miles away from us people were enjoying the nightlife of the capital. We made the decision to go and join them.

The harbour entrance was through a coral reef marked by red and green buoys, carefully obscured by the lights of the airport. We approached with trepidation, ready to retreat at any time. As in all things, there comes a point of no return.

Suddenly it was all over and *Breakaway* was inside the reef and enjoying a quiet, calm, tropical night. As we re-grouped and prepared to anchor, Christine put the kettle on. We finally settled a couple or 300 yards from a cruise liner. Drinking strong tea, heavily laced with condensed milk, Kirstie, Christine and I sat and enjoyed the sounds of a jazz band on the liner. What was all the panic about?

Olle P, our Dutch friends, and *Walkabout* were still out there. The radio reported the following morning that an American yacht, *Moon Shadow,* was driven up onto a reef in the Tuamotus. Everyone on board was safe but at that stage we did not know the fate of the boat. Out here the loss of the boat meant the loss of a home with all that entails.

Breakaway was now safely tied up to the quay wall in Tahiti but we worried about the others.

Tahiti 17 23S 149 22W

4th May 1998

Breakaway is still safely tied up to the yacht quay in Papeete. Fifty yards in front of us is the main road with a volume of traffic the likes of which I have never seen. The walkway in front of the yachts is the favourite place for the Tahitians to spend their warm, tropical evenings. Mums, dads and children, accompanied by their grandparents, appear every night to stroll past the boats. The fathers stop to explain to the children where we have come from. They point out the various rigs, explaining what we are all doing wrong. It's like living in a fish bowl. We love it. To find it boring would be impossible. This must be the best people-watching place in the world.

Behind the town the extinct volcanoes, covered in lush vegetation, rise up into the sky until the clouds obscure them. To our stern ferry boats and tugs move about all day. Last night a cruise liner entered the port to the sound of Polynesian music. This morning the passengers descended on the town to buy their souvenirs. We decided to treat ourselves to a cheap meal as it was Sunday. The restaurant was closed for lunch.

After two months at sea, with the three of us making our own way across the world's biggest ocean, there was a lot of excitement as we tied up at the town quay at Papeete. The sound of the traffic wasn't an aggravation as we slept the sleep of the just. Two days later the traffic fumes and airborne germs had taken their toll. Sore throats and headaches were the order of the day. A heavy cold soon followed. We had become accustomed to the fresh ozone of the ocean and no germs. The loom of the land with the city lights was blocking our view of the stars. *Breakaway* was becoming an apartment, not a boat.

The entrance to Papeete – reef breaking in the distance

We threw off the ropes and moved down round the corner, still inside the reef, looking for somewhere we could jump off the boat for a swim in clean, clear water. We found it. The locals paddle past in their outrigger canoes, big men covered in the most intricate of tattoos, moving their small craft along by muscle power alone. At night in a flat calm the anchor chain rumbles over the coral, the only other sound being the Pacific Ocean breaking on the reef that gives *Breakaway* shelter.

We catch the local bus to Papeete to shop. As the passengers climb on board the converted lorry, all the "Bonjours" are swapped. Arriving in the market, with the scent of flowers, it's more "allez oops" and "you are late today Bob".

The Tahitians are the most charming of people.

The wind is still blowing harder than it should be in the Pacific and *Breakaway* is ahead of most of the yachts. *Chinook II* lost their propeller coming through the Taumotu Islands. Leigh called me up on the radio when they were 80 miles out of Tahiti in strong winds. Darkness was falling fast when he was off the pass through the reef and it would have been dangerous for us to make our way through the coral to give him a tow. A German yacht *Tradewind III* tied to the town quay did the honours and went out and plucked our Aussie friends safely into the commercial harbour.

We missed the party. *Areaka*, another Australian yacht, still hasn't turned up. Ross is now officially reported missing. Nothing has been heard from him since he left Galapagos.

A young couple on an English yacht called *Casper* haven't been heard from for a few days. It is worrying because there is a baby on the way. Nancy is Dutch, eight months pregnant and would like the baby to be born in Tahiti. It's early days yet but the news of *Areaka* has sobered us all. Nick and Nancy have a lot of miles under their keel. No doubt they will turn up. Sometimes a yacht tucks in behind a mountain for shelter and the land blocks the radio signals. Let's hope this is the case with *Casper.*

Kirstie flew home yesterday. We are going to miss her, me in particular as she had taken over all the deck work. I nearly forgot how sails go up and down. The other good thing about her was the fact that she went shopping with Christine, taking the pressure off me.

You must understand I could now go on Mastermind with specialist knowledge of 'Supermarkets of the World 1996 – 1998'. How I hate it, the ways of women are beyond me. They pick up things, put them down, lift them again, examine the price, put them down once more, have a discussion and then say, "I never liked that". Would you even consider buying something you didn't like?

Another thing, they always steal plastic bags. If you just asked the girl on the till she would give you them, what does she care. Oh no, it has to be done surreptitiously. On my last visit to the supermarket the embarrassment was too much.

With my shorts filled with plastic bags, Christine said,

"Straighten up and walk quickly."

Never again. Anyhow, thanks for your help Kirstie. It was a good 5,000 miles.

9th May 1998

The day starts early out here. The local market begins at 04:30 with banks and other businesses opening their doors to the customers at 07:30. My first job in the morning is to head off to the local bakery for a French baguette and two chocolate croissants. The girls in the shop now know my order. Everyone wears a flower behind his or her ear. Behind the right ear indicates you are married, the left means you are available. They pick them from the bushes and trees growing in abundance along the streets. By the time I arrive, the market is in full swing with the ground floor devoted to the flower sellers and fruit vendors. It's a very colourful start to the day. Towards the back is the fish and meat section. Everything is spotlessly clean.

Christine
Good news, Nick and Nancy on Casper have safely arrived at Tahiti. The message had been passed over the airways so everyone can relax. We are enjoying the anchorage but are back to being thrifty with water again. Today our activity was snorkelling over the reef. It was a wonderful experience. The exotic tropical fish go about their business undisturbed by our presence and they are just my size, the biggest being six inches long and posing no threat whatever.
It's like floating on air because the ocean is so warm.
The suggestion is you swim during the day and not enter the water late afternoon or at night. That's when the sharks come in to feed. And don't swim in murky water – they might grab hold thinking you are a tasty fish.
We have just solved our water problem. Going along the shore in the dinghy, still in deep water, there was a small buoy attached to a hose. With the use of pliers you can have water in abundance. When we are ready to leave, Breakaway can be filled up with water from Tahiti, the only safe source as it is not recommended to take on water in the other islands. We learn all these tit-bits of life from the Pilot Books on board, necessary reading for our way of life.

Captain Cook's Bay, Moorea 17 30.16S 149 49.14W

Breakaway lives in a floating village of people; a community that moves around the world and of course we visit our neighbours. Tonight was *R Phurst*'s turn. A few nights ago they were on board *Breakaway* for a bit of Irish fun and a bowl of stew. This evening in a strong wind we went across the anchorage to join Bruce and Jean on their catamaran for a sundowner, what Americans call cocktails.

They had left home after their son of 17 had died of muscular dystrophy. In many ways they are living the adventures for a boy who never had a chance. Mark Twain wrote *Tom Sawyer* and *Huckleberry*

Finn for his son who died at an early age also, relating the adventures and dreams his child would never experience.

The wind was gusting through the anchorage up to gale force strength today and continuing to freshen. *Walkabout* is out on the ocean tonight along with the South African family on *La Rouche* who have to be in New Zealand for July to qualify for residency. The winds are blowing hard out of the south with a big sea running and neither yacht can lay a course for Tonga, the desired destination. They are taking waves into the cockpit and are cold and wet.

Walkabout's mainsail is in disarray again but Ian will muddle through. The one thing that never ceases to amaze me on this voyage is the close friends we make, all the yachts showing concern for each other. There are about 250 small boats circumnavigating at any one time, spread over the oceans of the world. It is understandable I suppose that when you meet another travelling yacht in an anchorage there is a get-together to recount tales of gales, the high cost of living in French Polynesia and where the next best place to stock up is.

The winds have now started to ease and *Breakaway* is moving around on her chain, gently pushed by the current. Bora Bora, 100 miles to the west of us, is reported to be the prettiest island in all of the oceans. That is a big claim to make, as it's unlikely anyone has seen all the others.

Our present anchorage in Captain Cook's Bay, Moorea, is hard to beat. The jagged mountains seem to continually change shape, from early morning when the first light from the east hits them, to the evening when the bay darkens and the sun slips out of sight, leaving the boat nice and cool after the heat of the day.

It's great to sleep covered with a
Olle P, our Dutch friends, just pulled
Papeete, Tahiti. Hans' wife, Mariann
a few weeks and his daughter Astri

They hired a car, inviting
Astrid especially wanted to s
waterfalls. The Fiat Panda is
off-the road capabilities. We
Italian engineering could go no
'shank's pony'.

Hans cut walking sticks to help us on
in the forest in search of the waterfall, the track an
jungle encroached. From one of the clearings we could
and Hans led us on. Now the Dutch have done this with the
before, causing all sorts of problems. Still we followed him.

Half an hour later the heavens opened. It was time to retreat to the car. The path we had climbed was itself a waterfall of mud and slime as we made our way down. Hans was the first one to go onto his back as his feet left him. Christine was next, followed by Astrid and myself as we slipped and slithered down what was a six inch deep river of mud, mainly using our backsides to support us. When we came to the gentle stream we had forded on the assent, it was now a raging torrent. Covered in mud we didn't care anymore, plunging into it and carrying onwards – at least it washed the mud off. As we arrived back at the car the deluge had stopped, steam was rising from the jungle, and us. It seemed prudent to stick to the roads for the rest of the day.

The houses on the island are beautiful, wooden pre-fabricated bungalows with roofs covered in palm fronds. The gardens are tidy - everything in keeping with the surroundings. The majority of the islanders live close to the shore, round the coast with the reef protecting them from the Pacific.

Dogs bark furiously as you go by, running out to protect their properties. When you get close they wag their tails, turn around and go home again. I am slightly wary of dogs even though we always kept them at home. I met a man with a dog once and asked him did his

dog bite? He said no
off, I berated him,
I though
That's
It pay
At t
complete
home.
Thin
inv
c

and his dog immediately bit me. As I fought it

you said your dog didn't bite."

not my dog," he replied.

to be cautious.

he bottom of each garden are a few graves, well cared for, with headstones. It seems out here you can get buried at Now this of course has certain advantages, mainly the cost. of the saving in funeral cars. It also means you don't get lved in a long carry around the town on a bad day, disrupting mmerce and traffic. The downside is tripping over your relations on the way to work every morning, never mind the problems that would arise if you ever wanted to move house. Do you swap great grannies with the new owners or do you take them with you? It doesn't bear thinking about.

The Pacific hasn't been an easy ocean for us to cross. This year we were not subjected to the normal weather patterns because of El Nino, but things are now starting to settle down. I have just talked to *Walkabout* and *La Rouche* on the radio. The winds have eased, the seas are settled and everything is OK with the boats. They will be in Tonga in a couple of days.

Christine
Bob is not feeling the best today. His ear problem is back again.
Usually every time he's been swimming or snorkelling a little vinegar goes into his ears and that seems to keep them right. The routine has lapsed and he is suffering as a consequence. Kees (pronounced Case), another Dutchman, our hippie friend from Happy Island, sailed in yesterday. He had the perfect cure for earache. Par boil a large, sliced, round section of onion, wrap it in some soft material and lay it on the ear while it is still warm.

'Very powerful things, onions," says Kees, "Look how they make you cry."
Bob is feeling a little better. Whether it was the prescription ear drops, the pain killers or the onion, or a combination of all three we

may never know, but one thing is for sure, I'll have the vinegar
ready next time he comes out of the water.

The Chance of Employment

25th June 1998

Most of the boats we meet sailing in the Pacific are under the British Red Ensign. Next in line has to be the Aussies and New Zealanders, closely followed by the Americans with the odd Canadian, then the Europeans and lastly the French, who have to be the sailors who do it with the most flair. Irish, well...there's not a lot of them about.

Nearly all the yachts have a card they hand out. It gives the name of husband and wife, or captain and crew, along with the boat's name. Most have the address in email, which to me is some form of modern hieroglyphics beyond the understanding of a man of my age.

I used to have a business card once. Initially I was very pleased with it, feeling it was an indication that I had made my way in the world. From the point of view of generating work it was unsuccessful. Christine eventually pointed out I had the wrong phone number on it. The best card I have seen out here so far was from Curley, Luke and crew of *Silver Harvest,* a converted fishing trawler we met in the Caribbean. The back of his card says:

'Boat sales, antique sales, whiskey, caviar, ocean safaris, wars fought, bars emptied, parties crashed. Orgies organised, birds pulled, revolutions started, virgins found, bribes taken, elections fixed, partners pinched, alibis supplied, dragons slain (24 hours' notice required), scrap metal dealt, salvage and demolition diving, sign writing, welding, Oxyacetylene cutting, chandlery bought and sold, Leatherman stockists and worldwide problems solved'.

They, like us were also out of work.

Now you can understand after all of this I was quite excited to get a call from Debra, the American single-hander on *Reverie,* asking if I could find some spare parts for her in Papeete. Her self-steering had failed because of two hydraulic lip seals. Debra gave me the measurements over the radio that night. It was hard to sleep with the thrill of it all.

Next morning Christine made me a sandwich and a flask of tea. I could not wait to go to work. The search for the seals was on. I walked 10 miles that day around every outlet in Tahiti, also all the stockists of outboard motors, suppliers to the car trade and forklift manufacturers, to no avail. Next morning on the radio I explained the situation to the boss. There was a pause and then she asked was Alan of *Incandescent* tied up close to me. I immediately went and told Alan to turn on his radio. She gave him the same instructions she had given me the day before. Alan said he would do his best.

After many years of self-employment, I had forgotten the trauma of being sacked. Now this is the man who held down 13 jobs in Canada in six months. That was a record, even for me.

The morning after, with the initial feeling of rejection, you wake up and then realise there is no urgency, turn over, have a scratch, eventually reaching out for the book you were reading the night before and take the day as it comes.

Alan did no better than me and Debra still hasn't got her parts. Being a lazy man, after one day's unsuccessful efforts, I was going to phone home and have someone send them out. Still, it was nice to be employed again, even if only for a short time.

After the stress of the day, we go to bed early. The night hours are long in the tropics. The head hits the pillow at 8pm or so, but we are up at five or six to face the new day. For a few mornings, I listened to the radio to see if Debra would reinstate me.

Thankfully she didn't.

Autonomy Day in Papeete

When we first arrived in Tahiti to clear into French Polynesia, it was still early in the season for this part of the Pacific. The winds were strong and the weather bad. Only 100 miles to the west Raiatea was experiencing winds of 80 - 90 knots, causing loss of life.

We didn't linger too long but moved across to Moorea. Marianne of *Olle P* was due back from Holland and carrying mail for us, so we came back to Papeete Harbour to meet her and catch up with the news from home. What a difference a few weeks make. The harbour was full of yachts of all nationalities, gathering for Autonomy Day in the islands, 14 years of self-rule.

The party starts on 29th June and finishes on the 14th July when the French celebrate Bastille Day. Anyhow, the day started early. The morning had a holiday feel as no shops opened and from the boat we watched the preparations and barriers being erected on the route, just like the Lord Mayor's Show but with a tropical flavour.

People were appearing in Papeete from all the islands in French Polynesia, arriving by ferry, air and outrigger canoe, for a weekend's fun. For months the islands and atolls have been choosing a King and Queen to represent them, villages preparing costumes since last year. The whole thing was taking on the air of a Caribbean carnival. We had an early lunch and then went ashore to savour the atmosphere.

The celebrations started with the officials being led to a viewing stand by tattooed warriors wearing nothing but a loin cloth. The dignitaries in their formal attire looked over-dressed as it became obvious that a couple of centuries of Missionary zeal had failed.

The parade of the islands then got under way. The first to arrive on the scene was a representation of the Royal Tahitian court of the past, led by the King. In those days the high society showed their wealth by being in a cloak of feathers and adorned by flowers. The courtiers and warriors then followed, one and all carrying spears and clubs carved out of wood.

The females were costumed in grass skirts and a coconut cut in half. Where they wore the coconuts, I'll leave to your imagination.

Next in line were the Marquesains, the cannibals of Polynesia. I can only say that for one day at least, they took a trip into the past, though at the end of the parade it was reported they all gathered in McDonald's. But at the opening ceremony, with a plethora of spears about, the dignitaries looked slightly worried.

After the warriors, each village was led by the Chief, followed by parents and children. Every sport on the islands was represented. Basketball, judo, roller blading, soccer, parachute jumping, tennis, mountain biking, to name but a few, and the motor cycle club.

The motor cycles arrived in a blaze of light as darkness fell. Japanese engineering of the highest standard, the local Hell's Angels on their Harley Hogs. For me these guys put on the best display of the show. The glistening machinery snorted and roared, just wanting to speed away as they slowly followed the badminton players at walking pace. Maybe they have got it right out here. Do your own thing but don't interfere with others.

The night ended with the harbour lit up by the outrigger canoes giving a torch light display, followed by a firework show that would have taken the light out of your eyes. The topical night was ablaze as we sat on *Breakaway* with some friends to watch the evening show, with the sunset over Moorea giving its own display.

We have to start moving soon, weather is dictating again. It will be a pity to leave these islands. They are wildly expensive but compensate with the kindness of the people and the beauty of the mountains, which climb out of the sea, the sunrises and the sunsets.

Next week we have to move towards the Cook Group or maybe American Samoa, depending on the breeze. I think we will do an overnight to Bora Bora first. That could turn into a fortnight.

The people of Polynesia are wonderful, good looking, charming and happy. They seem to smile continually, ignoring the French influence, and at every opportunity going back to their roots. Even some of the missionaries are reported to have enjoyed these islands. Tomorrow we point *Breakaway* west for the Cooks and Tonga. We will always remember Tahiti, not only for the landfall in paradise but for the kindness of the inhabitants and the nicest Hell's Angels I ever met.

Christine

For our last night in Tahiti we decided to treat ourselves to an evening meal and made our way to a large car park by the ferry terminal. There we found the restaurant vans where you can have your choice of cuisine. Tonight we opted for Special Chow Mein and watched our food being prepared on a wok over an open fire.

After dinner, music from the dance competition drew us to the arena and for £5 per head we joined the audience. Pricey stuff for the Breakaway's budget but it was magic.

The drums taunting the dancers to make wild, erotic movements. The girls wore grass skirts with a band of tassels at the hips to accentuate the movement. The other style is a short wrap-around skirt bunched up around the waist to give the same effect. Headdresses of flowers, feathers or elaborate grasses set off the flowing, waist length hair. Really beautiful, and the fellers weren't half-bad either - a wonderful evening to add to our memories.

Rarotonga, Cook Islands 21 12S 159 47W

24th July 1998

In 1768 a French sailing vessel arrived in Tahiti. A bare breasted girl brought her canoe alongside and climbed on board. Once on deck, she let her pareu fall from her hips. Dressed as she was born, she bid them welcome. The French sailors, after many months at sea, of course averted their eyes. De Bougainville, the Captain, wrote in his log,

"We are in the Garden of Eden."

So the myth of the South Seas began. Today things have changed and the only people taking their clothes off are the European tourists. But still the South Pacific continues to act as a magnet to the dreamers of this world.

Don Silk, the Harbour Master here in Rarotonga, is a fine example of a dreamer, leaving New Zealand 37 years ago on a 26ft sailing boat he and his mate had built themselves. Don's wife was also part of the crew. They arrived in Rarotonga, fell in love with the island and got no further.

A much larger yacht was wrecked on the reef. Don and his mate Boyd managed to salvage the wreck and turned it into an island trader, working the atolls of the Cooks. Using trading goods to negotiate for the coconut crops around the atolls, they went from strength to strength and were eventually the proud owners of two small cargo vessels that wouldn't have been allowed out of harbour in our home waters. But they did all right. Don is now in charge of the harbour and rules with a rod of iron in a very relaxed way. He has written a book about his adventures, *From Kauri Trees to Sunlit Seas*. We bought it. I suspect every Yachtie does to try and keep the harbour fees down.

Tom Neill, another Kiwi who ended up in the Cooks, also wrote a book, *An Island to Oneself*. Tom is now dead and is buried in Rarotonga but if you ever get a chance to read the book, grab it. Tom put himself into exile on the most northern, uninhabited atoll, Suwarrow. For 16 years he lived there, alone except for the occasional yacht calling in.

Don and Tom were mates, one a hermit, the other an entrepreneur - I would have loved to have sat beside them as they swapped yarns at Trader Jacks, the local bar. Yachts still arrive in these islands chasing the South Seas dream. That young vahine who created the fantasy 200 years ago has a lot to answer for. Still, some people find their niche down here. Others go home disillusioned.

Two weeks ago a report came in from a yacht that an English couple had been cast ashore on Tom's old atoll of Suwarrow. They had hit the reef and were living off the land; the local patrol vessel hadn't enough fuel to go and rescue them. A £20million Sheikh's motor yacht *Golden Odyssey* happened to be in Rarotonga harbour. The bold Don explained the situation and off he went on board the Sheikh's yacht to rescue the stranded couple. Don dismissed the whole affair as a storm in a teacup, though he did say *Golden Odyssey* had a very good wine cellar.

The Cook Islands are celebrating the anniversary of Christianity arriving in the islands 175 years ago. It also coincides with Autonomy Day when the islands achieved self-rule. They still live under the umbrella of New Zealand who look after foreign policy and defence. Tonight for celebration of the introduction of the Gospel, all the Churches got together to praise the Lord with song. Let's not kid ourselves, this was competition at the highest level. The audience, or maybe that should be the congregation, cheered, clapped and whistled, depending on who they were supporting. What a fine night everybody had.

Leaving, we met a Minister from Australia who is on Rarotonga for two years to look after the United Church of God. I said to him that the faith of the people was quite impressive. He told me at one time his parish was in the Australian bush during a time of drought. The ground was burnt barren north of the Geebung. The Murray River was running dry so they decided to have a day of prayer, asking God for the rains to come. That Sunday the faithful arrived. Only one little girl brought an umbrella. Now she had faith!

We had decided to delay our departure from Rarotonga because of the deteriorating weather. God makes the weather. It's up to us to decide what to do with it. We stayed.

Bob on *Loon II* left. A charming man from the west coast of Canada, he lived at one time in Australia and always wanted to go back. With this aim in mind he built his own gaff-rigged boat. Part of his life was spent as a commercial fisherman in Alaska. As he left that morning the wind was freshening. Before darkness there was a full storm. No one has heard from him since. He impressed me as a strong, capable man on a well-found boat. Let's hope the wind has taken him somewhere else. Twelve hours after he left the wind and seas were vicious, much more than forecast. That same night about

100 miles east of the Cooks another yacht was dismasted. We hope that in some quite anchorage we will hear Bob's story.

Christine
In three days we head for Tonga, 850 miles to the west. The weather is still playing up in the South Pacific. Last week a tidal wave hit Papua New Guinea leaving a death toll in the thousands. The Cook Islands are collecting to help with the relief fund. Rarotonga is safe but if a Tsunami hit some of the northern atolls there would be no survivors as they are so low lying. The local people are conscious of this. Still, we hope the weather is settled for the passage.

Tied stern to harbour wall in Rarotonga

29th July 1998
The Pacific weather continues to confuse us. These are not the islands of gentle breezes. The harbour was hit by 50-knot winds last night.

To put it mildly, all hell broke loose. We had cleared to leave for Tonga but it started to rain. At home that is not a good enough reason to call off a passage but we are now used to blue skies, so we decided to stay until the clouds passed. Reeds Nautical Almanac used to give old sailors' rhymes. One that sticks in my head was,

'When rain comes before the wind
Halyards, sheets and braces mind.
But when wind comes before the rain
Soon you may make sail again'.

The old seamen were right on this occasion, the rain fell out of the sky in torrents, then the wind started to come. Before the night was over, *R Phurst*, the American catamaran, had dragged her anchor and was on the reef. There was a container ship on the quay directly across the bay breaking her hawsers like bits of string. If she went adrift, all the yachts would have been crushed like eggshells. Don Silk, the harbour master, came on the radio,

"*Breakaway*, have you got a dinghy in the water?"

I had to tell him no.

"*R Phurst* will not survive if we don't get help to him," says Don, "and the weather is too bad to put swimmers in."

The plan was to take a rope to the cat and haul her off using ship's winches. I hijacked a dinghy and took a line from the ship across the harbour to the catamaran. The ship started hauling. The cat started creaking. We checked the bilges, she wasn't taking water. The ship took the strain, the rope stretched, the water flew off it. The umbilical cord held and *R Phurst* slowly came off the reef.

I made my way back to *Breakaway* and the sea was blowing smoke. Christine had the tiller hard over with the engine half ahead, trying to hold station and take the strain off the anchor. The wind was hitting us on the side but the stern lines to the quay were holding. The rest of the night didn't encourage sleep, that's the South Pacific for you. At least when the wind came it stopped raining.

Tonga is starting to look a long way away.

On Passage to Tonga

Breakaway is on passage again, bound for the Kingdom of Tonga, or the Friendly Isles. After five days of gales in the Cook Islands, we were ready to leave at the first signs of the wind abating. We had two anchors laid. I also dived down to attach a line to an old mooring on the seabed and there were three ropes securing *Breakaway*'s stern to the shore. We were glad of them all.

The morning of departure started early with a dive down to sort out the mooring and free a fouled anchor, leaving one anchor to lift. There was plenty of help ashore and the remaining ropes were cast off. The harbour mouth didn't look too inviting as the surf pounded the reef, breaking over the quay. Christine kept *Breakaway* in control while I cleared the decks for action.

If anything wasn't tied down we were going to lose it.

As we climbed up the first wave, *Breakaway* could have used the gearbox of a Land Rover 4x4 to get up the hill. White water was breaking 50 feet away on either side as the second wave took us up into the air again. The rudder felt light and the prop was cavitating, one more wave to go and we were free. The third was gentle, the sails were set. Honolulu to the north, Antarctica to the south and Tonga 850 miles west. We were out of there.

Once *Breakaway* had cleared the islands, after 12 hours the wind died. The engine was turned on and the fuel consumption for the journey worked out. It's now day four and we have 450 miles left to cover. All that is needed is a breeze for 24 hours and then there will be enough fuel left to make it. If not we will drift until it comes.

I came on watch at midnight. Christine runs the boat the rest of the time apart from a couple of hours in the afternoon and relieves me at about six in the morning. We both look forward to the evening meal with the one drink we allow ourselves before it, usually the only time we are in each other's company.

The night watches are lonely for both of us and the darkness is for a good 12 hours in these parts. You sit with your own thoughts as the yacht moves across the ocean, hoping for wind but not too much. People you have met and mistakes you have made in life roll across your mind like an old newsreel as you wait on dawn arriving - but as always dawn comes.

Day 7. Tonga is now less than 24 hours away. This could be my last night shift for a while. The entrance to Port Refuge doesn't look too difficult. We will arrive on the edge of darkness with two options. Take a chance and go into the unknown, or stay out at sea for another night. The moon is full. I think we'll take a chance. The Pacific is vast and every time we put to sea, days pass without the sighting of another ship. This time we haven't seen anything for seven days, just ourselves and the ocean.

Whales are reported in the area. So far we haven't seen any. The night before leaving Rarotonga they were spotted just outside the reef. At one of the hotels the guests gathered to watch a mother playing with her young. The visitors of all nationalities applauded and cheered as the sun set and the family moved out into the ocean. The problem for us at night is the chance encounter of whales sleeping on the surface. They could bring *Breakaway* to a sudden stop, or worse.

Day 8. Tonight we arrived in Neiafu, Tonga, to a welcome from Hans and Marianne of *Olle P*. Hans was waiting there is his dinghy to hand us a mooring line. We were tired but the adrenaline was still pumping - another ocean passage without incident. *Olle P* and the 'Breakaways' went ashore for a meal. Christine sang a song with the resident group. The group was great. We'll sleep well tonight in a very safe anchorage.

By the way. Bob of *Loon II* is lying at anchor not too far way. All's well that ends well.

Christine
As we were making our way to Tonga, contact with the outside world is through SSB radio. The yachts ahead of us are a reliable source of information and give us a run down. They report on the weather situation, if there are any changes to navigation, what to expect from the officials, where you go to tie up and what to avoid. All useful stuff and it certainly makes your landfall a lot less nerve racking. Every island has its own little foibles. In Tonga they remove your fruit and veg as there is a harmful fly that lives on the Cook Islands and they don't want it to take up residence in Tonga. We only had some scallions and a shrivelled up lemon left for the gentleman from the Department of Agriculture. He was a little disappointed but cheered up when I gave him the Australian Women's Weekly dated November 1997 he had his eye on.

Neiafu, Kingdom of Tonga 18 39.29S 173 58.55W

The Kingdom of Tonga is one of the best cruising areas in our opinion - whales playing to the west of the islands and sheltered water for anchoring.

It's not surprising that two of the world's biggest yacht charter companies, Sunsail and Moorings, rent their boats out here for people to enjoy the holiday of a lifetime. Both companies have provided their own charts of the area which most of the cruisers and liveaboards have surreptitiously photocopied.

Tied up alongside – Neiafu, Tonga

Not to be outdone - tonight we are in anchorage number 11. The boats all talk to each other in numbers. It's like ordering a Chinese carryout. It's nice to go sailing again with easy instructions.

Now down here the Post Office is lovely. They don't have a postman, they have cardboard boxes. The idea is simple. You go down to the Central Post Office, which is the only one, with your cardboard box. There the Post Master General gives you a nail and a hammer. You write your name on the box and nail it to the wall. Your mail is put into the box until you call to pick it up at your convenience. Simple, effective, cuts down on labour and it works.

I asked the lady behind the grill if I could take her photograph. She looked embarrassed and then said, "If you send me one." At this stage I hadn't realised that there are no means of developing photos on the island. Something so normal and every day to us becomes special and unobtainable. Of course she'll get her photograph eventually, as will the wonderful lady in the market who answered every question with, "I have 10 children".

The Tonga group of islands has a charm all of its own - a very special people with their own culture that is still very much alive. Can you imagine a land with no television, nearly but not quite untouched by the outside world, where history is related by storytellers sitting around the fire. In saying that the youngsters are highly educated, equal to any European standard. They just have different values.

Breakaway is anchored at the moment in an isolated bay with a small beach fringed with coconut trees. The moon is old and as darkness falls the only light comes from the stars. You can feel the jungle around you.

Last night a beast started roaring ashore. The primeval sound would have made the hair stand up on the back of your head. As daylight broke the cause of the noise became clear. There were three cows walking along the beach. It was their moo-ing we heard. It was just the jungle playing tricks on us. We haven't heard a cow since leaving Ireland. What is normal at home becomes unusual when you haven't experienced it for a while.

Pigs are certainly in vogue out here. They run about the street and are treated like dogs, and like dogs they will stop to be petted and stroked. If you happen to go into a waterfront cafe for a meal, more often than not a pig will come under the table and lie with his head on your feet looking for a bit of attention. A couple of days ago I was eating a bacon sandwich, feeling guilty as I gave its nephew a pat.

The pigs are quite self-sufficient. As the tide goes out they wander up and down the shore looking for crabs above low water mark. I am told they also swim after fish and in the shallow water have been seen to dive down and catch them. This is what I have been told.

Christine

*We are anchored tonight in sand, a thin layer over a bed of coral.
As you lie in your bunk you can hear the rumbling of the anchor
and chain. It is very disconcerting, so in these conditions I always
put the anchor alarm on. Bob doesn't like it because it tends to go
off at night just when you've managed to go to sleep. I'm happier
when it's activated so it's my job to reset it. Fair enough. I am so
grateful for the modern navigation aids we have on board but have
great admiration for the old adventurers like Captain Cook who
successfully navigated these low lying islands. We have it easy, but I
can live with that.*

The Garden Party

Today has been great. At first light we lifted anchor to come round to
Neiafu, the centre of the universe in Northern Tonga.

Youngest son Jamie arrives in six days. To sail down and meet
him would take three days so off we went into town to see what could
be arranged with the Royal Tongan Airways.

Jamie is now flying to meet us.

While booking his ticket we were told that the King himself
was in town today to open the proceedings for the South Pacific and
Asian Parliamentary Conference. Now through the grapevine we
heard that, with the help of a pair of long trousers combined with a
shirt and tie for me and a long skirt and blouse for Christine, we might
be allowed to participate. Also, no hats to be worn.

Off we went to join the celebrations. With Christine swinging
on my arm, the pair of us walked into the enclosure as if we had every
right to be there. Fortunately nobody stopped us. The grass enclosure

had tents to protect the dignitaries from the heat of the day. We sat down in one and nobody seemed to mind.

The ladies were dressed in their finery and the giant Tongan men clad in suits. Now their suits are unusual, the top half is the same as we would wear, the bottom half is a wraparound skirt. Underneath the suit jacket is tied a woven mat made from pandanus leaf and looking like an apron. The mat is worn as a sign of respect to the King. At times of funerals they wear a larger mat. Today everyone was dressed in the good suit and it was reminiscent of a Masonic Lodge on ladies night. Anyhow, we tried to look as unobtrusive as possible.

The band, also in traditional dress, was playing tunes from the fifties, 'Let's go to the Hop', 'Rock Around the Clock' and similar pieces of classical music. We clapped our hands and joined in, then silence, his Majesty was arriving. We all stood as the biggest King in the world made his appearance. He, along with the Queen, Princess and entourage eventually got themselves seated in the Royal Tent. The local Archbishop was the first on stage with the longest prayer I have ever heard. The King replied - a lovely speech by a lovely man.

Next was the Chinese representative talking in English. I'll not dwell on that. They were all there, Thailand, China, Vietnam, the Japanese taking pictures, the Micronesians along with the representative from Fiji - who made the King look small - with his face covered in a fearsome beard.

Next was a troupe of some 400 dancers. The custom out here is if you enjoy a particular dancer you can walk out and put some money down the front of her blouse. Meanwhile the King sat on his throne enjoying the whole thing as much as us. Next out was a statuesque dancer covered in coconut oil. She danced mainly using hand movements that told a story. The Royal Princess was the first up to stick a bank note on the skin of the dancer. It was held on by the oil. All the courtiers followed suit; the dancer was starting to earn a few bob. A tapa cloth was then presented to the King - a thing of beauty that took 12 women to carry it because of the size. As the King left, the cloth was lying in the middle of the field along with many ceremonial gifts. Then came the tea and buns – I couldn't believe it – every one of us was served and it just kept coming.

It's a pity Jamie missed all the excitement by a week, still there will be lots to see and we are just looking forward to seeing him.

After all the festivities we moved *Breakaway* around to Ano Beach on Panga Motu. As we arrived, there were two other yachts at anchor. One of them told us to get ourselves settled quickly, as the King was about to arrive for his daily swim. We were going to get our chance of a 'special photo' after all.

In the village about half a mile away a changing tent had to be erected. The King left it with a robe over his swimming costume, climbed into a small boat to come to the beach where we were anchored. It is isolated with no connecting roads. His inflatable boat stopped, he entered the shallow water surrounded by eight other swimmers in lifejackets. Off he went floating along gently on his back. He ignored us and we ignored him, as it should be. After 15 minutes or so it was back to the boat and off to the tent. The locals sang songs of welcome. It made me think that maybe that is the way our Royalty was able to act in the past. Everything fairly low key, the family and friends out for a day on the beach and of course no photographers to spoil the occasion as yours truly had run out of film.

King Taufa'ahau Tupou IV is now 80. His eldest son is first in line to the throne but is in his 50s and never married though it is rumoured on the islands that he has plenty of heirs. Number One Son will be passed over and his younger brother will take on the mantle of King as he has a wife and children.

The islands of Tonga move at a slow pace. This week's headline in the paper is about the installation of cats eyes on the main road, causing great debate, with the paper explaining how they work, along with little diagrams so that drivers will be prepared for the onslaught of modernisation. There are no traffic lights, no doubt they will come next, let's hope it's not for a long time. The main street of Neiafu is like something out of the Wild West. The pavements are covered by verandas to shade you from the sun. The old wooden shops are full of customers sitting on long benches awaiting their turn, or maybe just in for a yarn. The tick books are piled high beside the old fashioned tills. Cash registers as we know them are something else that hasn't arrived. They smell like shops should. Most of the goods aren't packaged except for stuff that comes in from New Zealand on the island trading ships. Those of you who remember shops before supermarkets would find Neiafu a stroll down memory lane.

Christine
The Kingdom of Tonga is the first country in the world to welcome the dawn of each new day. So it will be the first country to see the first dawn of the new millennium. The local people are very proud of this fact and 'Tonga 2,000' stickers are everywhere. Tourism is low key here but I hope the idea of 'Tonga 2,000' catches on and brings the islands some much-needed publicity.

The Arrival of Jamie, Our Youngest

26 August 1998
Christine and I set off for the airport to meet the youngest heir to the money we are spending – a highly charged, emotional time. Vava'u International Airport has to be seen to be believed. There's a cluster of huts with two wooden benches outside under the shade of palm trees. There we will sit and wait in sight of the one runway, with an old Land Rover as the emergency backup vehicle.

Several days ago Jamie had left Belfast, changed at London Heathrow, New York, Los Angeles, Honolulu, and Tongatapu – now the culture shock of Vava'u.

We heard the small plane before we saw it. Flying into the wind heading for the runway it weaved and wavered along the path cut out of the jungle. The Land Rover had gone ahead to chase the pigs away and the Pilot seemed to know what he was doing. Tyres burnt rubber and the plane shuddered to a halt. Our own personal art student appeared with a shaven head except for a blond forelock. After two years, sight unseen, I didn't care what hair style he had. Christine shed a few tears and to tell the truth I did too.

The taxi man got into the act as well. Still we got Jamie back to the boat as he tried to adjust to the strangeness of it all. The temperature was down, only about 85 degrees. As the taxi pulled up at the harbour, home was waiting in the shape of *Breakaway*. The Yachties were all aware of the situation and everyone was there to say hello. What was good - Jamie realised we were all right and we realised he was too.

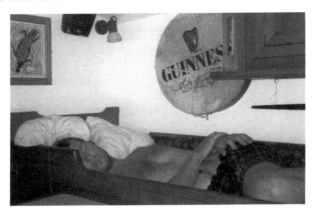

28 August 1998

Breakaway and crew left harbour for a day sail. The Yachties had organised a Bar-B-Q. We arrived in the bay but turned out again. At the moment company is not needed. The moon is not yet full but in another week the three of us head for Fiji. It is only 450 miles away – a short passage to give Jamie a chance to settle in.

Suva, Fiji 18 07S 178 25W
(Half way round the world)

The crossing to Fiji was lively to say the least, but with son Jamie on board and dodging a couple of reefs in the darkness his young eyes made a difference. The moon was almost full and visibility reasonable. Clouds were scudding across the sky as we approached the main island of Viti Levu - our destination – in a strong wind and dawn a long way off. Discretion being the better part of valour, we hove to until daylight. The moon set, the sun rose and it started to rain.

From five miles offshore we could not see the island. Under sail we worked our way towards the harbour entrance. With all the modern aids of navigation, the entrance to Suva harbour was marked by two wrecked ships, which alone would be inclined to make you rather nervous. Once – twice – we backed off for another look – Jamie on GPS, Christine on the tiller and me having a good worry.

I had celebrated my 58th birthday two days previously and was suffering from a form of male depression. Just as we closed the reef, with the surf surging beside us, Christine told me I was only 57. Happy days – a younger man was in control. The anchor finally went down and the boat was safe.

David from another yacht, *Anda*, brought us the first pint of fresh milk we had had in two years, along with a loaf of fresh bread that bore a passing resemblance to the loaves we knew and loved from home. As always after a passage, that first night of uninterrupted sleep is just wonderful. The Bureaucrats of Fiji had to be faced so the next day the three of us set forth into the fray - Customs, Health, Immigration, Agriculture and Port Authorities.

To clear in only took a morning as I had learnt a new trick. The forms are in triplicate and there were many of them. The small office was crowded with other yacht crews filling in forms, leaning on the back of the person in front of them and asking for help from the officials which neither side could understand. I went up to the desk and asked for help. After instructions were issued I played my trump card holding my hand behind my ear indicating deafness. The forms were filled out for me and I was free to go. There were only so many times you could say "pardon" without causing offence so it was better to claim no hearing at all. The little ruse was to help in many of the countries where language was a problem.

We were now free to savour the delights of downtown Suva. The sea behind us, we were determined to enjoy the land. Photos needed to be developed and sent back to Tonga as promised, markets were there to be visited. What was on at the cinema? Is there a good cheap restaurant? We found them all. Fiji was fun. Where else in the world do policemen wear white skirts with a jagged sharks tooth hem?

Suva has to rank, along with Papeete in French Polynesia, as one of the great cities in the Pacific, but with items at a fraction of the price. The market under a multi-storey car park had to be seen to be believed, with countless stall holders selling their wares. Everything was there from a wooden cannibal fork for eating the brains of the enemy, to the Fijian boomerang, a vicious throwing club. If the warrior throwing the club missed, the enemy picked it up and threw it back, hence the name boomerang. As we all know, the Australians call a boomerang that won't come back a stick. We were having to look ahead and not overstock because New Zealand was next on the agenda and importation rules regarding food were very strict.

Fiji was a good place to give *Breakaway* a rest along with us and also do some work on her as there was a tough passage ahead en route to New Zealand. Still – we were half way round the world and having the time of our lives.

Other yachts were gathering in the anchorage and all were of the one opinion - navigating into Suva harbour had been a nightmare. All had made it, but some had scars from close encounters with bits of reef that were not shown on the chart. *Woody Goose*, a 55ft wooden ketch, was driven up on the reef of Suva. Under full sail she had landed between a rock and a hard place, lying on her side 100 yards from deep water. The call went out,

"Mayday, Mayday."

Dinghies were launched and the small crafts went out to help. It was like Dunkirk all over again. The rescue had started. *Woody Goose* had a bit of a 'past'. She was imprisoned in Gibraltar accused of drug running and then sold off at auction. Anita and Roger from Yorkshire bought her. Anita, with the onset of MS, and Roger with a dream that looked like it was finished on a reef in Fiji. The dinghies from the other yachts could not do a lot except strip the boat of personal possessions, loading them onto an Australian yacht, *Bimbimbi,* that had offered to stand by as a support vessel in deeper water close by. *Woody Goose* was not insured.

Daylight came as we tried to secure the yacht from pounding herself to death on the coral. She was more than a yacht. It was a home being wrecked. Anchors were laid, cockpit cushions put under the hull to try and protect her from the reef. We started to lighten the boat in the hope that she might float again. It was doubtful as *Woody Goose* had been sailed up onto the reef at high tide.

The tide was dropping further each day as the team of helpers raced against time carrying gear to the edge of the reef and into the dinghies. Then the local help arrived in the shape of a tug boat offering a rescue for £30,000, a lot of money for people with no insurance. At this stage the weather was also deteriorating and that was not going to help. Roger did not have the £30,000 and the tug retreated to harbour. We continued to unload *Woody Goose* trying to save as much as possible while the vessel continued to pound herself to destruction.

The next day a Fijian Naval vessel was coerced to help. They ran a tight budget that only allowed them to put to sea 10 days a month. The Navy tried to put a line to the boat with the use of a rocket but it failed. A high powered inflatable was launched to take the tow line over the surf. The boat capsized and was driven towards the reef wall with the three crew members tossed out and both boat and crew ending up on the reef itself. The Yachties on the reef swam out to rescue the Navy personnel. The bedraggled sailors and then their craft were saved, all a bit the worse for wear.

Another rescue had to be aborted and it did not seem possible that the yacht could survive another night of abuse as we continued to strip her. Another salvage team came on the radio with an offer to help at a more acceptable price of £4,000. Next morning they appeared. A tow line had to be attached to *Woody*. After many attempts a line stayed attached and the tow boat took up the strain.

The Yachtie team had worked wonders to attach the 1,000 feet of line in extreme sea conditions. The salvage vessel, a small fishing boat, did not have enough power to move the stricken boat. They were soon to join the Navy in the harbour. The deal had been struck under Lloyds Open Form, 'No cure, no pay', *Woody Goose* was still stuck. In the early hours of the fourth morning I was awakened to be told,

"Organise a tow into the harbour Bob."

A Fairy Godmother was on her way. A vessel called up at 03:00, the Captain saying he was 30 miles away and if he could render assistance he would divert. As daylight broke *Maupiti* appeared over the horizon. On the lines of an off-shore oil rig supply vessel, she had been rigged out for luxury ocean cruising. The multimillionaire owner and his family were on board. It turned out he had done a bit of sailing himself and had offered help.

The Cavalry had arrived – *Maupiti*'s Captain took over the operation. Their dinghy was launched and a rocket line was shot through the surf to *Woody* where the Yachties prepared a bridle round the yacht to attach the tow. The bridle broke. The Captain came on the radio again. Four rockets later at a cost of £450 each *Woody Goose* was still digging her own grave in the coral. Time was now of the essence but the owner of *Maupiti* had an appointment elsewhere and had to move on. The Captain had the painful task of calling the operation off. There were tears shed as everyone listened to the conversation. The Yachties stood around, not quite knowing what to do next. The last chance had gone. Half an hour later the radio cracked into life.

"The owner has forgone his appointment, we will stand by for three hours until high tide and give it one more try with the last rocket on board."

The tide crept in. The tow was attached, this time with 3,000 feet of line *Maupiti* took up the strain. *Woody Goose* was being dragged off the reef. It was sink or swim from four feet of water into 400 feet. Norm, the unemotional, tough old Aussie, was screaming,

"She's floating in deep water."

Woody was back in her element, scarred but only taking a little water. I went out on a Canadian yacht to take over the tow. A fleet of dinghies was there like a pack of Border Collies, the owner of *Maupiti* cracked open a bottle of champagne. The Captain reeled in his 3,000 feet line.

The feel good factor was running high. The British yacht *Woody Goose* was towed into the anchorage supported by 'International Rescue' as they had become known - a Canadian, South Africans, Kiwis, Australians, Swedes, Norwegians, French and of course the Irish. *Maupiti* was given a resounding three cheers. She turned and disappeared over the horizon from whence she came.

International Rescue

Horns blew as *Woody* dropped her anchor, four days and four nights late, damaged but still afloat. Her strong wooden construction had saved the day. There would have been very few boats that could have survived what she had been through.

That night at the Royal Suva Yacht Club, all recounted tales of daring do. Roger, *Woody*'s owner, bought a raffle ticket. He did not win. They had just used up a lifetime's luck.

Christine

The drama was not over for the day. As the yachts were celebrating the success of the mission, a call come over the VHF radio in the Yacht Club that Woody Goose was dragging her anchor. Breakaway's crew was first away from the dock but was soon overtaken by the faster dinghies as International Rescue got underway. Taking us from all sides they were soon out at Woody Goose, leaving us gently rocking in their wakes.

Bob, Jamie and I pottered after them. What happened was that Woody Goose had dropped her anchor straight into a bucket on the sea bed. Of course the anchor couldn't take hold and the rescued boat in a crowded anchorage was heading for more trouble. The anchor was re-laid, minus the bucket, and all was well once again.

Suva to Musket Cove

Back at anchor in Suva, the rain had been slowly getting us down, it was time to move. The island of Viti Levu in Fiji had a strange weather pattern. From east to west there was a dramatic climate change.

The east was mostly overcast with the storm clouds always looming. The west was a tropical paradise, just as you picture the South Pacific, with white beaches and palm trees swaying to gentle breezes.

On passage we experienced all the weather of the islands, from strong winds to a lightning storm of immense power accompanied by heavy rain. The black night sky was lit up as the forks of lightning danced over the sea round *Breakaway*, illuminating the surf on the reef a couple of miles away and reflecting in Jamie's spectacles as he sat out in the cockpit on watch. As daylight came and the storm passed behind us, the next problem was to find a passage through the coral. The Admiralty chart stated,

'CAUTION – do not use satellite navigation to plot a position as the pass through Navula Passage moves South-West at a rate not yet determined'.

So - we cheated again, but when the anchor went down in Momi Bay the three of us were quite satisfied with the results. Over the radio we heard more about *Woody Goose*. She was slipped and under repair in Suva. They had been lucky, but not so everyone on the high seas.

The Pacific that year had been hard on yachts. *Aureaka*, the Australian yacht that had gone missing off the Galapagos Islands, was found drifting 600 miles south of Acapulco in Mexico, the sails in shreds and the vessel stripped. Had the single hander fallen overboard or was it pirates from the coast of South America? The family held a remembrance service for Ross. It would have been his 60th birthday. The yacht was still drifting as the cargo vessel that found her could not take a tow because of an impending cyclone.

It is not all high drama on the high seas. There was also a lot of fun to be had. Wherever cruisers got together, events were organised, especially races amongst the yachts. There was a major race every year – a 2,000 mile run to Australia from Fiji.

Unlike any race I have ever heard of the rules were as follows:

- Rule 1. If the weather is poor at the intended start it will be put off until a good day
- Rule 2. There is a prize for the biggest fish caught on passage
- Rule 3. Each yacht must carry 'spiritus' liquor to the Race Committee's satisfaction. The Committee reserves the right to remove samples for analysis
- Rule 4. If the wind becomes light, the engine must be started
- Rule 5. Line honours will automatically disqualify unless it can be proved that blatant cheating occurred
- Rule 6. Matching oilskins and a refrigeration system that works will not even be considered
- Rule 7. Points will be awarded to yachts carrying the following - an iron and ironing board, washing machine, pot plants, more than two pairs of pyjamas each, children, photocopied charts
- Rule 8. Each yacht will be awarded a first prize plaque
- Rule 9. Small boats can leave up to two weeks before everyone else but they will miss the Pig Feast

It was a good way to make an ocean passage. Some of the yachts got so carried away they went to Australia just to be part of the race even though their original intention had been to sail to New Zealand.

Breakaway was bound for New Zealand and nothing was going to deter her. My sister and family had lived there for many years and after so many sea miles my sights were still set on sailing into the Bay of Islands, North Island, New Zealand. It was time to knuckle down to some real work.

Breakaway was going to Vuda Point Marine on the south east corner of Viti Levu to be lifted out. When they built the airport, a quarry was created by digging out the coral and using it to form runways, leaving an unsightly hole in the ground. A local businessman saw an opportunity and transformed the eyesore into a safe haven for yachts. Pontoons were built, services supplied and a channel dug out into the sea. We were now in a part of Fiji favoured by the big hotel groups and tourists were a common sight. There was a complex nearby serving food, so we made our way along a sandy path lit by torches as the sun set somewhere over Australia.

A night off was on the cards before work on *Breakaway* started. A Fijian singing group entertained us, big men in skirts playing guitars in time to the beat of the surf pounding the reef. What a night out - three drinks and a large Italian pizza each for £3 a head.

The next day work started on *Breakaway* as she was lifted out of the water. The last time we dry docked was Trinidad in the Caribbean and I always worried when she came out of her element. Still the weed on her bottom had grown like grass. As the hull became dirty we slowed up considerably. A clean boat could take a day off the voyage to New Zealand when, for the first time in a couple of years, *Breakaway* would leave the tropics. The land of the Long White Cloud runs down to the roaring forties where the low pressure systems of the Southern Ocean are ruled by the God of Storms.

We had to prepare the boat for that voyage. *Breakaway* was parked outside the fence of the First Landing Beach resort, the grounds were our back garden. One of the grounds-men put the gate on the latch for us so that we could come and go as we pleased.

Each evening the Captain Cook Sunset cruise arrived with its full load of Japanese tourists to enjoy our back garden. They waved at us when they saw Belfast on the stern. Photos were taken. A little railway engine trundled past pulling flatbed trucks loaded with sugar cane – another side of Fiji. The field workers earn £3 a ton to cut and load.

For the first time in our travels I became an employer - to tell the truth for the first time in my life. I encountered labour problems immediately. Not with Joe, the local lad who was paid £7 per day – I know it was scandalous but he needed the job and that was the local rate. The problems were arising in the works canteen run by Christine who worried about Joe. The union had formed. Joe ate bacon sandwiches and drank cups of tea supplied free while I sanded the bottom of the boat. To be fair Joe occasionally stopped eating long enough to advise me where I had gone wrong.

That evening was the firm's party, but Joe couldn't come, he had another party to go to where Kava was served. Kava is a root grown in the high lands of Fiji. It must be bought in the market and offered as a gift to the chief of any island you visit. The gift is accepted and you become part of the community. The drinking of kava is a ceremonial affair. The kava is pounded to a powder and then wrapped in a rag. Next it is immersed in a traditional carved wooden bowl filled with water. Another little bowl is dipped in and passed around the assembled guests. In early years the kava was chewed by selected maidens. Softened by saliva it was then spat into the bowl. The effect of the drink is slightly narcotic leaving the mouth numb and the brain dead – the colour of the drink is dishwater grey and dishwater also describes the taste.

Back to the firm's night out – we joined in with the Japanese taking photos. One young couple frolicked on the beach in the beautiful setting. Next morning there was a beach wedding for the romantic couple, the groom in full morning suit and the bride's white wedding dress spilling across the sand. They looked a picture and there were many taken.

Fiji was proving another hard place to leave. Body shape did not matter. Shirts were worn rolled up so that bellies could be admired and my tummy was not big enough to be beautiful, and it was getting smaller by the minute with all the hard work on *Breakaway* in the tropical heat.

We enjoyed the people and I enjoyed reading the local papers as they were written in English. On every page was a smiling Fijian. They had the most wonderful smiles even when the circumstances were not happy ones. One smiling girl was pictured lying in a hospital bed with her father smiling beside her. He had been interviewed. The little girl had been on the outside toilet when a tree crashed through the roof, injuring her. He was asked for his opinion on what had happened. He said, and I quote,

"It just goes to show you can't trust trees."

The last week we spent in Fiji, my sister Geraldine, her son Graydon and brother-in-law Gary joined us. The plan was for Gary to sail down to New Zealand on board *Breakaway*. The first day after our emotional reunion we set forth back to Musket Cove, which offered a chance for swimming in clean water again and all the trappings of a tropical resort. Halfway there 'with six on board' I realised we needed a bigger boat. Fortunately the following day the alternator failed and we had no way of charging our batteries to run reading lights at night or even start the engine, so it was a quick retreat to Vuda Point to regroup. The family booked into the First Landing Hotel, a nice little chalet, taking a lot of strain off *Breakaway* and bunk space. The rest of the week was great as we re-explored Fiji.

There were three brothers called Abdhul who ran the local taxi service. To save any confusion they were known as one, two and three. Each day we would go with one, two or three into Lautouka, the nearest town, to adventure.

Not everyone was as lucky as Christine and me when it came to family relationships. A couple from Ukraine were working on the islands off Western Samoa. Newly married and deeply in love, money didn't matter as long as they had each other and were in the islands of paradise. A German yacht, single handed, sailed in and offered our young lovers work aboard his ship, she as cook and he as deckhand. The three of them set sail for Suva and the delights of Fiji.

After a few weeks of idyllic cruising among the coral atolls it was time to sail from Fiji to Australia. The captain accompanied by the cook set off to do paperwork while the deckhand prepared the yacht for sea. On their return, the cook told her beloved that there was a small paperwork problem with Customs that only he could sort out – off he went.

The authorities knew of no problem so back he came to the boat. On the dock was a plastic carrier bag containing some of his clothes. Captain and cook had disappeared over the horizon leaving husband without a passport and penniless. Now, as you can imagine, Consulates representing the people of Ukraine are few and far between in the islands of Polynesia. He was probably better off without her but what do you do with no money, no passport and no paperwork.

While we were anchored in Musket Cove holiday resort, a father and his young daughter drifted past in a little sailing dinghy they had hired on the beach. Shortly afterwards I noticed they were over the surrounding reef and heading for the wide, blue Pacific. Off I went in our dinghy to give them a tow to safety. He explained to me it was very hard sailing into the wind and appreciated my help.

Musket Cove

As I went back to *Breakaway* I realised we had 1,200 miles of sailing into the wind on our way to New Zealand ahead of us, taking a possible 10 to 12 days.

After seven days' holiday, sister Geraldine and nephew Graydon flew home. It only took them three and a half hours. Brother-in-law Garry helped Jamie, Christine and me prepare for the trip south, with last minute shopping for food, filling the water and fuel tanks, while I serviced the engine. After this it was up to the top of the mast to inspect the rig. As I get older the mast seems to grow taller.

The journey to New Zealand was to be the first time in two years we were moving out of the tropics, heading south to dodge the cyclone season, but there was a chance of gales brewing in the Tasman Sea. A few yachts were also preparing for the journey and the talk revolved around isobars being squeezed between high-pressure systems and tropical depressions, but no one seemed able to foretell the weather.

My horoscope in the Fiji Times predicted me going on a long journey midweek. That was as good a forecast as any, so we left on Wednesday to the good wishes of other Yachties and a final farewell from our Fijian friend and helper Joe, sporting a snazzy new personal stereo with his earnings.

Christine

Preparing Breakaway for the voyage to New Zealand was a complete change of routine. Instead of piling on food, we were aware of restrictions ahead so we all began sharing our diminishing supplies among the boats. In the stifling heat of Fiji, we had to rummage into the darkest recesses of Breakaway to hunt out socks, jumpers, trousers and jackets. We had been warned that the temperature would be dropping drastically at night and to be prepared.

The warnings were right. I am the proud owner of a very special sailing jacket with built in buoyancy, a harness and a thermal lining and at times I wondered was I right in the head bringing the bulky thing with me, but it turned out to be just the job.

As I came off night watch it was a simple matter of passing the jacket over, knowing my relief would be warm and secure in the cockpit. I could then go down below and pinch his bed.

On Passage to Bay of Islands, New Zealand

Plan A was to do a small shakedown cruise to Momi Bay, drop the anchor at this isolated beach to spend a quiet night before going out into the ocean. We moved straight to Plan B. With a heavily reefed mainsail, *Breakaway* turned to port, negotiated the reef and pointed in the general direction of New Zealand. Why put it off, we were as ready as we were ever going to be.

Breakaway arrives in the Bay of Islands

Russell Radio is a voluntary service run by two retired Kiwis, Des and Richie, who communicate with yachts on ocean passages giving advice on weather and informing people on shore of the yachts' whereabouts. They came up every morning and evening to offer advice and comfort.

Two days out the wind died and *Breakaway* drifted. Now the idea was to use the easterly trade winds to get far enough west and south, putting us in a position north of New Zealand where the prevailing south westerlies would be of advantage.

Des advised me to start the engine and run a rhumb line course for our destination at the Bay Of Islands in North Island New Zealand. A rhumb line is the shortest distance from departure to arrival. Des was right, we motored for the next seven and a half days with no breeze to fill the sails. On Thursday afternoon, Guy Fawkes Day, nine and a half days out of Fiji we spotted New Zealand. At one stage we were starting to wonder did it really exist. Then, on the horizon, landfall; the Bay of Islands, to the north and south of us were headlands. We couldn't see the gap in between as the rest of North Island was hidden in the sea mist.

Breakaway tentatively closed the shore towards the land of the Long White Cloud, so called by the original Maori explorers on the way across the Pacific in their canoes. Their landfall was probably easier than ours. We had to face customs and the man from the Ministry. Customs was easy.

"Have you anything to declare?"

"I declare this is the most beautiful country in the world."

"Pass friend."

He was from Liverpool.

Next was the Scotsman from MAF, the Ministry of Agriculture and Fisheries,

"Have you any onions, honey, popcorn, wood carvings, shells, coral, baskets, cats, dogs, meat from England, cheese, cloves of garlic?"

He paused for breath and then continued, "Have you any oranges, apples, are you importing drugs, liquor, cigarettes, guns, do you carry or transport any tropical diseases, has everything on board this vessel been put on by yourselves?"

By this time my nerves were wrecked. We had almost everything except the cat and dog. Christine started to sing a few bars of 'Oh Flower of Scotland', he stamped and I signed the forms, we offered him a wee dram. Welcome to New Zealand.

In the midst of all this trauma, an old friend Dennis of *INTI* appeared to bid us welcome and invite the crew of *Breakaway* for a meal aboard his boat.

Now Dennis at one stage was a Russian interpreter to Tony Benn of the British Labour Government a while back. Dennis originally came from British Guyana, South America and went to Russia at the age of 16 years where he met his wife Martina from East Germany. They got married, but the new bride couldn't leave the Eastern Bloc for one year after the wedding. Bureaucracy doesn't mean much to Dennis.

Did I mention Dennis is an Arawak Indian? At this stage the man from MAF gave up.

New Zealand

Not everyone had as good a crossing from Fiji to New Zealand as *Breakaway* and crew.

A week later the weather broke as an early summer gale swept North Island. *Woody Goose*, the yacht rescued from the reef in Fiji a couple of months ago, was driven onto the beach at Great Exhibition Bay, an isolated area just south of North Cape, the most northerly part of New Zealand. Help came quickly in response to the mayday call. As the rescuers arrived at the scene, the yacht was high and dry and Roger was searching for his wife Anita. She was found on the beach shortly afterwards and had drowned in the surf.

The local Maori community put a taboo on the beach as a sign of respect to the dead. This meant the yacht was safe from petty theft. Anita is now buried in New Zealand, the yacht is abandoned and Roger has returned to England. A sad end to a sailing adventure.

The sea hadn't finished its destruction. A few days later, fearsome winds struck again gusting up to 75 knots. There were still a lot of our friends out there battling to get to New Zealand. A yacht on its way from Queensland, Australia capsized and was dismasted. Two of the crew were drowned. An American warship rescued the owner and his wife. On arrival in New Zealand she was hospitalised with head injuries.

Two more maydays went out 80 miles from the coast of New Zealand; American yachts on their way from Tonga were in trouble. *Freya* was spotted by a rescue plane. A helicopter then reached the stricken yacht. A diver was dropped into the ocean and then dragged on board the yacht. The father and son were winched to safety, followed by the wife and rescuer. The rescue took place in 30 foot breaking seas with 60-knot winds. They were taken to Whangarei suffering from hypothermia.

The second yacht, *Salacia*, was not so fortunate. A French crewed merchant ship went to their rescue. They managed to get a line across to the man and woman on the sinking vessel. He was pulled to safety; she slipped out of the life ring and was lost. The ship circled again for another attempt but the yacht was gone along with the woman. The captain of the ship stated that they might have hit the yacht on the second attempt. Still if he hadn't tried they both might have been lost.

The Pacific had taken its toll that year. Pacific means peaceful. That's a myth. We were glad it was behind us.

Auckland

Sailing into Auckland

12 November 1998

The morning after we had cleared Customs in New Zealand we moved to the Town Quay at Opua to obtain fuel, water and fresh food for the trip down to Auckland. The general store was built out over the water, resting on piles with its own dock leading to the back of the premises. The Post Office was next door with the Post Mistress standing at the entrance bidding everyone the time of day. They all replied, "Good morning Post Mistress". It was like the village of Trumpton come to life with Postman Pat, Fireman Sam, and Policeman Plod all as real characters thrown in for good measure. The Post-Mistress called over the veranda,

"Robert of *Breakaway*, your sister's on the phone."

The phone call from sister was to find out our ETA in Auckland. Now I knew an estimated time was no use as my mother was waiting and I would have to be 'dead on'. As it turned out,

Breakaway was half an hour late. Not too bad considering we had been travelling for two and a half years. Sailing up to Auckland Harbour Bridge, where the family was waiting, was a wonderful experience - we had made it – now all we had to do was turn round and head back home.

Fortunately brother-in-law Gary had booked us into Westhaven Marina in advance, as Auckland, the City of Sails, had introduced a policy of no liveaboards. That's us. In our case, they overlooked it, giving *Breakaway* three months berthing while staying aboard the boat. It is nice to get tied up securely with no worries of wind and weather.

New Zealand is hosting the America's Cup and this will attract the mega yachts of the world, small ships owned by the likes of the Aga Khan, the Getty Family, Sean Connery and Kevin Costner to name a few.

Westhaven Marina, Auckland

When I arrived in New Zealand in the 1960s, a family who happened to be cousins of mine arrived on the same ship, Johnny Johnson, his wife Lily and their young son Sidney. Sidney was five or six going to a new land. He is now a paramedic on a motor bike riding an awesome BMW fitted out to give early emergency medical help. His helmet is like something an astronaut would wear, with built-in microphones electrically wired to a screen on the consul of the motor cycle. There is no pillion seat. The area is used for a machine that stops cardiac arrest immediately.

If anything is wrong medically, Sid is fully trained to kiss it better. The idea is that the brave Sid can shoot off through the traffic to give critical First Aid until help arrives in the form of an ambulance and then the patient is taken to hospital.

He was telling me the first call was very exciting as he weaved his way through the rush hour traffic like the Good Samaritan going to give aid. With all lights flashing, he skidded into the driveway of the patient. Weighed down by electric leads still attached to the motor bike, Sid ran to the front door while the bike sat with the blue light flashing, giving a warning to all the neighbours that there was a serious medical emergency going on. Sid knocked the door. The wife came out. Sid tried to explain. The wife said,

"If you think my John is going to the hospital with pains in his chest on the back of a motor bike, forget it."

Christine
Bob and I are settling down to life onboard in Westhaven Marina.
It is much cooler here than in the tropics and the continental quilts
are out again. Youngest son Jamie has left us for a while to earn his
fortune cherry picking in New Zealand's South Island, along with
friend Steve who flew out to join him for the summer season. He has
been in touch, raving about the beauty of the country and especially
the Abel Tasman four day hike.

Settling into Life in New Zealand

Some of the travelling boats have decided to make New Zealand their home, mainly South Africans who have left their country and are making a new start. Immigration acceptance is worked out on a points system. Now £1 million adds up to all the points anyone would ever need. They are also awarded on your age, technical skills, talent and children.

Christine and I haven't any points, but those who have are settling in already. The live-a-board children are happy as schools have stopped for the summer holidays. Meanwhile the fathers are out job hunting, while the mothers are doing the rounds of schools trying to find one willing to accept their children, and find a house, hopefully all in the same area.

We are doing other things. Top of the list is knocking *Breakaway* into shape for the return trip. For me the Chandlery shops are like Aladdin's Cave. Since leaving home two and a half years ago we haven't had a chance to buy anything for the boat that has served us so well. During this period, yachting technology has moved on in leaps and bounds and there is so much equipment I would like to buy or update the old systems on board.

Breakaway may have to continue as she left – without the modern updated equipment but down below she is like brand new. I have been busy renewing the seals round the hatches. One of the boats, which went down off New Zealand this year, had its hatches torn off by the sea. A happy ending to that story though – this was the 11 year old boy and his parents who were winched to safety by a rescue helicopter just before the vessel sank.

When you hear of such events it makes maintenance work all the more necessary. Christine has touched up the varnish work and we have installed proper curtain tracks. Curtains serve two purposes; they give us privacy and help keep the boat cool in the heat of the day. I'm back to making shelves for more storage. Gary, our Kiwi brother-in-law, has got himself involved in the project, which makes life a lot easier.

Christine
Back home you rarely see exclusive vehicle number plates but down under they seem to be readily available. It certainly makes your car journey more interesting. Ahead of us the other day was a glamorous lady wearing designer sunglasses, driving an expensive soft top sports car, her long blond hair blowing in the wind. The registration plate read 'WAS HIS'. Not too hard to guess the story behind that one.

Westpark Marina, Clearwater Cove

Christine has run away from home and left me to my own devices for a week. She, along with Jamie, is off to Coromandel on the East Coast of North Island to spend a holiday with our friends and relations in a bach on the beach. Now a bach is a Kiwi term for a weekend house, a small retreat in the country where you escape from the pressures of the big city. Bach is an abbreviation of bachelor. When the young male Kiwi fled the nest for the first time, about two weeks after earning his first pay packet, he went to live in a flat with his mates.

I suppose you could say I am baching. Christine has left me tied up at Westpark Marina where liveaboards are welcome, with a full list of jobs and instructions on how to feed myself. The job list is creating a problem. Feeding myself is easy.

Christmas and New Year is holiday time - summer in the Southern Hemisphere - and the Kiwi sailors are down at the marina listening to weather forecasts. While the husbands check out the nautical aspects of things, the wives are inviting me on board for dinner. I hope the holidays are over before Christine comes home to *Breakaway*. My street cred will be gone. I am really the man who sits with a blanket over my knees while my wife sails the boat. Still, at the moment I am enjoying the fame.

Now on the up side, Jamie, our youngest son, who has sailed with us from Tonga, is suddenly in demand as an artist. After four years of study, his work is highly sought after. Unfortunately he flies home in a fortnight to be a prophet in his own land. At the moment he's selling paintings as fast as he can produce them.

While Christine is off gallivanting, one of my top priorities is an engine service. We are only half way round the world and *Breakaway* has a long road ahead of her. About the month of May we set off for Aussie. There are two ways to approach it, straight across the Tasman Sea or back up into the tropics and the French islands of New Caledonia. A bit of sunshine drifting again before heading for Brisbane and the delight of Queensland wouldn't hurt and the Tasman has a reputation, a bit like the Irish Sea and the North Channel. The only difference is it's about a 1,000 miles across.

It's strange having to spend so much time in one place after two and a half years of wandering like sea gypsies but as always weather dictates our itinerary. On land people are confined by the hands of a clock, but the movement of the sun across the sky controls us. What we will do on our return to Ireland is often discussed. Two people who have now lost all the land skills, more used to looking at a night sky as the boat crosses oceans. Even here where Bar-B-Qs don't require too many social graces we attack the meal like two camels preparing to cross a desert.

Christine and Jamie will no doubt return in a day or two. Meanwhile I work at the boat making a mess during the day and tidying up in the afternoon. Now to be honest, it's not all doom and gloom. There is the continuing flow of visitors all bringing their carryout and wanting to spend an afternoon sitting in the sun and enjoying the feeling of being afloat whilst safely tied up. When all the guests go home, I tidy up and settle down to an evening watching the borrowed television, some good, some bad but I have control of the remote control. I flick through the programmes happily, they are for the most part the same as we have at home, just a few episodes out of date, but then I'm out of date and enjoying catching up.

Well there you go, me on my own. I hope Christine and Jamie, who is out here spending his inheritance, don't arrive back and find me enjoying myself.

Christine
Well my wee holiday is over and I'm back to Bob asking me where his specs are, what's for dinner and such like.
Jamie and I had a great time lying about on beaches, having a refreshing swim in the sea and enjoying a cool drink at the vineyard down the road – our favourite spot.
After the free wine tasting session you could purchase a glass of your favourite and sit in the shade under the kiwi fruit vines.
It was a chance to learn more about our New Zealand family, Jamie's cousins Nicola and Graydon, his Auntie Geraldine and meet their friends, and for me to spend some time with Bob's mum who had come over from Northern Ireland especially to greet us sailing into New Zealand.
A very pleasant few days and, dare I say it, a bit of a break from Bob and his lost spectacles.

A Very Special Delivery

Auckland, as cities go, is very spread out. Because there is plenty of land, the buildings go sideways instead of up. It also has a large population of Polynesians. New Zealand is the protectorate for a lot of pacific islands, the Cooks, Niue, along with others. The islanders come down to the mainland to search for work and a new start for their families.

While we were visiting Rarotonga, or Raro as the locals call it, we were asked to bring medical supplies to Aitutaki, 160 miles to the north. We were willing but the weather at that time was far from favourable. The chances of a landing on the small atoll surrounded by reefs, being pounded by seas built up thousands of miles to the east, were slim. Unfortunately we had to say no and allow the reliable island trader to do the delivery. Eventually it put to sea, hit a reef and sank on the way there.

Our old friends Tom and Dee had stopped in Palmerston where they were treated to the hospitality that only the Pacific islanders can offer. They had to anchor outside the surrounding reef and be ferried ashore in the locals' boats and were not allowed to go back to their boat again until fed and watered and entertained on the small atoll until it was time for them to leave. A few nights ago they joined us to stay for bed and breakfast on board *Breakaway*. Their yacht *Axe Calibre* is tied up in the far north of New Zealand in Whangarei.

They were people on a mission. The locals of Palmerston had asked them to deliver a parcel full of presents to their friends and relations in Auckland. The parcel was meant for Christmas and Tom and Dee were a few weeks late, but the islanders work on island time and Santa Claus can come in late January. The only address they had was Otura in the south of Auckland. Out came the phone book and the family was pinpointed. Not a problem because everyone living on Palmerston has the surname Masters. Off we set, at one point we stopped to ask directions to be told white people wouldn't be welcomed, as it was a very rough area.

Christine and Dee said they could handle a bit of rough so we continued. As we cruised the streets of the suburb with me driving Tom's beat up Ford estate searching for our island friends, children and their mothers waved at us.

We only made one mistake. Seeing a man pulling out of his drive and desperate for directions I pulled in behind him to ask for help. As I struggled with the column gear change trying to find reverse, Tom got out waving his road map and the driver of the other car accelerated. Unable to continue down the driveway because I was blocking it, he had to drive over the grass, knocking down a hedge and a garden fence in his effort to escape. Tom ran after him still hoping to catch him before he made the road but to no avail. Wondering what had caused his panic we could only assume that he was making a quick getaway from persons unknown who were obviously going to serve him with a summons.

Eventually we tracked down the migrants from Palmerston where we were given a tremendous welcome. Dee had photographs of their family up in the islands. A few tears were shed. Not only had she photos but the big parcel of presents. As I sat among these people who offered us their kindness and friendship, I could only wonder what they were doing living in a suburb of Auckland when the palm lined beaches of their very special home beckoned them.

Christine
Clearwater Cove where Breakaway is moored is in the fruit and vegetable growing district and the roadside outlets for these products are very impressive.
Corn is abundant at the moment and you can buy ten cobs for two dollars (about 66p). Served piping hot with loads of butter, it is a meal in itself. Seafood is abundant and the shops sell the famous green lipped mussels, 'Alive, Alive Oh'.
They are very good to eat and especially beneficial to arthritis sufferers. My tip for today.
Store-bought mayonnaise, add a squirt of tomato ketchup, a dash of Tabasco, a squeeze of lemon and some freshly ground black pepper. This makes a tangy sea food sauce, but go easy on the Tabasco.

News of Daughter Kirstie

It seems a long time ago since we ran in front of a gale off the coast of Colombia heading for a safe haven in Cartagena de Indias. We were looking for a secure harbour to give us shelter from the easterly gales prevalent at that time of the year in the South West Caribbean. Drake and the Freebooters of centuries past plundered the same seas.

It was there we met Andy for the first time, a single hander on board *Voyager*. Every day he snorkelled and spear fished for food. Sometimes in the evening he would join us for dinner where he contributed his catch of the day.

We were bound for Panama and a transit through the Canal to face the Pacific. In Panama our daughter Kirstie was there to join us for the 3,500 mile passage to the remote islands of the Marquesas. Lying at anchor, supplies were taken on board and we were waiting for the weather in the great ocean to ease before starting the passage when Andy on *Voyager* turned up.

It was like a Mills and Boon story. Daughter took off in our dinghy and Andy wasn't spear fishing. Christine and I worried, you know, the way parents do. Still, he had his own boat, that is as good as a house, and he could feed her with fish, and with our lifestyle, who are we to point the finger.

Eventually the time was right to leave; the anchor was lifted as the three of us set off into the Pacific for the long haul in search of French Polynesia. Emotions were high as Andy set off, also for the Marquesas but via Mexico and other places fore-bye.

Thirty two days later we arrived at Hiva Oa and Kirstie went searching for a telephone only to find out that Andy had lost his boat off the coast of Guatemala.

Twenty miles offshore *Voyager* was taking in water at an alarming rate. In the darkness of the night he managed to slow up the flow and after hours of bailing he beached his boat on an isolated palm lined beach in Guatemala. There, like Alexander Selkirk who gave Daniel Defoe the inspiration for the book *Robinson Crusoe*, he effected repairs. But the 10-ton yacht was impossible to launch again without help and there was nothing he could do but set off into the jungle and look for a friendly village, hoping the local people could do something for him.

After a two-hour trek he found what he was looking for and arranged for a fishing boat to pull him off, but when arriving back at *Voyager* he found his boat stripped of all his possessions. Not only his personal effects but everything was gone. All the internal fittings of the yacht, the mast, toilet and cooker had been stolen. Even the electric wiring had been stripped out, leaving Andy with only a hull, no engine and minus the keel that had been removed for the lead ballast.

Kirstie eventually left us in Tahiti to fly home by way of Paris. Word came back to *Breakaway* that Andy had met her in Paris and they were getting married in August 1999. Meanwhile we were stuck on a South Pacific island with only the dancing girls for company whilst daughter and a ship wrecked sailor were enjoying the sights of Paris with no thought of us lying at anchor in a tropical paradise, lonely and emotional.

During our travels, we had met up with Leigh and Deb circumnavigating on *Chinook II*, 42 feet of ocean going splendour. They had been drifting around the world for 10 years and were heading home to suburbia and stability. And their boat was looking for a good home. The upshot of the whole thing is that Kirstie and Andy have bought *Chinook II* off the Australian sailors, to everyone's delight.

What does this mean to us? We will lay *Breakaway* up in Townsville in the Northern Territories of Australia and fly back to England for a wedding this year. After the nuptials, it's the four of us back to Australia to pick up the two boats. From there we will make our way back to the Northern Hemisphere.

Kirstie told me on the phone the other night that she and Andy are going on a five-year honeymoon. Who do they think they are? What a silly idea. Starting off married life enjoying themselves while they are young enough to do it. You are supposed to wait until you get old and past it. Anyway we are both very happy about the two of them.

Our youngest son Jamie has just left us after five and a half months sailing in the Pacific and touring New Zealand. When we sailed out of Carrickfergus the ropes were thrown off and the adventure started. People asked us at the time how we could leave the family. This obviously worried us also and there were tears shed as we sailed towards the open sea on the road to anywhere. As it has turned out, we have spent more time with our children than we possibly would have done at home.

Our eldest son Neill joins us in a few days for a two week holiday from work. The last time he was with us we sailed the seas off the Windward Islands in the Caribbean and visited Antigua, Guadeloupe and the wonderful clear waters of the French islands, Les Saintes. We will also be spending a lot of time with daughter Kirstie and Andy helping them prepare their new boat for sea.

Back to the present. At the moment the tide is out and *Breakaway*'s keel is buried in the mud of Auckland Harbour but shortly, when the cyclones in the north move in, we have to go sailing again. Do we cross the Tasman, the sea of storms or go up island to the French group of New Caledonia previously not visited?

The hazardous Coral Sea is ahead of us and also the Great Barrier Reef to be avoided before Townsville is reached. There are winter gales to face en route but with good marine weather information available on the radio we'll be doing our best to avoid them.

As we move into the winter months, your weather will be improving. Hope you have a good summer.

Ken's Car

Lil Cook was a teenager in Belfast during the War when she fell in love with a New Zealand navy man. A three-day engagement and then they were off to Dublin on the train for the two-day honeymoon. On the way south the newly married couple sat facing each other in the carriage. Lil said,

"You are very quiet, Ken."

"I'm always quiet," he replied.

A few days later Ken was on a convoy heading into the North Atlantic and bound for Russia with supplies. I first met them in the sixties when I was working in New Zealand as an electrician after emigrating down under on the £10 scheme. At that time they had a weekend house at Red Beach where I would visit at weekends. It has now developed into one of the most desirable homes you could wish for with a patio leading straight down to the beach and the constant sound of the Pacific.

In 1972 Ken bought an Australian-made Holden Automatic Estate. The couple had a family of four, three boys and a girl now nearly my age, none of whom are allowed near Ken's classic, which only has 60,000 miles on the clock. He lent it to us. Now the car is in pristine condition and about the length of a bus.

Everywhere we go people give the double take. Complete strangers talk to us, retelling their adventures as young couples taking their family on camping holidays in a similar car. But it goes beyond that. The young surfers stand in awe as we pull into the beach car parks. They give us the high five and shout "Yo Bro" thinking Christine and I are two old surfies from the sixties. It's quite nice being icons for a short time. Ken has already told me that on no account is a surfboard going on the roof of his car, not a problem, we can't surf anyway.

What a pleasure to drive a car with automatic gears, no power steering and none of the confusion of stalks sticking out of the steering column controlling multiple electrical gadgets that aren't needed. Ken is still quiet. I think he is worrying about his car. Thank you Ken and Lil.

The New Zealanders have proven to be a very hospitable race. Shortly after we arrived, complete strangers offered us their home for three weeks over the Christmas period. We are invited to countless Bar-B-Qs. To tell the truth, if we accepted all the invitations, we would never be in.

Where *Breakaway* is based at the moment in the upper reaches of Auckland Harbour, the marina is surrounded by houses second to none. The homeowners come down to their yachts and motor boats at the weekend to party. This marina is home to about 100 liveaboards who get up every morning to go to work.

By eight o'clock the car park is cleared. After work the pontoons fill with people discussing their daily toil over a cold beer, so they see us as slightly special as we sail our boat. I bask in the glory. Hopefully after this long lay-up we'll remember what ropes to pull.

Christmas with our NZ Family

Our son Neill has joined us for a couple of weeks so we are doing the tourist bit. It's good to see him and catch up on all the home news. Since we arrived here Christine has purchased a laptop computer, but I am not giving up my pencil.

Neill is going to put us on the Internet. Can you imagine this, me in an Internet café with a pencil. Everyone assures us this is the modern way of keeping in touch with the rest of the world. No doubt they are right. I will give it a go anyhow. Meanwhile the computer is Christine's, an area of the boat in which I am not allowed and a piece of equipment I dare not touch.

When the words 'what I write' are transposed to the PC it blips and beeps in confusion as the spell check is run through trying to sort out the Ulsterisms.

Rotorua

Son Neil is with us and we are on our holidays. His time is short, only 11 days down under but still it is a good break from the wind and frost of the Northern Hemisphere.

Breakaway is the family home, a floating house which evolves for the different conditions and climates we find ourselves in. We are unaware of the changes, like all things in life, they creep up on you.

Neill's first night on board we caught up with all the news and gossip from home. Next day it was off to explore, before jet lag caught up with him, down to Rotorua and all the delights of the geo thermal regions of New Zealand - booking into the Kauwai Motel.

What a joy. Hot water piped up from the bowels of mother earth for our pleasure. Each room had its own spa plunge pool to languish in. Mineral waters piping hot with the ability to cure all ills - now this was good. To me it also had the bonus of an armchair and a television hooked into Sky. I took full command of the remote control. Never mind the changes to *Breakaway*, do you realise Ena Sharples isn't very well.

Now New Zealand invented bungy jumping along with many other adventure sports, one of which is white water rafting. While they were working at that, Ulster came up with the ejector seat and the vertical take-off Harrier Jump Jet. Now I have no desire to be hurled out of a jet at 5,000 feet or to bungy jump, but Neill and I decided to have a go at white water rafting. Could the kids not stay at home?

Like most adventure sports they are graded to levels of difficulty. White water rafting starts at one, progressing to five plus. Six is recognised as commercially unacceptable as participants can be injured or even killed. Neill decided on a five plus. Christine said I had to go along to look after the child.

We arrived at the riverhead to be met by three young Kiwis smoking rolled up cigarettes, all bronzed with muscles popping up in the strangest places. We were fitted out in wet suits and crash helmets and informed to brace ourselves in preparation for a trip over a 21 foot waterfall in a rubber dinghy. Another "Oh my God" situation for the 'Breakaways'.

Neill, two Americans, a terrified English girl and myself humped the rubber boat down to the water. By this time the English girl and I were bonding, fear is contagious. At the arrival on the banks of the surging river, the Kiwis stubbed out the cigarettes and started a course of instructions. They told us not how to paddle our craft but how to survive when it smashed itself to death on the rocks and we were flung out.

If under the waterfall curl yourself up in a ball and go with the flow. Try not to lose the paddle. If the raft upturns, hang on, if possible, at all times hang on to your paddle. If you are stupid enough to fall off whilst in midstream, lie on your back with your feet pointing forward and go with the current. If, in this position, you accidentally go over a waterfall before we can save you, curl yourself up into a ball and hang on to the paddle. Paddles must be expensive in New Zealand. Anyhow, off we drifted down the gorge with the cliffs rising hundreds of feet above us.

The instructor shouted orders, we paddled, and everyone seemed to be getting the hang of it. The man at the back steers. I was in the front. The first couple of drops were quite exciting. Wet but safe, we had shot the rapids and come out the other end, gently drifting in a pool of clear water. I couldn't understand what all the fuss was about.

Then we hit the big one. The five plus and there was me at the front. The rubber raft hurled itself into space, hung about for a moment and then fell into a maelstrom. I was three feet under, the back of the raft bent over the front and then we surfaced totally out of control. Things were so bad that one of the instructors lost his paddle. We were lucky. The next raft capsized. We pulled them out of the water, them with broken noses and other associated injures.

It was good to get back to the armchair.

Christine

Most of the travelling yacht community use e-mail for keeping in touch. I must admit to being in awe of their ability to sit down at a screen anywhere in the world and manage to transmit a message home. Neill convinced me it was time I had a go.

The places where you can find the e-mail facility are known as cyber cafés here. It all sounded very scary to me but I was keen to try. We were directed to a screen and Neill began showing me how it worked. I was amazed. We logged on and then sent messages. The next day in another town 100 miles away, in another cyber café, I was informed on the screen that four messages were waiting for me. I managed to retrieve them and can't wait until I'm next in town to have another go.

Bob thinks white water rafting is tough. Getting up the nerve to surf the net is much more traumatic. I think I'm hooked.

The KISS Method – Keeping it Simple, Stupid

When *Breakaway* sailed out of Carrickfergus Marina in June 1996, she was a well-found yacht. A year had been spent preparing her for her travels. So far she has proved herself up to the job. At that time we worked on the K.I.S.S. principle. Keep it simple, stupid.

At the start of our adventure we were equipped with all the needs of a sailing boat - self steering gear for the oceans, a radio for communication and a GPS to tell us where we were - oh - and a pencil and paper.

Then we started to encounter the offshore cruisers and a world of technology beyond us. Yachts were equipped with generators, powered by the wind, electronic charts, radar and computers linked up to everything, with the capabilities of giving weather forecasts and tides for any harbour in the world.

Our stopover in New Zealand has changed the KISS idea in everything but the pencil and paper bit. I refuse to give that up. One of the first things we bought in New Zealand was a laptop and printer and it belongs to Christine, a thing of complete mystery to me.

Technology has reached a step further. Now the computer has the above mentioned tidal and weather programmes entered into it. The poor old boat is as confused as I am. In bad weather the computer can't be used in case it gets wet and that's just when you need it most. It isn't a lot of use. As for the tide, if the seaweed on the rocks is still wet the tide is going out. If dry, it's coming in. One of the great secrets when entering a new harbour is how to know if a seagull is swimming or paddling. This may not be of great importance in general terms; to me it's crucial. If you get it wrong the seagulls are inclined to smirk at you.

We also have a new echo sounder fitted. So far, *Breakaway* has managed reasonably well with a bit of string and a weight tied to it - the so-called lead line of old as used by Cook and Francis Drake. You throw the weight over the side until it touches the ocean bed. Pull it back on board and measure the bit of string that is damp - simple.

Not now. We send a sonar beam to the bottom, which tells us exactly the depth of the seabed the boat is crossing over. It also indicates any fish that may be about, and informs us the exact depth we are in as we go aground. Since we draw six feet, I already know that.

Next on the list was a radar - the all seeing eye - once again sending out beams. In theory when it hits a target a signal is sent back to make us aware of the danger.

So what stage have we arrived at now? Do I sit at the chart table and monitor all these new devices or do we continue to sail the boat by the seat of our pants as before. I think we will stick to the old ways and use the new devices, along with the old skills.

Part of the problem is the instruction manuals talk in a language I don't understand and to run the boat we would need a 12 year-old on board. For instance, after installing the radar I couldn't turn it on. Wouldn't you think they would equip it with a simple on and off switch?

Another purchase was a new hand-held radio that seemed like a good idea at the time. It made sense as a backup to the main system. Not so. Now when I go ashore Christine can monitor my progress. She calls up with demands for shopping. A tube of toothpaste, two toilet rolls. At the moment I really don't mind. New Zealand is an English speaking country, but when we arrive in New Caledonia my sign language is limited. Toothpaste I can handle.

Only six weeks until we point *Breakaway* north on the journey home. Christine and I are looking forward to it but that is going to take a couple of years with the Tasman Sea and the Indian Ocean still ahead of us. The smart battery charger is now flashing an orange light. I'd better stop and investigate it. Why did Neill have to leave and go home? We could be doing with him.

Christine
Bob's electric connection box is now like a plate of spaghetti with all the new additions to the electrics. As for Breakaway's interior, I have resisted buying too many souvenirs because there isn't room and a small space can soon become cluttered. By the same token we would like items round us that evoke memories. There is a nice new painting on the bulkhead given to us by son Jamie depicting our favourite scene - a tropical island bar under a palm tree with the sea gently lapping the shore. A few items are stowed away.
A Tongan priest's stick, which has great powers or so I was told by the shopkeeper and a Fijian war club that could come in handy if we are ever boarded.
Mind you, we already have a deterrent, they will probably fall over Bob's electrical wires.

Gulf Harbour

Belfast Lough lies about 54 degrees north of the Equator. The Arctic starts at 65.5 degrees north. Each degree is 60 nautical miles and a nautical mile is roughly one point one land miles. So we only live slightly less than 700 miles south of the Arctic Circle. Is it any wonder our weather at times is poor. Auckland is at 38 degrees south of the equator which puts it somewhere between 1,600 and 1,700 miles north of Antarctica.

There is a subtle difference. We have protection from America, the landmasses in the Northern Hemisphere are greater. Down here there is no protection. The winds of the south blow from the west with nothing to stop them. They are called the Roaring Forties, the name for gales in the Southern Hemisphere that the square-riggers of old searched out to achieve speed, but at the cost, hellish conditions for sailors and often the loss of ships and crew.

Autumn has now arrived in New Zealand and it's time for us to move again. The weather is still fair, though today it rained and blew a bit. In three days we start moving north towards the sun.

So it's up to Whangarei for the next few weeks to prepare *Breakaway* for New Caledonia, the last of the Pacific islands before Australia. Whangarei offers good shelter as the anchorage is 15 miles up a river. There we will meet with old friends from the Pacific. Some are staying here for another season, a few are moving along, much in the same direction as us.

An offshore cruising yacht is usually easily identified in a marina - everything on deck is lashed down. The aft end is adorned with solar panels, wind vane steering gear, wind generators and sometimes a few potted plants. On occasion there's a mongrel dog pacing up and down or a cat climbing the rigging. The weekend sailors can spot the breed immediately and stop for a yarn, usually inviting us out for a drink or a meal and more often than not a night ashore with all the luxuries of toilets, showers and a bed that doesn't move. You know the beds I mean, the ones that don't rock you to sleep.

Today was spent turning *Breakaway* into a boat again. It has been a country cottage for the last four months. The sails are holding up well. There were a few stitches needed but they should certainly hold up for the next leg to Australia. By then they will have to be looked at again. The main sail is ready to be hoisted with two reefs tied in. All the lines are singled up. We managed to photocopy a chart of Kawau Island. The forecast is reasonable - just - we are out of here

166

at first light. It's not a big passage, only 15 miles or so, but it is our first little step moving back up into the South Pacific.

As we work our way north, the clock is counting down, departure from New Zealand is only a month away. The onslaught of winter is near and the storms up in the tropics are just about past. It will be nice to swim again off the coral reefs.

The down side of all this of course is leaving friends and family. The hospitality of the Kiwis has been second to none. Sister Geraldine and family are coming to join us on *Breakaway* over Easter.

When we finally throw the ropes off I can imagine a few tears will be shed.

Christine
We had a family day out last weekend. The whole team of us had been given tickets for a cheese and wine tasting event. The weather was glorious, which suited the outdoor venue.

On our way in we were given a wine glass, ours to keep. We could then sample wines from all the regions of New Zealand and other countries.

The food on offer was wonderful. Samples of crab cakes, fish chowder, lamb kebabs, venison, ostrich, it was all there, even some cheese. Passing a reverse bungee jumping machine, Bob and niece Nicola decided to have an adventure and give it a go. We all went to watch.

By the time the rest of us struggled out of the car, they were back. At £10 a turn they decided it didn't warrant an adventure after all.

Whangarei Town Basin   34.43S 174.19E

Now I said last week and the week before and the week before that, we were leaving New Zealand. It still has not happened because of particularly nasty weather. Still the deadline is approaching fast with a wedding of the daughter to attend in August and Christine and I have made arrangements to fly home from Australia, so it really is time to move on.

Yesterday it was 'preparing to go to sea' day. Christine had done all the last minute washing whilst I checked the engine, filled up with fresh water, what we now call sweet water, and tidied up the deck. All the survival equipment is stored in cockpit lockers with the life raft strapped on the stern, alongside the flares and survival kit and a large container of water not quite full so that it can be thrown over and still float. We also keep a panic bag lashed down close at hand with a knife nearby to cut it free.

Now the panic bag is the ultimate survival kit. Different people fill it with different things. We carry matches, toilet paper, batteries, spare GPS, a chart of the area, torch, flares, glow sticks, sun cream, glucose sweets, high energy biscuits, pears soaked in chocolate sauce, 20 cigarettes and of course a hip flask with whiskey in case the situation becomes extreme.

So now picture the scene. Christine is down below putting all the gear away. It has to be done carefully, otherwise items rattle and roll and keep you awake when off watch. So Christine packs the gaps with whatever she can find and then goes off to collect the washing. I am outside in the rain stowing the lockers with ropes, spare water, and fuel, along with anything else that comes to mind. That is when I notice the leak. The boat is slowly sinking from under us. One of the sea cocks had failed; the means of closing off the holes in the hull to prevent water coming in. Boats only float if you keep the water out. I had just found a failed valve.

The movement of boats is restricted in Whangarei by the height of the tide so the lift out facilities two miles down the river were out of reach at this stage. Now we have a strange situation. A boat sinking but not quite as it is sitting on the bottom but as the tide comes in she can escape, but then she can sink. A betwixt and between situation. The cry went out for help.

Tom of *Axe Calibre* arrived along with David of *Anda*. Temporary repairs were effected and Christine made a cup of tea. Customs had to be informed that *Breakaway* was not leaving the Land of the Long White Cloud just yet. The boat yard and yacht hoist were going on overtime standing by for high tide. Two hours before the flood, ropes were thrown off and under engine we moved downstream with *Breakaway* suffering from a severe case of rising damp.

David had borrowed a car so he could meet us and take our lines. Tom was on board having a good worry along with us. Then we went aground on a sandbar not marked on the chart. I was starting to despair. Tom said it was his fault, I'll never know why because I was driving. The blame could not be laid at Tom's door. At least with the boat high and dry it was not going to sink.

The last of the tide lifted us off and we eventually made safe harbour and David threw his ropes, the crane lifted us out, the rain came on again like you have never seen. Christine and I fell into bed mentally and physically exhausted to sleep the sleep of the just with *Breakaway* sitting on hard land.

The rain continued the next morning but the repairs could not be put off. The faulty sea cock was removed and a new one purchased. To fit it meant my crawling into the locker and taking up a position with a two-foot wrench. At this stage my knees were up around my ears somewhere, with my right hand, which was holding the giant spanner, below my legs trying without success to exert enough pressure to remove the faulty but stubborn hull fitting. I tried to move my head to stop the rain pouring down my neck and that was when I caught my excess fat between my ribs.

"Deary, deary, me," I exclaimed.

The pain was excruciating and there was nothing could be done to relieve it, as I was now in a position only possible to an expert practitioner of yoga who had achieved a state of deep meditation.

Christine was only trying to be helpful as she draped a canvas cover over my head to keep me dry. This had the effect of plunging me into total darkness. Not only was I suffering severe chest pains, I had now gone blind. The "deary, deary me's" were coming thick and fast. I never read about this type of stuff in the yachting press.

The repairs were eventually completed and the rain continued to fall. The next day *Breakaway* was back in the water but with five inches of rain falling in three hours I am not sure if she ever left it.

All is well that ends well and we hope to move back into the warm tropical seas on Wednesday. For the last month, the low-pressure systems have been chasing each other across the Tasman Sea. The situation seems to be easing at the moment with a weather window appearing in the next couple of days. Let us hope that is the case. I am just about adventured out and a gentle sail to start the journey back to Carrickfergus wouldn't hurt. This trip is the beginning of the second half of the world, still a long way to go. It seems as if we are starting out all over again.

Dinghy Dock - Whangarei Town Basin

Christine
Word travels fast in these parts. I came up to drop off one load of washing when Bob told me the bad news about the leak. I was the first to hear of it but by the time I had walked back to the laundry room to collect the second load a complete stranger said to me, "sorry to hear about your bit of trouble."
Amazing – how did he know? Still what is truly amazing is the way people help you out. The first night of the drama we were picked up by car, then rowed across to Axe Calibre and treated to a three-

course meal. Feeling extremely cold and wet, the first thing our hosts did was hand us a pair of woolly socks each. Whangarei is also the place where travelling yachts made every effort to get to when babies were due. In fact one of the yachting community was a midwife and during our stay she could be seen dinghying between four boats looking after her charges – all new born - twins on one boat and a boy and a girl on the other two. It also meant the babies had dual citizenship, a much prized commodity.

Voyage to New Caledonia

Nouvelle Caledonie, New Caledonia, so named by Cook on his voyages of exploration, lies to the west of Isles Loyaltie and the Pacific Hebrides. Cook was enamoured by them as they reminded him of Scotland and home, even though he was an Englishman who sailed out of Whitby. New Caledonia was our next destination, the last of the Pacific Islands before we move into the Coral Sea and Australia.

Leaving New Zealand has not been easy, what with weather and family. My sister Geraldine came up to Whangarei to wave farewell, also delivering her only son Graydon and son-in-law Karl into our care. The boys had taken the King's shilling for the voyage north. After the emotional farewells, family set off south for Auckland and we prepared for the next morning tide to take us north.

The four of us enjoyed our last happy hour, but retired early in preparation for the next day. As it happened, it turned out to be a day of retreat as we tried to push *Breakaway* against 35 knots of wind over tide around Bream Head. It quickly become a no-go situation. As Churchill once said, "It was a glorious retreat." So we made our way up the river to a sheltered berth to rest up and prepare to face the fray again the following morning.

Next day with the seas easing but still a fresh breeze we managed to clear Bream Head and point *Breakaway* north for the first time in three years. The journey home had started. There was a low-pressure system lying to the south and a high to the north. What with the highs moving anti-clockwise and the lows clockwise down here, the reverse of the Northern Hemisphere, I was in a state of mild confusion. But as long as the highs did not meet the lows, everything should turn out all right.

Noumea in New Caledonia lies about 870 miles north of New Zealand, a voyage of eight days or thereabouts. To forecast weather so far in advance is impossible. After three days you are in the lap of the Gods. New Zealand's 'Des' of Russell Radio was there again to help us. He is one of the unsung heroes of ocean sailors. On a strictly voluntary basis Des starts works at seven o'clock each morning.

"Russell Radio, Russell Radio, this is *Breakaway*."

"Good morning, Bob, how are things with you?

"Not too bad."

We then give our position, boat speed, course, barometer reading and cloud cover. He then gives his predictions and advice. It might be to hold your course or move more to the east or west for better winds. It would only be a fool who didn't take his advice. The whole talk show starts up again at seven in the evening.

Des is not only a good forecaster, he is also an easy listener and as the yachts report in with their positions he has the ability to give comfort from the radio shack on land hundreds of miles away. I look forward to my twice daily chats to him with pleasure.

10 May 1999   22.17S 166.25E

The passage to New Caledonia has so far given us reasonable weather and we are both looking forward to the tropics again. Every day north is a 100 miles closer to the sun and the temperature increases daily. As we cleared New Zealand, the rig of the day was full oilskins and no one on deck without a harness. Each day becomes easier. The oilskins are away and it's summer gear again, shorts and T-shirts.

Karl caught a fish today, another first for *Breakaway*. In the midst of the drama Karl stood on the autohelm knocking the boat off course. At one stage I think the fish had him by the throat. Karl eventually won the battle, the cockpit was covered in blood, though the fish looked unharmed.

Now you must understand I am the type of man who buys meat in the butchers and I do not necessarily want to be a witness at the execution. But the evening meal was good and the fish could not have been fresher, even its relatives didn't know it was dead.

Breakaway now has only 100 miles to run to the reef-strewn coast of New Caledonia. We do not want to enter in the dark even though the passage through the coral is well marked. On our present course, and if we can maintain our speed, Breakaway should enter Bourail sometime tomorrow afternoon. From there it is a torturous route through the coral reefs up into the capital Nouméa.

If all goes to plan customs will have cleared Breakaway by tomorrow night and then we can enjoy all the delights that the French colonies can offer. At the moment Karl and Graydon have the French phrase book out trying to master the language overnight. French with a New Zealand accent is not the language of romance. At least they are making a stab at it. I have to stick to sign language.

Christine
At last we are safely tied up at the marina in Port Moselle. The yacht club's motto is Le Bout du Monde, 'the far end of the world' or 'a piece of the world' depending on who translated it for me. All four crew members of Breakaway are very taken with the place as the weather is perfect, dry and sunny with a cooling breeze, no mosquitoes and we are right in the middle of the main town, handy for anything we need. The fish and vegetable market starts early and I'll be visiting it as soon as I have mastered the value of the French Caledonian Franc. Trouble is I am converting it into New Zealand dollars, our currency for the last six months, and then sterling, torturing myself trying to see whether I am getting value for money.

Port Moselle, Noumea, New Caledonia 22.24S 166.25E

On board a fishing boat certain things were not allowed: white bone-handled knives, swan vesta matches, red headed women and whistling of course was out of the question.

At one time in Girvan, a Scottish port on the Ayrshire coast, a priest or minister, depending on your allegiance, was newly appointed, or anointed. He came down to the quay to 'Bless the Fleet'. They turned their backs on the man of God, retied their ropes and went home to the red headed women, because the day he chose for his blessing was seen as a curse to the fleet.

Isn't the world a strange place? Out here in the Pacific you cannot give a woman a small black pig. It can be taken out of context and you have to marry her. Another no-no is to pat a child on the head. You know the way you do. Not out here. This can allow the child's soul to depart and cause all types of confusion in later years and certain death to the one who did the patting. You cannot be too careful in Tonga. It is a terrible offence to wear a hat or carry a rucksack. But the world is full of superstitions. Things we all worry about. Don't walk under a ladder, don't step on a crack on the footpath or the devil will have you. Stories and fears go back before the age of Christianity, back to the times of myths and fables.

Today we went shopping for a couple of new T-shirts for me. On the return from the expedition, the Aussie yachts were coming back into the harbour in retreat, a wise seaman-like decision.

The Pacific is a big ocean. The Pacific people were the travellers of the seas and land became dangerous. The reef fish caused illness, but deep-water fish were good to eat. Because of the lifestyle controlled by wind and weather, the fables were built up and now the superstitions are truth and so they should be. With a full moon the tides are higher and sailing a canoe becomes more difficult.

We are now preparing to bid farewell to the shores of New Caledonia. The boys have caught their flight back to New Zealand. Customs has been cleared. Immigration has been informed. The

Harbour Master has shaken our hand. There is a full moon in God's heaven. And the tide through the pass in the coral reef is fair at nine o'clock in the morning. Then - in the words of an old sea shanty - 'We're bound for South Australia'. Well not quite, we are heading for Queensland where the weather is a bit better at this time of year.

When we arrive in Australia we have to start all over again with the Customs, Immigration and Port Authorities there. They have another unique set of rules. Before we could obtain a visa, proof of income was required. Income, what is that? We managed to duck and weave to overcome that one and were bid welcome - plus I had a note from my mother.

We are now running down our stocks of dried food, honey, popcorn, fresh vegetables, eggs of any shape or form encased in a shell, tins of British beef and of course wooden souvenirs and baskets. Everywhere we go, the rules change.

It seems the Aussies are quite liberal on the amount of booze we can bring into the country. Unfortunately we haven't any – it all ended up in a tip in New Caledonia taken ashore as rubbish by mistake. Will we never learn?

The trip across to Brisbane is 800 sea miles or about seven to eight days on *Breakaway*, though with a good ocean current behind us and the south east trades, the passage could be faster, which could mean overtime charges from the Customs men. The arrival time has to be very carefully judged. Australia is the only country to charge a yacht on arrival, and time and a half on weekends.

This is our last port of call in the Pacific and then it's the Great Barrier Reef and the Coral Sea. We look forward to it with anticipation and a degree of apprehension.

Christine
Why is it when you are looking forward to going somewhere, folk have to tell you horror stories? This one is about crocodiles. Hunted almost to extinction, they are now protected in the area we are heading for. Their numbers are increasing and they have lost their fear of man. One attacked a woman and, as is their way, put her under a ledge in the larder. The Police found the body and

placed it into their boat for a proper burial. The crocodile, not pleased to be losing his lunch, climbed into the back of the boat and took it back off them. What with deadly poisonous snakes climbing on board to bask on your decks and sharks just waiting for you to go for a swim, it is all a little off putting. More cautionary tales are in the front of the Pilot book for cruising in Queensland and I quote:

'Entanglement in the tentacles of the sea wasp is almost certain death. Sea snakes are mostly deadly. When swimming, choose sandy-bottomed lagoons so that you can see the sharks. The death adder lies in sand and strikes when trodden on. The cruising person must be doubly cautious when in the wild. The taipan snake will attack without cause and has the most deadly venom'.

That would certainly put an end to any idea of a swim off an out-of-the way beach or even a walk to stretch the legs.

The Coral Sea

Breakaway's decks cleared for passage making.
Extra fuel and water tied to the 'granny' bars' at the mast.

The Atlantic Trade wind route is known as the Milk Run, the Pacific is sometimes called the Coconut Milk Run. As boats travel the world they use the winds and currents that are available. We stepped off the beaten track and chased our dreams to New Zealand. One of the problems is getting back out of there. For us the route was via New Caledonia, the next leg being Australia.

Day after day we watched for the weather window to allow *Breakaway* to point west. Full of confidence and ignorance I decided the day was right. I was wrong and the poor old boat, along with me and Christine, slogged to windward for two days.

Now windward work means going in the direction that the wind is coming from which is contrary to where you want to go. But the wind backed, we eventually could fill the sails and head in the right direction. The change came on the third day out of New Caledonia and the crew settled down to life on the ocean again. Watches were set, three hours on and three off. If conditions change and the wind freshens, waken the other crew. You crawl out of bed, slide over the table, gather yourself, attach a harness and go onto deck to sort out the problem. A rogue wave smashes into the boat, the decks are awash, you are awake and coming to life.

The oceans are a strange place, hard to describe. It is your turn to take the deck, three or maybe four hours of watch-keeping. The moon is on the wane but the stars are giving a good light. You look down below where the world is full of peace and calm. But you are on watch, a lonely man with lonely thoughts.

The time goes past slowly on the night shift. Usually not a lot happens. The self-steering gear points the boat in the general direction, the sails pull her along and when the wind is steady *Breakaway* gets on with it, knocking off the miles slowly but steadily.

Meals are something to look forward to. At times they can be basic. In rough weather I do most of the domestic side of things. I am one of the lucky ones and cooking I can handle in most conditions. Even with the boat heeled at an angle of 30 degrees I manage to put a meal together. If conditions are good, we allow ourselves one drink in the evening before the meal. It is the one time of the day when we both sit in the cockpit together. The sun sinks over the horizon, one goes to bed and the night shift starts all over again.

On the passage to Brisbane, Australia, another yacht came into sight a couple of miles from us. I called them up on the radio. *Capricorn* was bound for New Caledonia against the prevailing winds and conditions were not easy on board as the comfortable following seas *Breakaway* was experiencing were breaking over *Capricorn*'s decks as she went to windward. The skipper turned out to be a man from Cork who sounded very tired and disheartened. They were not going anywhere very quickly. Ships that pass in the night - he went back to work - I went back to looking around me, their light was soon lost in the three-metre swell.

As we closed the coast of Queensland, more traffic started to appear, mainly in the shape of oil tankers plying their trade on the oceans of the world. If one of them hit us, it would not feel the bump. As their lights appear on the horizon, we become more alert, preparing *Breakaway* to alter course if necessary. They also have watch keepers and are aware of the small yacht. Depending on who has right of way, the other alters course. We call them up on the radio as it is easier to change direction on *Breakaway* than it is on one of these giant ships. They usually say,

"We have you on radar, hold your course."

Breakaway entered Moreton Bay in Australia a couple of hours after first light. The ocean chart was put away and the new one brought out of the chart table. The fairway buoy was where it was supposed to be and from there we picked up the shipping channel. It was relatively easy and there was a ship just being boarded by a Pilot. We tucked in behind. A Belfast Pilot was once asked did he know where all the rocks were. He replied,

"No, but I know where they are not."

The ship soon left us in its wake and the next 30 miles to Scarborough was spent hopping from buoy to buoy, avoiding the sandbanks and shifting shoals that give the bay its hazardous reputation. Nightfall comes quickly in Australia and we were pushing hard to find the marina in Scarborough before darkness. As *Breakaway* approached, a prawn fishing boat moved aside to let us pass. I waved thanks and he waved back.

Welcome to Australia. The yellow quarantine flag was flying in the breeze. As *Breakaway* entered the marina, we were told to go onto the quarantine dock and if we required clearance that night there would be an overtime charge. The following morning was time enough for us. A full night in bed sounded very attractive.

Christine and I tied *Breakaway* up with a fence between Australia and us. Various sailors came down to say hello and swap yarns through the barred gate. Them on one side, us on the other.

That night the lights on *Breakaway* went out early. No more watches, no more tankers, no more reefs for the foreseeable future. Tomorrow morning customs and the quarantine inspection service will be down at nine o'clock to make sure there are no animals or infectious diseases on board.

If *Breakaway* gets the all clear we are then free to roam Australia at will, an island continent big enough to set Europe in. Australia we look forward to with pleasure.

Australia

Christine
The first thing I noticed waking up the next morning, our first day in Australia, was the beautiful clear song of the bell bird. It is a wonderful feeling, the sounds are strange and foreign and you cannot wait until you are free of all formalities so that you can go exploring.
Things taken for granted in everyday life for us have a special importance, especially your first shower after seven days at sea. Pure luxury.

Breakaway is now parked at Aquatic Paradise, 10 miles to the south of Brisbane in what is known as a canal development, one of the last in this state. They are now frowned upon by the environmentalists for whatever reason.

The yacht is tied up to a private dock. Our pontoon is fitted with electricity and water for the boat and a table adorned and shaded by a sun umbrella. The foreshore has palm trees and a magnificent plumage of crimson flowers along with other exotic plants to be enjoyed. About 20 paces away is a swimming pool with a Jacuzzi to supplement it, big enough for a family. We have a key to the side door of the house, giving the owners and us privacy, and have also been provided with a television for entertainment in the evenings.

Our new friends Del and Evan were determined to run a television aerial down to *Breakaway*. This of course would have allowed us the use of Sky, along with countless other programmes. I had to call a halt to their generosity. Two nights ago one of the neighbours came on board along with a drop of whiskey and a set of car keys. Roger put the keys on the saloon table. He offered the use of a car and we helped him drink the whiskey.

How did we get here? Over the Christmas festivities at my sister's house in New Zealand a lady called Del turned up and invited us to stay at her and her husband Evan's dock in Moreton Bay.

So here we are. Evan is unfortunately down with the flu at the moment but he dutied off his friend Roger to Pilot us across the sandbanks of Moreton Bay from Scarborough to Aquatic Paradise. That is a story in itself. Roger steered the boat and I became chief cook and bottle washer. I am looking forward to Evan getting better as he built a 42 foot steel yacht and has a lot of sea time behind him.

A couple of days later we set off in Roger's Mitsubishi with Christine navigating and me driving a car with more buttons than a piano organ. Air conditioning came off and on, rear view mirrors kept changing the view and the windows continually opened and closed at will, but we eventually got the hang of it.

We were off to Noosa in search of Irish Immigrants. My Aunt Peggy was always a very adventurous woman. Peggy and Jackie now live in Noosa, Queensland. They joined the Canberra on her maiden voyage as she sailed out of Belfast for New Zealand and the Southern Hemisphere. After a few years in their new home, they moved across to Australia and all the delights of the sunshine coast.

They now live in a retirement village called Noosa Outlook Retirement Resort.

What a pleasure to see them both. Jackie and I sat out on the back deck having a smoke and a beer catching up on old times while Peggy made lunch and met Christine for the first time. Lunch was a big bowl of Irish broth. There were tales to be told and memories of Belfast to be remembered that night. The next morning Jackie made an Ulster fry - if there was something unusual about the whole thing, it was the cook standing at the stove dressed in a pair of shorts wearing an old fashioned pinny.

But it was time to return to *Breakaway* in the Japanese electronic nightmare called a four-wheel drive, though I was getting the hang of it and starting to enjoy the experience. We took the scenic route. It was time now to explore the harbours and anchorages, which we would explore on *Breakaway* in the near future. As sailors looking out to sea from a harbour you notice the rocks and reefs; all the hazards out there trying to catch you unawares. *Breakaway* has only been a short time in Australia but we still look at the escape routes.

Eventually we made our way back to Aquatic Paradise and all the comforts of *Breakaway*. Del, our hostess came down to say hello, claiming she missed our company. The three of us sat in the cockpit as the sun went down. The new moon was rising with Venus bright and clear above it. It was good to be home after a couple of great days.

We are enjoying Australia.

Christine
The Sunday markets in Brisbane are something else.
I have been to a couple and enjoyed wandering around. There is the second hand/gadget type of market were you can buy anything from an electronic restraining collar for a dog to a receptacle for growing worms to release into your garden – fascinating.
We visited a craft fair today and there were so many things I wanted to buy but the restriction of living on a boat stops me dead, to Bob's great relief. Where would we put the lovely frog doorstop or the large wooden box for your potatoes and onions, the ceramic pots, bread bin and the quaint old garden bench? I came away empty handed. But on the way home we passed a market garden. Fresh vegetables were laid out on an unattended stall with an honesty box. Finally I was able to spend some money, so it is cauliflower cheese tonight.

King of the Road

Australia is the land of everything on a grand scale, sheep stations and ranches, many of which are bigger than some European countries, roads that run towards the horizon with a stretch of straight highway 100 miles long. Out here the last of the frontier men are the truck drivers, kings of the road carrying loads weighing up to 250 tons.

Daughter Kirstie and fiancé Andy's boat *Chinook II* is lying 800 miles to the north of Brisbane in Townsville. We wanted to go up and check it out before the wedding. You understand we wanted to have a good nosy, but the distances are so vast the cost of flights or train rides were prohibitive, so back to the truckies. We managed to hitch a ride north with Jim, not exactly a king of the road, more a pretender to the throne.

Off we set into the night following the Bruce Highway in the head lights beam. Eight hundred miles without rest except for the occasional pause at a comfort stop to wash our hands and fill up with food and diesel. The Aussie breakfast is a big one. We were there to keep our driver company and I dozed as Jim talked to Christine, trying to keep her awake.

The truck thundered on towards the tropics, the verge of the tarmac attracting kangaroos. After the heat of the day, dew forms on the road, this runs off onto the verge making the grass green and sweet for the animals of the bush. Unfortunately it also attracts them to the main long haul highway in Australia where the trucks take their toll. The roadside is littered with road kills, big and small, kangaroos, wallabies and dingoes.

All the vehicles are fitted with crash bars on the front, an Australian invention to break the impact and save the car or truck. They seem to work.

Then we hit sugar cane country, the home of snakes and the venomous cane toad. We continued without incident passing over Last Goodbye Creek, a massive riverbed with no water flowing and trees growing in the middle all waiting for the big wet. For eight hours at 60 miles per hour there was sugar cane. Sometimes we had to stop to allow a train to cross the road. They were filled to the top with sugar, each train pulling up to a 150 cars. One was so big that it had another engine in the middle to help take the load.

Daylight came eventually, Jim had put 700 miles behind us, time for another comfort stop. In the past the cane was cut by hand, gangs of men working with machetes harvesting the crop. Before they started work, controlled fires were lit to burn off the surplus vegetation and drive out the snakes and toads.

Only a 100 miles left to Townsville and *Chinook II* and they still burn off the cane fields. As the sun rose, the mountains appeared - colours changing by the minute as the light moved higher in the sky. The bold Jim dropped us off with our sleeping bags and packs. He had only 200 and something miles to cover to Cairns, his destination. He kept on trucking.

A new town for us and a new adventure so off we went looking for a place to rest our heads. Then we met Karen and Ian, the couple from *Walkabout*, our old friends from the Caribbean and Pacific. They gave us a bed for the night along with a few drinks and a good meal. On top of all that they took us sailing out to Magnetic Island just inside the Great Barrier Reef. We anchored in Horseshoe Bay.

Inside the Great Barrier Reef

In Australia today it is frowned upon if you kill anything, including sharks. At one time beaches and bays were surrounded by shark nets to protect the swimmers – no longer – today they lay hooks with bait attached to distract 'Jaws' and feed him so he won't eat the humans. None of us went for a swim.

Incandescent another cruising yacht, dropped anchor close by, more old friends from the Pacific. For two nights we told the old tales again, fought the gales, outdid each other with our bravery, sails ripped, rigging failed, lives saved by great feats of seamanship. But when it was all said and done we have one up on them. We had travelled with Kiwi Jimmy, 'King of the Road'.

It was time for *Walkabout* and *Incandescent* to sail north for Cape York, the Torres Straight and Darwin before heading into the Indian Ocean. Ian dropped us at the beach and we waded ashore to catch the ferry to the mainland. My fantasy daydream was of the ferry captain suffering a heart attack with the call going out for someone who could drive a boat to volunteer. I was ready, sitting in my seat like a coiled spring. The call did not come.

When we arrived back in Townsville after bidding farewell to *Walkabout*, our first priority was to find accommodation. We also wanted it be within walking distance of the boatyard where *Chinook II* was stored.

The first place to welcome us was the Republic Hotel. We made our reservation in the public bar that was reminiscent of a saloon in a John Wayne movie. Our intention was to stay for four nights. The barman suggested we only pay for one, which should have been a bit of a hint. Up the rickety stairs, along a long corridor with brown carpet that used to be some other colour, we found a room with a view. The other residents grunted "hello" and a few girls were still dressed in their night attire. I must say they appeared friendly enough.

Christine did not seem too happy when she came back from the ladies toilet stating that the seat had been left up and that there appeared to be what looked like peepholes in the partition.

We spent the rest of the day clambering over *Chinook II*. The honeymooners are sure to enjoy it; a well-equipped boat designed for the oceans. We were tired after a walk back to the Republic, eating a carry out of fish and chips, having decided to give the hotel dining room a miss. The view from our room was over the beer garden. The tropical sun went down and the patrons arrived to enjoy themselves below our window. One of them had a continuous hacking cough that rent the night air, giving the impression he was not long for this world, accompanied by his mates shouting "shut up" in between choruses of 'Tie me kangaroo down sport'.

Occasionally some of the singers would break off to go for a walk with one of the female residents; they could not have gone far as they were usually back in about half an hour. It turned out to be a long night. The next morning we moved out.

Townsville, Queensland

185

Backpackers' rooms are cheap and clean in Australia. Just what we were after so next stop was the Adventurers Resort. Backpackers is youth hostel type accommodation; we had a double room with shared cooking and toilet facilities. From the outside it looked like San Quentin Correctional Institution but after a quick inspection we decided to stay. There did not seem to be a lot of young people about, but of course it may not have been the right time of year for student travellers. The next day we discovered why - the majority of the rooms were occupied by people on welfare with their bed and board being subsidised by the State.

As the following day was a public holiday, our neighbours were at home. Just because you are on the dole does not mean you are not entitled to a day off like everyone else. As the night wore on, each landing had Bar-B-Qs blazing as the inmates broke all the rules. On one side of us a Maori family were dancing the Haka, struggling to make themselves heard over the sound of a didgeridoo from the level above us.

Then a stranger stopped to talk, his name was Mick. He lived down the street in St Vincent de Paul's. Full board there was only £2 per night, but you were not allowed to drink or smoke and had to be in bed by nine o'clock - a place for people who had fallen on hard times. As Mick explained all this to us he kept bringing one knee up to his chin and lowering it, repeating the exercise with his other leg like an athlete at the start of some great race.

Now Mick also spoke with a lisp, add this to a strong Australian accent and things were becoming confused. His ambition was a career in a hotel, hopefully as a receptionist. Suddenly he brought his wrist up to his face and looked at it, he was not wearing a watch, with one bound he was gone, it was five to nine, lock up and lights out time down the street.

As we travel around the world we invariably encounter shopping malls – each one the same as the last, filled with franchise holders for international companies selling their products with the same sales pitch. If you travelled and only stayed in the Sheratons or Hiltons all you would experience was the Sheraton and the Hilton. Normally we are off the beaten track with our home *Breakaway* to go back to at night. Townsville was different, the accommodation was not five star but as least it was a novel experience and the natives were friendly.

Christine
Leaving Australia, we flew home to Kirstie and Andy's wedding.
An un-scheduled visit but very welcome for all that. The wedding
was great, all the family was there and Bob and I even managed a
trip back to Carrickfergus, our home town. Of course all the talk was
of the new boat Chinook II and the plan was for Breakaway to sail
up to Townsville, help the newlyweds sort out their new floating
home and then both boats would sail down to Brisbane to avoid
cyclone season in North Queensland.
As Bob said, "I suppose it is not so much losing a daughter but more
like gaining another boat into the family."

Queensland Coast

Five days ago we finally managed to get out of Moreton Bay with a 50 mile run up to the beach resort of Mooloolaba where we had been told there was a good anchorage. Good it was - and unusual. As we approached, a coastguard vessel was coming in too. He must have noticed our home port on the stern as he called up on the radio.

"Is this your first time here? – follow me, you are a long way from Belfast."

He then proceeded to give us a guided tour of the area,

"To your port is a new canal housing development - over to starboard is the Yacht Club Marina, the beers are cold - just ahead, there is a pontoon where you can get fuel and water – come more to port, it's a bit shallow on that side – just go ahead of us now and drop the hook wherever suits. Enjoy your stay."

What a nice way to enter a strange harbour. In the wee small hours of the following morning we slipped down the river in darkness, no one awake to notice our leaving. Once clear of the harbour with sails set and a course laid, Christine retired and I stood the first watch. Daylight soon came and we were both up for our next challenge, the entrance through Wide Bay Bar. The chart warns:

'Wide Bay Bar should not be crossed without local knowledge. The directional leads on Fraser Island and Inskip Point may alter as the bar shifts'.

Calling up the local Coastguard watch officer, he informed us their lifeboat was out on a training exercise and were more than happy to train with us. We had just got our local knowledge. Off we went again following the volunteer Coastguard being escorted in safely and shown the sights along the way.

Continuing our journey, Frazer Island is the biggest sand island in the world and the sea bed reflects it. With strong tides throughout the area, when the tide ebbs, it leaves sand banks exposed throughout the channels. Everything is very well marked but with the constantly changing sand bars the authorities have trouble keeping the buoyage updated.

Christine
It has been quite a day. We are now safely anchored off Kingfisher resort. With the dinghy launched we went to explore our new anchorage. It is a totally different world onshore. No cars are allowed on the Fraser Island ferry. Only 4x4 vehicles as the ferry deposits the vehicles on the beach. Bars, restaurants, swimming pools and shops are all tastefully hidden away among the eucalyptus trees with connecting wooden walkways. One sign caught my eye,
* 'Do not feed the dingoes, they may have different tastes'.*
Kingfisher Resort rents out cabins in the bush and I can see why it is so popular. Built along the lines of the early settlers homes with tin roofs and shady verandas, they are close to the amenities but private and secluded - a very restful spot.

Townsville Motor Club Marina S19.15 E146.49

It has been an interesting week. We are tied up in Townsville Motor Boat Club Marina. It has turned out to be the most expensive marina we have stayed in to date. But everything has a bonus, we are five minutes' walk from town and our neighbours are a couple of travelling vets from Brisbane. They are moving around Australia on a concrete boat called *Bedouin*. Peter fills in for vets on holiday, earns some money and then they move on – a James Herriot of the outback.

The practice he is now working for loaned him a car along with a weekend off so he invited us to join them on a safari. We did not have to be asked twice. The sandwiches were packed and the flask filled, the Harpers were bound for Ravenswood.

Now Ravenswood at one time was the major town in North Queensland and all because of gold. The American gold rush had petered out just about the same time as the first strike was made in Aussie and so Ravenswood was created, from a prospector lifting the magic metal on his shovel. The dreamers flooded in chasing wealth. Some found it, most didn't. Ravenswood boasted 75 pubs and 70 brothels. The Catholic Priest gave a sermon saying,

"Some people pray at Church on a Sunday and some people prey on their fellow man the rest of the week."

He was right but it did not change anything. They chased the gold as usual, and if lucky, spent the money foolishly. Today Ravenswood has 200 people, two hotels – or Aussie pubs – a court house, a school along with an historical society working hard to sustain those buildings that are left. The gold mining still goes on but under the auspices of a company that employs people. Somehow the vision of a man in work clothes driving a Japanese 4x4 does not compare with the image of a prospector arriving in town with everything he owned being pushed in front of him in a wheel barrow.

The Old Gold Mine

But even today this near ghost town has its charms. You breast the hill and stop under the shade tree, the dust settles and shimmering in the heat is Ravenswood, two hotels with bat wing doors, few customers and the mine workings of the last century just as they were left.

First stop, the cemetery where all history finishes - dry, parched ground with no rain to disturb the lonely graves. The gate creaks as you open it, the entrance to the real history of the town,

'Jean aged two, always missed.'

'Simon, 18 months, taken to heaven'.

So the list goes on in this sun-scorched field, headstones of marble worn down by wind and dust, bleached by the hot sun. You feel you are standing at the graveside with the mourners of old. Most of the memorials are to the young in this lonely paddock.

All the gravestones give birth and death details but what is unique to the Irish families is the extra information on where they were born - Kilkenny, Kildare, Newry - people still hanging on to their heritage in a land far away.

Then there was Mrs McGrath's shop. A structure of wood with a corrugated iron roof filled with things that are no use but all great - just bits and pieces with no commercial value - each and every one a treasure reminding us of our youth. Washing boards and tin baths, you know the type of stuff, carbide lamps along with a wheelchair with one wheel. Essential equipment. Then I spotted a wind up record player with a record. One of the old 78s, it scratched and screeched. It was obvious the needle was blunt.

"I have more," she said.

"Get them out," I said.

Fitting a new needle, Christine sang along with Mrs McGrath, 'the night that you told me those little white lies', trying to fight her morbid curiosity and not looking at a series of photos of a cat being devoured slowly by a python.

From there, across the road, was the 'Star of the North,' now making up 50 per cent of the hotel accommodation in Ravenswood. An old Queensland structure - verandas to give shade, a circular bar where the stock men gathered to prop their elbows on the polished wood counter, relax and tell each other of the massive drives when they moved cattle on the hoof down to Adelaide, 1,500 miles across and with little grass for the poor beasts to eat.

Then sheep came to the area, an idea brought about by the civil war in America and the abolition of slavery - no workers - no cotton. The continent of Europe needed wool as a substitute. Gold was getting hard to find but the land was not suitable for sheep. The fortunes of the town fell by the wayside and other centres sprouted up leaving Ravenswood behind. But it is on the way back. The efforts of the few remaining locals and tourism have brought a revival and there is still gold in 'them thar hills'.

The 'Star of the North'

Well, that's my news for today. Tomorrow morning we have to move *Breakaway* around into Ross River and six o'clock comes early, particularly in Australia. We are 10 hours ahead of you.

Christine
We were to see more of Australia's uniqueness on our visit to the old gold mining town. As our friends took us up a track to a lookout point en route they spotted a wallaby with her joey, almost as big as she was. Disturbed by our presence, the baby jumped into its mother's pouch and they stood there wondering what we were going to do. A little bit further down the road, looking as if they had been ordered to pose for us, were three emus, while across the road was a camel. It was like driving through a wild life park. Ant hills were also part of the landscape, built so that they lean towards the north – a navigational aid for lost travellers.
I am also glad to report that Bob and I will soon be heading out to the airport to pick up Kirstie and Andy and take them to Chinook II. (The boat's name is a Canadian Indian word for a warm breeze). The feel good factor is very high at the moment.

The Creek

Sailing around the world involves periodically calling into repair shops or boatyards and putting yourself and your boat into the hands of the Philistines. They lift you out and smile, "Welcome to Peaks or Powerboats in Trinidad" – "Hello to Vuda Point Fiji" – "We are so glad to see you in Landas Auckland."

Breakwater Marina, Townsville 19.15S 146.49E

Now of course there is Rosshaven in Townsville, Australia. Like all the rest of them the rules are 'No cash, no splash'. These people want to take money off you at an exorbitant rate. If you don't accept their terms, you don't go back in the water.

Also in nearly every anchorage there is the alternative approach to boat repairs, known wherever you travel as the 'creek'. It works on the self-help co-operative basis. There are always endless cups of tea in the creeks of the world, also experts planning the next project. Each phase of the operation is discussed in fine detail, mainly involving financial out-goings and how to avoid them. The purpose of all involved is for one person at least to escape the creek, on a craft of great beauty, heading for the sun-drenched anchorages of the seven seas.

The method of building usually favours concrete or ferro-cement, as it is known in the sailing clubs – a much-maligned material with no real faults except for the people who apply it. The Rosshaven creek committee is taking the traditional approach. It seems that big Mick's wife's sister's husband's cousin used to do a bit of building and was still a dab hand with the mortar board and float. Now the fact that big Mick left England 50 something years ago, abandoning kith and kin, and hasn't been back since, did not deter our friends in the least, it just changed the subject under discussion. For a while it was time to reminisce. Big Mick had gone off to fight the Germans and had never returned home, ending up in Aussie.

This started Harold off. In today's politically correct world Harold would be classed as vertically challenged as he only ever grew to four feet eleven inches. Harold wanted to join the Australian Army as a lorry driver taking troops to the front in the Korean conflict. This was not to be, as his feet did not reach the pedals. Any mention of the American Automotive Industry at all sets him off. He is, however, full of praise for the Japanese as they make cars to fit his size perfectly.

Rocky IV came back into the conversation at this stage. He had got his name because he owns four boats, none of which work. Between them there is not one that floats or moves forward, but to be fair the meeting was being held on Rocky's boat *Affinity* which was parked on land overlooking the river.

Rocky had been in the galley making another cup of tea and had overheard parts of the conversation concerning conflicts long past. He claimed that whilst he served in Australia defending the continent from Japanese invasion in the forties, (the Germans were not a worry because they could not get past big Mick), the powers that be put bromide in the tea of the Aussie soldiers, at one time a common practice to take the minds of the troops off matters of a sexual nature. It slowed down the urges so that they could concentrate on the job at hand which was killing the enemy. At this stage Mick said,

"D'you know, I think it is starting to work."

The professional boatyards do not have this calibre of people on their payrolls.

Two hundred yards away is where *Chinook II* is having her refit before facing the oceans of the world. Each morning Brian the yard manager appears, gives a sharp intake of breath, shakes his head and tries to fill us with doom or despondency, the only solution being the expert help the boatyard can offer. "Thanks Brian" but no thanks.

Chinook II is slowly coming together, in fact the launch day is so close we have moved *Breakaway* out of the Creek and into the Marina to prepare 'our house' before cruising the coral coast.

The marina is about two miles away but it is a world apart from Crocodile Creek – full of plastic racing yachts, gleaming in the sunshine, just waiting for their owners to arrive. As we slipped our mooring in the creek things became a bit emotional. From the bank the committee waved, "Good luck", "Bon voyage", "God Bless", "Come back and see us." I intend to. The Australian equivalent of *Last of the Summer Wine* is alive and well up a creek in Townsville.

Christine – 1 January 2000
Happy New Year!
Cockroaches are not the only bugs on board Breakaway. The millennium bug had inhabited my second hand personal computer. When I switched it on to see what would happen, it had returned to the day it was born – 1980. Not too much of a problem except in the tidal programme. All was resolved, as Andy is a bit of a whiz with computers and soon had the system up and running again. Living on a boat means you are self-sufficient in a lot of areas, making your own power, carrying your own supply of water and fuel, so the media warnings to stock up with life's necessities in case the millennium bug caused havoc, was not too difficult for us.
Today Bob and I walked into the town. The ATM machines were in full swing and McDonalds was serving breakfast. All was right with the world.
ps. While I was in collecting the latest batch of photographs, I overhead the pharmacist passing on a tip to a customer who was enquiring about what is the best thing to take to avoid diarrhoea when travelling abroad and finding yourself in less than sanitary conditions. "Eat some yoghurt every day," was his advice.

The Launch of *Chinook II*

2 January 2000
It is not unusual for me to be slightly behind the times but here we are in the new Millennium – Christine and I have moved into the 21st

century with a sunrise in Australia. None of it really matters, we will all continue with our own concerns about work, family and friends; it's nice that while technology moves on, people remain the same.

Chinook II, the other half of the fleet, is now in the water, tied up in Breakwater Marina on the other side of the dock from *Breakaway*.

Andy and Kirstie are like any other young married couple in their new home, although instead of painting and papering they are rubbing down the decks, varnishing the bright work and checking the rig. This 'house' has to cross the Indian Ocean so the seaworthiness of their new home is of first priority. She is a very pretty yacht.

When the boat was launched, the engine fuel system had to be bled, as do all diesels after major overhaul. Whilst Andy looked after this problem, we lifted floorboards and checked for leaks. She was only sinking slowly plus the engine would not start. The man on the boat hoist stood by. The leak was stopped. The man on the hoist said,

"Goodbye, they do not pay me overtime."

We were cast adrift. As his car started, so did *Chinook II's* engine and we motored out into the river, he with traffic lights to contend with on his way home and the four of us setting out into the unknown.

Chinook II is now safely tied up. The first day in the water caused stress, but it also gave a lot of pleasure as she cleared the pier heads and into the roads of Townsville waters. The wind freshened, there was a ferry coming in from Magnetic Island full of holidaymakers. Andy gave way to port - the passengers waved - the spray threw a rainbow over the bow - Kirstie picked up the leading marks for the marina - Andy swung the wheel. The swell was slight, the day was warm.

Christine put out the fenders and Kirstie organised the stern. I looked after the bow. As we entered the walls protecting the marina, a fisherman pulled his line in. The new 'house' had found its first temporary home – only a short voyage but one we will all remember.

As *Chinook II* pulled up to the dock, a man who we had never met before was there to take the lines. Six foot two, wearing an Aussie bush hat over a bandanna and an earring displaying an ivory dolphin, our soon to be good friend Graham shouted, "Welcome."

The heat in the boat yard had been untenable, what with the temperature in the high 30s and 90 per cent humidity. Black dust covered everything and endless hours were devoted to cleaning *Chinook II* in preparation for a day's work. But all that is behind us now that she is afloat.

The marina where we are staying is close to the town. There is a sea breeze to cool things down, a swimming pool only two minutes away and a lovely shore walk around the bay. A boat's proper place is in the water and although the facilities are good in Townsville we are all keen to be on the move and see how *Chinook II* performs.

Christine
After a disturbed night due to the heat and humidity, Bob and I were jolted into action by a knock on the side of the boat.

"Breakaway, how about a swim in Alligator Creek?"
Our boatyard friend Irene, who loaned us her car on several occasions, had called to take the crews of Breakaway and Chinook II out for the day. So with a picnic packed off we set up the Bruce Highway into the Bush, passing mango orchards along the way. It was a popular spot and we were lucky to find a place to park the car and also a vacant picnic table under a gum tree. On closer observation we found it already occupied. A kangaroo was lying in the shade, totally unconcerned with our presence. What a treat, we staked our claim and then walked the short track down to the creek.

It was wonderful; there was a large pool of deep clear water which was just cold enough to be really refreshing, fed by a small waterfall. What with sharks, sea snakes and deadly jellyfish in the sea it was great to be able to swim with no worries, secure in the fact that there are no alligators in Alligator Creek. Irene and her family gave us a great day out and on our way back we stopped to buy a tray of mangoes, the last of the season - delicious.

Rosslyn Bay

16 January 2000

The two boats had to get out of the cyclone belt and head south. Unfortunately the prevailing winds are from that direction so it made it a bit of a slogging match at times. Tied up to a berth for the night brings a much needed rest. As we pulled into the marina, people came to help with our lines,

"Hello *Breakaway*, nice to see you back."

We had stopped at this spot three months earlier on our way north. Two days later it was Australia Day, the 26th January. It is a national holiday so we decided to stay and join in the fun at the Capricorn Cruising Club, after all everyone needs a bit of a break and *Chinook II* had caught up with us. Andy was always glad to stop and work on the boat and Kirstie came with us for the sail past.

The holiday morning started early with the yachts dressed overall, standard procedure for a celebration, with signal flags being hoisted in their proper order. Most of the Aussie boats flew homemade bunting and *Breakaway* hoisted the flags of all the countries she had visited. The occasion was the Blessing of the Fleet. A Minister of the Cloth stood on the yacht club pontoon as each vessel passed he called our her name and then,

'God Bless all who sail in her'.

The first in the sail past was the island ferry, an extra bonus for the passengers and then the local yachts, motor cruisers, the Coast Guard and finally *Breakaway*. It says somewhere, 'the first shall be last'. He gave us a special blessing welcoming the Irish and asking for the light to shine down on us. We all felt quite emotional. Christine wanted to blow our fog horn but I felt it was inappropriate to honk for Jesus.

Christine

As Breakaway sailed down the coast of Australia we left ahead of the other half of the fleet, Chinook II. After a few hours, however, she hove into sight and it didn't take the larger boat long to overhaul Breakaway and show us a freshly painted red stern.

As the night came we enjoyed a full moon and the comforting glow of Chinook II's stern light ahead of us. It is good to have company sailing, it also means when you arrive at your destination there's a chance of fresh milk and bread waiting for you and perhaps even an invitation to dinner. Coming in last has its appeal. We should be meeting up with the other long distance cruisers soon. Some have been hiding from the cyclones in Brisbane and further down the coast at Sydney and there will be a large number making their way over from New Zealand after Easter when the weather is more suitable. It will be great to see our chums again.

Burnett Heads

30 January 2000

Breakaway sailed through the night from Rosslyn Bay to Burnett Heads at the mouth of the Burnett River, which is navigable as far upstream as Bundaberg. The passage was quiet except for some fishing boats that surrounded us at one stage, going about their business.

There were not too many of them as the government has put a quota on catching prawns so that the crustaceans can re-group, and the fleet has been laid up for three months. The conversations on the VHF radio as the various skippers discussed politics and government were colourful. Most of their comments were unrepeatable.

Next day we arrived in the river planning to anchor but a marina berth looked attractive after a night with little sleep. *Chinook II* was a day behind us so we set off to explore and pave the way for them. The township of Burnett Head is not even a crossroads, it is only a T-junction. The top of the T consists of the Post Office, a bakery and a butcher's shop. Across the road is the pub taking up more acreage than the rest of the town. Nobody has bothered to build anything on the other corner and the road disappeared among the cane fields running straight as far as we could see. A bus comes once a day to take you to Bundaberg but not on Saturday and Sunday. It does not necessarily return once a day. There was a sign on the bakery window,

'Due to Yvonne's maternity leave, bread will only be available in the morning. In emergencies the butcher will be able to provide some in the afternoon'.

Who was responsible for Yvonne's condition, we don't know, but the Post Office was full of speculation.

The main source of entertainment was the Blue Water Sports Club overlooking the small Marina, well worth a visit. It is full of local colour with men in heavy boots wearing shorts, singlets and stockman's hats. The lady behind the bar was lovely, handling the hard men of the cane fields with soft words. The fishermen started to appear and a pool competition got into full swing. We left to head back to *Breakaway*. In the middle of the road a dog was feebly scratching itself. It was probably safe enough. The next day was Saturday so it didn't have to dodge the bus for two days. The excitement was too much for us so we planned to move up the river to Bundaberg the following day as soon as *Chinook II* arrived.

The river is well marked with buoys but we planned to move up on a rising tide. This meant that if *Breakaway* touched the bottom the rising water would allow her to float again. As it turned out, we cleverly followed a local boat so the journey was without incident and the two of us could relax and enjoy the scenery and the wildlife - sea eagles and pelicans - and motoring through the cane fields, a brilliant green of new growth, was amazing.

Bundaberg is certainly more exciting than Burnett Heads. Both boats are tied up five minutes' walk from the main street. I use public libraries a lot, they are always air-conditioned and you can read the papers and magazines for free. On my last visit the librarian made me welcome but asked me to avoid the area where there was a guest speaker lecturing the Society of the Chronically Fatigued. I couldn't help but stick my head around the door. Almost everyone was asleep.

Billabong Wildlife Sanctuary

Christine
It's against the rules to 'cuddle a Koala', or so the notice said, but Junior took a liking to Kirstie and before the keeper could do anything about it he was in her arms. The problem is they have very sharp claws for climbing trees and they are not as cute as they appear. However Junior's manners were impeccable and he was the highlight of our visit.
There was also a lot of worthwhile information handed out on the conduct of crocodiles, which is good to know as Breakaway has to anchor in their territory.

Time to Regroup

Our big job this week was sorting out charts for the journey back to Ireland.

Indonesia alone is an archipelago consisting of 13,677 islands, though now with the loss of control of East Timor it may only be 13,676. The charts for the group are not easily obtainable but as the whole area is unsettled with civil unrest we may choose to avoid it.

If this is the case, *Breakaway* would leave Australia later in the year for the Indian Ocean going straight across the middle before turning right for Sri Lanka. We would then have the option of a last quick sortie out into the Pacific to visit Papua New Guinea and the Solomon Islands, then back to Australia via the Torres Straits to restock in Darwin in preparation for all points west.

As this was not part of the original scheme, we now have to plan the route and buy the charts we need. So far on our travels we have managed to swop charts and Pilot books with other sailors but it is proving difficult in Australia as most people are heading in the same direction. There is still the option of photocopies but they are not always good enough for shallow waters and inshore work.

It would be nice to go into the Pacific one more time as it is unlikely we will ever travel as far by yacht again. Papua New Guinea, the Solomons and Borneo are all a bit off the beaten track. Borneo is now known as Kalimantan. However 'The wild man of Kalimantan' doesn't have the same ring to it.

In the approaches to the Great Sandy Strait

Tin Can Bay, the Great Sandy Strait 25.48S 153.12E

Breakaway and *Chinook II* decided to dodge the weather and find shelter in Tin Can Bay. What an odd name for what turned out to be a charming place. It is really a misuse of an Aboriginal word for the dugong.

The dugong is similar, if not the same as, the manatee of the Florida Keys except it has an Aussie accent. Up in Florida the poor old manatee is being driven to extinction, the main danger being fast powerboats damaging the slow mammal with their propellers. We were fortunate in seeing a few of these gentle creatures. They greeted us on our way into Tin Can Bay, gently moving with the waves. The old sailor men thought they were women who lived in the sea, creating the myth of the mermaid. Those poor sailors must have been a long time at sea and a long way from home.

The marina entrance was fairly tight, but like everywhere else someone was there to help. Christine was on deck and I was driving – a kick astern and *Breakaway* responded. Christine passed the lines ashore to our old mate Laurie Piper of the gaff-rigged schooner *Atlanta*. The last time I talked to Laurie was on the radio as he headed for Rarotonga in the Pacific,

"I am storm rigged and on a sleigh ride, sorry Bob I have to go on deck – OUT."

That conversation took place a few 1,000 miles ago. Since then Laurie and *Atlanta* have come home to regroup. *Atlanta* is now running charters in the waters of the Great Sandy Strait.

We found ourselves falling into the lifestyle of Tin Can Bay fairly easily, living in the Tropics is inclined to relax you. They say that after four years of going 'troppo' you really are not much use to anyone – especially an employer. Laurie offered me a job. Unfortunately the rules of Australia do not allow me to work as a deckhand or anything else for that matter.

Our friend arrived early the next morning to take us up to his property, about 40 acres of the prettiest country side you are likely to see, especially since it had rained solid for two weeks. Before the rain it was parched and dry. At the moment the grass is a lush green – the dam was full and the cockatoos were singing songs. Kirstie and Jana, Laurie's daughter, rounded up two of the horses on the farm and took off trekking among the gum trees.

They had to be back at one o'clock as that was when Kev the

farrier was arriving. Kev arrived and the horses didn't, at least not for a while. He didn't seem to care. Talk about laid back. In between cups of tea and cigarettes, the story unfolded. At 14 years old, Kev went to work out west on a big property, well not that big; just about the same size as Ulster. Anyhow about a week into the job the owner and stockmen were going out to muster the brumbies, the wild horses of Australia, running free for the taking. Kev was only an apprentice stockman so they left him behind. The boss told him to shoe the horses.

"Shoe horses...how?"

The horses were running around in the paddock and the necessary tools were lying about.

"Just get on with it."

Many years later Kev is an expert. I always thought that horseshoes had five nails on one side and four on the other, not according to Kev,

"We get the shoes made in Malaysia mate, Korea makes them but you get no wear on the bitumen with theirs 'eh? Sometimes we put three nails in both sides or maybe four 'eh? A toe clip forward on the hoof and one on each beam back aft 'eh?"

Kev was now talking to a sailor. This was a big man not designed for bending over. Homo sapiens, the ape that got up and walked - his back was hurting. Kev has spent his life bent over examining horses' feet. He walked carefully with his bushman's hat and a leather apron and a mouth full of horseshoe nails.

"Don't ever look a horse in the eye 'eh? They are not hunters, they are runners, look them in the eye, what have you got mate, confrontation 'eh? What happens, they run and I am left with a shoe in my hand 'eh?"

Kev would then wander back to his little propane forge to adjust the Malaysian shoes to fit each customer taking all the time in the world, never quite finishing the story, leaving you in abeyance waiting on his next words of wisdom.

"Drive the nail in the right part of the hoof mate, don't go into the quick 'eh? White or light coloured hooves are softer, that makes them easier than dark ones to drive a nail into - but don't buy a horse with four light coloured hooves – eh?"

Kev loaded his portable forge and anvil into his Ute and rolled a cigarette. I would have loved a smoke. Did I mention I have given them up?

"Have a good one 'eh?" says Kev.

"You too mate," says I.

Laurie had stopped drinking months ago, but made an exception on this occasion.

"A beer mate," he said.

"Seems reasonable 'eh?" I answered - I have started to talk Queensland. "We'll stop down in Tin Can and catch the sunset eh?"

Christine
Tin Can Bay had still further delights to offer. At high tide just off the Coastguard Station, dolphins would come in close to the shore. They were there waiting for the land dwellers to feed them. In the past a black Labrador used to swim with them. They would all head off together across the bay and the dog would return exhausted but happy. Some of the locals were not pleased about this strange liaison, concerned that he would hurt the dolphins. One day he mysteriously disappeared from his home. For a while the dolphins didn't come back, they missed their chum.

Aquatic Quays, Brisbane 27.29S 153.13E

Cyclone Steve has just passed through Cairns in tropical Queensland leaving chaos in its wake. Townsville, where we were based for a few months, missed the full strength of the winds but flooding caused extensive damage. It was because of the approaching cyclone season that we moved the two boats south.

Breakaway is safely tied up in Brisbane, well outside the Cyclone belt back in the canal system of Aquatic Paradise at the bottom of our friends' garden - Del and Evan Jones. Andy and Kirstie came in a few days later to moor *Chinook II* next door, courtesy of the neighbours. The Jones were heading to New Zealand for a family wedding and wanted us to house sit for them.

Del, Evan, Andy and Neighbours at Aquatic Quays

For us it will also be a bit of a holiday moving back into suburbia, with the added attraction of the use of a car. The whole escapade promises to be good fun. Christine is in charge of the interior making sure everything runs smoothly – on the downside she may get used to a dishwasher and all the other labour saving kitchen appliances and I will have to prise her away when the time comes.

My instructions are to look after the swimming pool, situated just outside our bedroom, access is through the French window and across the side of the Bar-B-Q area. It really looks after itself. Every other day I put a cupful of hydrochloric acid into the water. Don't ask me why, I am just following instructions. Living in the house clears *Breakaway* for a bit of maintenance. Her varnish work is starting to look a touch weary again.

Meanwhile next door an upholsterer was coming to look at *Chinook II's* main saloon. Days have been spent looking at materials, far too many colours and combinations to make a choice. The whole thing is very complicated. The colour must be light to make the area look larger but that means you could stain it easily. Cotton is cool but polyester is tough. Down in this part of the world they try for cool, up in our latitudes we want a feeling of warmth. I make every effort to avoid these types of discussions. You could be blamed later if things don't turn out as expected.

After our arrival in Australia, Christine and I both signed up to Medicare. There is a reciprocal agreement for British passport holders for free health care. Both of us have suffered good health since leaving Ireland but here was a chance to get things checked out and so we called into the local clinic.

Melanoma or skin cancer, caused by the sun, is a big threat out here and someone of my age spending lots of time in the outdoors is obviously at risk. The doctor started to search my head and face for the dreaded signs. Christine has often said I need my head examined.

It was decided that some dubious looking bits of flaky skin would have to be burnt off my scalp. For this they use liquid nitrogen to zap the offending area. I was nuked five times. My lady doctor assures me there is nothing to worry about. I am booking for another zapping session in two weeks. So you can understand my lack of interest in soft furnishing materials. It is hard to concentrate with your head looking like a pizza. This from the man who stopped smoking for the good of his health. You can't win, can you?

Christine

It's a bit strange sleeping in a king size bed when we have been used to lying on a bunk. Oceans of room, but I still cling onto the edge. Old habits die hard. Bob is not coping. In the middle of the night he gets up and goes back to his shelf on Breakaway but I still have company. Poohs, a Burmese cat of 15 years, likes her comfort and snuggles in beside me. At her great age I am watching her very carefully, I don't want anything to happen while she is in our care. I have never had a dishwasher but am now completely sold on the idea. It is absolutely marvellous, I love it, what a great labour saving device. I wonder if we can fit one on the boat, along with a microwave, washing machine, drier, fridge, television, bath, etc...

A Fridge at Last!

We are now safely ensconced back on *Breakaway* after our house sitting adventures. It is good to have a full night's sleep undisturbed by strange noises – cars starting up, dogs barking, phones ringing, dishwashers going through their cycle, neighbours talking and alarm clock radios coming on. Then there are the bins to be put out and the grass to be cut.

On the boat you are rocked gently to sleep uninterrupted except maybe for the splash of a fish jumping. Our alarm clock is the sea birds giving the wakeup call as their day starts. The living space on *Breakaway* would not be considered enough room even for the smallest lounge in a house but it is what we are now used to.

Youngest son Jamie is coming out to join us in a few weeks to give us a hand to spend his inheritance. He will get the good room up forward, commonly known as the fore peak. He lived there for six months in the Pacific so knows what to expect – a bed just long enough for his frame with four small open lockers for his worldly goods.

Under the bunk 30 gallons of water is stored along with other bits and pieces in deep storage – a bag of woolly jumpers and sweatshirts, socks and blankets and stuff that really should be thrown out but we can't bring ourselves to do so, using this area the way householders utilise attic space.

Before he arrives, we want to take *Breakaway* out of the water to clean her bottom and paint it with anti-foul. She has a little garden growing below her waterline at the minute, which makes her very slow as the growth causes drag. As soon as Jamie arrives we will give him a week to acclimatise and recover from jet lag then we are on our way. The route will take us north to Cape York and over the top of Australia heading for the Indian Ocean via the Torres Strait and the Arafura Sea. With Darwin our last stop in Australia. This should be a leisurely trip of about 2,500 miles, hopefully spending most nights at anchor. It is important for the boat to be efficient and able to achieve her full speed over these types of distances otherwise we would add days to the journey.

One of the other projects being undertaken on *Breakaway* at the moment is the installation of a refrigeration system. We are one of the few boats without one. The Americans in particular are shocked to discover *Breakaway* has no means of freezing food. Aussies are dumbfounded that we cannot chill our beer. For a while I got around this by telling them that our fridge was broken down, this they could understand and sympathise with but Christine refuses to live the lie any longer.

Aided and abetted by son-in-law Andy, they ripped out my tool storage area under the navigation seat. Andy then extended the seat and installed a hand built box, which he sealed with epoxy. Around this interior box was a four inch gap which he filled with self-expanding insulation foam from aerosol cans. At one stage events got slightly out of hand as the foam expanded more than any of us had expected, creeping out of the sides of the new structure like something out of *The Quatermass Experiment*. Andy kept calm in the midst of panic keeping things under control.

The finished result is a thing of beauty. The next stage is to fit a cold plate, which will be supplied by a compressor under the chart table, all very clever. Now instead of eating fish straight out of the sea and fruit straight off the trees, we will be able to browse around the frozen food sections of the supermarkets with the best of them, looking at the sell by date of the products. Well you don't want to have anything that is not fresh do you?

So you can imagine things are fairly busy on board *Breakaway* at the moment.

Christine

Through Del, I had been invited out into the country for lunch with a group which meet every fortnight called 'Bitch and Stitch' who have a common interests in stitching, needlework, embroidery, knitting and such like. Our drive took us up into farmland as flat as a pancake, past road signs saying,

'Beware Koalas crossing – we live here too'.

The weather was perfect, a sunny day but not too hot. The area we were heading for is prone to flooding and the road has markers along it showing up to a metre in depth, but this is the dry season and there were no such problems for us. After a great lunch and a chat, and we were not being bitchy, honest, I had a chance to wander around and soak up the atmosphere. The area was mainly vegetable crops and the parcels of land were small, being close to the city I suppose.

Glenda, our hostess, keeps horses and uses the place at weekends, with the intention of building a house to retire to in a couple of years. As the sun started to go down, the shadows stretched across the land and the colours were magnificent, orange, yellow and cream – so soft for such a harsh place.

Son Jamie is Back Amongst Us Again

Son Jamie arrived a few days ago. We had borrowed a car and set off at three o'clock in the morning to collect him from Brisbane airport. The plane was on time but Jamie did not appear for another hour. Customs had decided to have a closer look at him.

When anyone is coming to join us, Christine always asks for stock cubes from home. So when questioned by the Customs Officer, youngest son broke down under interrogation and confessed to carrying herbs, all in neat little squares wrapped in silver paper. Mind you for a while the authorities thought they had cracked an international drug ring but they eventually let him and his stock cubes into the country.

Jet lag has taken its toll and he falls asleep at the strangest times and then can't sleep at night. This is one of the drawbacks of air travel.

Jamie catching up on his navigation

Breakaway's speed does not create any problems. Someone said one day's travel on a boat was an hour in a car or a minute in a plane to cover the same distance.

Tomorrow *Breakaway* will be lifted out for a bottom job and then Evan and I are going on a little sailing holiday for a few days. We will go up the coast as far as Mooloolaba. It is our way of paying them back for all their kindness. After that Rodger and his twin sons are joining me for a little excursion. Hopefully out to Lady Musgrave reef if the weather permits, a round trip of about 400 miles.

They are the neighbours from the other canal who have shown us great hospitality. Rodger and Evan are both New Zealanders who moved across the Tasman Sea. This is not unusual with Kiwis being allowed full rights of employment and benefits in Oz. Rodger has taken Australian citizenship. He claims the operation was not too painful.

Christine
With Bob away and Jamie visiting Chinook II to help get her ready, I have only myself to entertain. Staying in the house with Del we had an early start this morning helping a friend out by driving a van and delivering 75 flamingos to a Brisbane household. A first for me I have to say. It was a 50th birthday party and the idea was to sneak into the garden and set up the pink plastic flamingos and a large sign so that when the birthday boy woke up and looked out of the window he got a lovely surprise.

I would think it is quite a nice way to earn a living and the good thing is you get paid for making someone happy. Everyone was excited to see us and there was a great atmosphere of conspiracy, lots of whispering and knocking things over trying to keep quiet. We stuck the wire legs into the lawn and when finished it looked incredible, as if the flamingos had landed in a flock out of nowhere. It was first light but worth the early rise. Trouble is, we have to do it all again tomorrow morning, as the flamingos' disappearance has to be as mysterious as their arrival. Our hosts have been so good to us and Breakaway will be heading North and the long run home very soon. I have a feeling Del and Evan will make it to the Northern Hemisphere one day where we can repay their hospitality.

Mooloolaba, Queensland 25.35S 153.39E

5 May 2000

Tonight the winds are raging off the coast of Queensland. Down on the Gold Coast the beaches are being washed away. Up north the tropical low is travelling towards Yeppoon, the anchorage where *Breakaway* was blessed by the Pastor – the Priest – or was it the Salvation Army Chaplain? Anyhow at this stage the power of the blessing for fair weather is in doubt.

Meanwhile in Mooloolaba the harbour entrance is untenable, outside the ships of the world are lying to their anchors and the Pilot boat cannot get over the bar at the mouth. All beaches are closed to public access. I went for a stroll today along the strand with the spume and the spray pounding the shore and the lifeguard in his little hut on stilts, cleaning the windows. As you approach the beach there is a sign: 'No dogs, no tents, no cars, no bicycles, no skateboards, no fires'.

As I walked along, an illegal dog joined me for an illegal stroll. I threw a stick - he brought it back. I retrieved it after a bit of a struggle while the canine pretended that he was a killer and any attempt from me to gain possession of the stick meant instant death. I threw the stick again. By this time the lifeguard had cleaned the windows as Rover and I came past.

"The beach is closed, sir."

"Right," says I.

The dog buried the stick, the storm raged, the dog went home and I went looking for Christine. She was in the email café printing out news from the cruising fleet.

Walkabout is at the entrance to the Suez Canal ready to make her transit north to the Mediterranean. *Papangayo* is sheltering behind an island in Egypt. Their passports have been taken from them by an Egyptian gun ship, a common practice and nothing to be too alarmed about but still a bit of a worry.

Tom and Dee of *Axe Calibre* are leaving the land of the South Sea Poms (New Zealand) to make passage to Australia. Alan of *Incandescent* is back in the Channel Islands repairing the plumbing in his house while the boat rests up in Thailand.

The dog had dug up the stick and walked down the promenade of Mooloolaba with us. Dogs have to be on a leash.

"Is this your dog?"

"No," I said to the policeman.

"It seems to be with you."

"No, Officer, I am with it."

There were two young skateboarders going by wearing helmets. Well you can't be too careful can you? On the subject of brushes with authority, George of *Tortilla Flat* is like all the Yachties, too many days at sea as Captain under God, as long as your wife gives you permission.

Anyhow back in the mists of time, when we were in Panama, George hired a car to source some parts for the boat. So off our Austrian friend went with French Roland for company. George missed the turn off and did a U-turn around a traffic policeman. Roland closed his eyes. The policeman called ahead for help to track down the traffic violation. Eventually George was captured by a motorcycle cop, blue lights flashing. The fine was $150. George tried bribery,

"Would you accept $10?"

The policeman was shocked, "That is not how it is done, you pass me your licence with the money in it."

George apologised and passed over the licence. It came back empty. The man on the motor bike then escorted George to find his car and made sure he was back on *Tortilla Flat* safely. They shook hands - honour was satisfied all around. Afterwards George was relating his adventures in the Yacht Club bar when someone interrupted,

"It's people like you who are destroying the system – the going rate is only $5."

Back in Mooloolaba the waves are still crashing on the shore. The international boats are waiting to move north - *Chinook II* and *Breakaway* along with them. We have applied for our cruising permit for Indonesia, from there it is north through the Straits of Malacca, maybe with a stopover in Borneo.

The Malacca Straits are renowned for piracy but if they leave us alone we won't set George on them. Then Singapore, Malaysia, Thailand for Christmas – catch the North East monsoons to Sri Lanka or perhaps India. From there to the port of Djibouti at the bottom of the Red Sea. It is French, the old British port of Aden will not let us in to stay.

I did not mention the Seychelles or the Maldives, *Breakaway* might slip in there for some rest and recuperation. Next week the compass points north. We are half way around the world, and also half way back. The storms shall pass and in less than 18 months we shall – hopefully – be moving up St George's Channel, the Celtic Sea, the Irish Sea and the North Channel for home. How can Thailand or other places in the Indian Ocean compare? We will soon find out.

Christine
You do the best you can. Make sure the washing is up to date, stock the boat with food supplies and then...wait. Queensland has never known such a prolonged session of wet windy weather. The cyclone season is supposed to be over but they are still forming. I think it will be a few days yet before we move on and then there will be a last minute panic on my part to do it all over again.
Still, I have the new addition of a fridge so there will be more variety in our offshore diet. We can extend the fresh vegetables we carry to

broccoli, cauliflower and even a lettuce, some vacuum packed meat and a few packets of bacon for a tasty snack or the basis of a meal. I am already feeling the benefit as there is very little waste food now and I do not need to go to the shops so frequently.

There is only one problem. I can only hope Breakaway's batteries hold out – two problems actually, because of the fridge, Bob has lost his tool box area and he is not too well pleased.

The Queensland Coast

Si-Ju the Finnish yacht, was on her way back to Australia after suffering damage. Customs was there to meet them when they entered the marina, then they came to *Breakaway* to relate their story. They were sailing along, not hard going but 380 miles of windward work to go to their destination of New Caledonia. Daylight had come and Juorma went down below while Siv harnessed in to take over the deck. The boat virtually lifted out of the water with the force of an impact. Juorma joined Siv on deck to see the cause.

The water was brown as the blue ocean mixed with red blood. They had come into contact with a whale and obviously both sides were suffering wounds. The boat was taking water and one bulkhead (the supporting wall) had moved half a metre. There was a long rent in the side of the boat.

Three whales surfaced a short distance away and then they headed for the yacht again. As they got close they dived, our Finnish friends hung on tight. Two passed underneath, the third rammed them hard. Hard enough to move the toilet off its mounts and destroy the saloon table. The whales surfaced and looked at *Si-Ju*. A third charge would finish the yacht. Siv was by now on the radio, but to no avail. The whales continued their scrutiny and then turned and swam away.

Was it a mating pair with calf? Was it a male with two females? We will never know - an unusual event which Siv and Juorma were lucky to survive. With a large rent in their hull, they retreated to Australia, 400 miles away, to do repairs. Going this direction meant the damaged side was out of the water, but it was a nightmare journey for them.

Most cruising yachts don't carry comprehensive insurance cover. The companies see us as too big a risk. We have a third party liability from a German company, just to cover others, not ourselves. Anyhow the Finns had a policy that only paid out for total loss, mind you in a total loss situation they were unlikely to collect. A quick phone call to Finland, the broker who hails from the same arctic island as Juorma said,

"Get it fixed or replaced and send us the bill."

This company normally insures farm machinery. I like their attitude. Hopefully Siv and Juorma will catch up with us before we leave for Indonesia. *Si-Ju* was the boat who passed us a bottle of whiskey mid Pacific; we wouldn't want to lose them.

It is a pity to leave Mooloolaba but leave we must, the gearbox is working, sometimes, so I planned for slack water to make our departure to lessen the risk. Jack of *Miclo III* and Terry of *Argonauta* were there in their dinghies to act as tugs if things went wrong.

Breakaway, Whitsunday Islands

So with an Englishman pushing and an American pulling, we left the berth like the *QE II* and moved out to anchor to await the tide at four o'clock the following morning. This really is the first step on the long journey home. Waving goodbye, we were conscious of the fact that there were people we would not see again.

Some yachts will be heading back to America via Hawaii; some to New Zealand by the stormy Tasman, others to Papua New Guinea, the Solomon's, Vanuatu and other places. All will be seeking adventures, all remembering the good times and forgetting the bad.

Christine
At the 'Goodbye to Breakaway' party, the topic of discussion was Juorma and Siv's whale encounter.
"Did you hit the whale, or did the whale hit you?"
As it was a side collision, the general consensus was that the whale attacked. We were all keen to know what kind of a creature it was, the description was about 30 feet long, black with no other colour obvious and a flat nose. I have a book on the northern whales but no information on those south of the equator. From the description no one could come up with a name. Juorma remarked, "I know one thing for sure, I won't be going whale watching for a while."

Escape River, Near Cape York 11.00 S 142.40E

19 July 2000
"Tiger country mate, tiger country."

So said Aussie John back in Townsville, inferring great danger ahead (as everyone knows, tigers are the one thing Australia doesn't have but we understood what he meant). John was retired and lived on a motorised catamaran. He knew the coast of Australia well, having sailed it man and boy. When he heard *Breakaway* and *Chinook II* were heading over the top he was shocked.

"No place for the likes of you, used with the comforts of Europe. It is a place of legends, Australia as God made it – untamed and unspoiled by man's intrusion – tiger country."

Well, this afternoon we are anchored in Escape River, the last safe haven about 20 miles from the top. There are a couple of crocodiles sunning themselves on a sand spit about a 100 yards away. The crocs are now a protected species. At one time they were hunted but since the ban a crocodile attack is more common than a shark. Sometimes in mangrove river areas near the sea you can get crocodiles and sharks in the same waters which does not do much for the tourist trade.

The Escape River is so named because of the escape of Jackey Jackey, an Aboriginal guide. At one time the river was a natural divide between the Jardwadjali Tribe to the north and the Djagaraga to the south. The northern mob were fierce and warlike, their southern neighbours peaceful and placid. Anyhow the bold Jackey Jackey was leading Edmond Kennedy on an exploration trek to Cape York. Kennedy was killed by the tribe to the north and Jackey Jackey escaped and that is how the river was named.

A couple of weeks ago we sailed past Endeavour Reef. That is where Captain James Cook put his boat *Endeavour* up on a rock and the name lives on. Things have not changed a lot since those early times of exploration. However, there is now a marked shipping channel wending its way down the coast inside the Great Barrier Reef.

Breakaway and *Chinook II* also visited the Flinders Group. A cluster of islands of outstanding beauty named after Matthew Flinders, the man who led the first circumnavigation of Australia in the 1700s. A lot of the exploration work undertaken by Flinders is still in use on today's charts. Stanley Island, the recommended anchorage in the Flinders Group, has Aboriginal cave paintings, some dating back to before the birth of Christ, others recording the arrival of the white man's ships.

The British Admiralty left goats on some of the islands and planted palm trees. The idea was a good one. If sailors were cast ashore, they would find food and drink, the drink being milk in the nuts and the food – goats.

One such island is named Morris, marked on the chart by a single palm. Here is the classical desert island loved by cartoonists, a little hummock in the middle of the sea with its one lonely palm tree. Under the tree is a grave of an un-named pearl diver from the not so distant past. The divers ranged far from their home port on Thursday Island. Away for months on end, deaths among the crew where dealt with on the spot and graves were dug wherever possible. The only other inhabitants on this particular island are the pelicans and seabirds who nest here - a lonely final resting place.

Each day we try to achieve 50 or 60 miles between anchorages. Before darkness the anchor is down somewhere. As we drop the hook, prawn trawlers who have rested during the day go out to start the night shift. As we leave at first light they arrive back in. The further north we go, the less traffic. The anchorages now don't even have fishing boats or names for that matter.

Coast Watch, a branch of the Australian Coastguard, patrol the coast by air - every day flying over us. They call *Breakaway* up on the VHF radio and ask our intentions. We are now a fixture as they recognise the boat but still call to say hello. Their main job is to try and stop the influx of illegal immigrants entering Australia by sea. *Chinook II* is also easily identifiable, being red with a couple of white stripes.

Tomorrow it is around Cape York and into the Torres Strait and all that this entails, with strong tides and currents and a profusion of reefs - a stretch of water that prevented the discovery of Australia from the north. The Dutch East Indies or Indonesia as it is now known and Papua New Guinea lie 150 miles away but the turbulent seas kept visitors away. Cook travelled across the Pacific and found Australia and then went back to England through the Indian Ocean, stopping at Indonesia for repairs, a route we will be following. Tomorrow we leave the Coral Sea and the Pacific bound for Darwin, last stop in Australia before the trip to Bali in Indonesia. An option is to pull into Gove, a small mining town on the western side of the Gulf of Carpenteria. It is only about 350 miles and halfway to Darwin. It would break the trip nicely.

The only signs of habitation where we are now are oyster beds, laid by man to produce cultured pearls. Someone must look after them but we haven't seen anybody. The tropical north coast of Queensland is mile after mile of uninhabited golden beaches and mangrove swamps. Just offshore the coral reefs are scattered across the ocean. The mainland is mostly unexplored and lots of the reefs unchartered.

By the time we leave, *Breakaway* will have covered about 5,000 miles of coastal cruising and not even seen a fraction of this vast continent. At night the Escape River is in darkness with nothing moving except for the odd splash along the banks as something catches dinner. The crocodiles on the sandbank have just slipped into the water. I am happier when I can see them.

"Crocodile country, mate, crocodile country."

Christine
No one was in a hurry to launch their dinghy after we had dropped anchor in Escape River. We looked over at Chinook II and they looked over at us. We take it in turns to save fuel but no one was in any particular rush to go ashore on this occasion. I finally managed to entice Kirstie and Andy to lunch with the promise of fresh baked bread, but they kept well clear of the shore and the inhabitants on the mud banks. Dire warnings had been given out about the wild life in these parts and I have to state that every word is true.
Tip from the Kenyan Settlers Handbook,

*'When butter becomes tainted or rancid, place in a bowl, pour a
solution of bicarbonate of soda dissolved in water over it and
leave for an hour – drain off the liquid. The butter is restored'.*
It works!

Red Island

This area is Mecca for the four-wheel drive enthusiasts who travel
from all over the continent, across the dusty outback, along dirt roads,
towing trailer tents. They are loaded down with spare fuel and water
and the inevitable tinny (an aluminium boat) lashed to the roof and
the outboard mounted on the tow bar beside the mountain bikes.

The main inhabitants of Red Island are Torres Strait Islanders
and mainland Aboriginal people. The islanders resemble the people
of the South Pacific from the Melanesian culture. There are five
different groups or tribes in the areas – three islander and two
Aboriginal, each run and controlled by their own elected council.
Everyone and everything is heavily supported by the state, the only
work being in the service industries – education, health, fire service,
police, park rangers and the odd entrepreneur.

Providing a service is Jean. She is the local taxi company and
her limousine is a Nissan Patrol 4 x 4 fitted with kangaroo bars. It is
as dirty inside as out. We had called on her services to take us to the
nearest hotel known as The Canteen. There was no way of telling
where the road stopped and the carpark started as everything was
coated in red dust. The magnetic anthills disappeared into the
distance in straight lines pointing due north. Cook may have
discovered Australia in 1770 but no one has done too much with this
part since.

We went to the hatch and made our purchase. Because of the
problems of alcohol among the indigenous people, the bars in some
areas can only sell hard liquor to be taken away, two days a week. This
law did not seem to apply to us as we purchased the Aussie wine boxes
with no trouble at all. The four-wheel drives were parked up for the
night in the campsite. After all you can only rough it so much.

Breakaway has to leave tomorrow. The small supermarket had
a poster up advertising a Saturday market to be held on alternate

weekends. The venue was 'under the coconut trees'. Somehow that has a better ring to it than the council car park. Unfortunately we were going to miss the event.

Christine
Red Island was the treat I had been looking for. There was a great atmosphere ashore - everyone was very friendly and as we walked around getting our bearings, we found communal showers, fresh water, fuel and gas supplies. In fact everything a travelling yacht is looking for, as well as somewhere to dump the rubbish collected over three weeks of sailing and of course the supermarket with a wide range of goods - happiness. The ladies in the laundry told me it was not a problem to use the facilities so Jamie dinghied out to Breakaway at anchor and brought back all the bedding and dirty clothes, telling Chinook II on the way about our good luck. As we hung out the last load of washing, the first was dry and it was wonderful to sleep between clean sheets again.

Black Point, Port Essington 11.09S 132.06E

The Gulf of Carpenteria and the Torres Strait boast the strongest trade winds in the world. They blow in from the Pacific and are squeezed between Indonesia, Papua New Guinea and Australia. I don't know if the claim is true but three days out it started to blow and blow hard. Darwin radio was giving a forecast of 30 to 35 five knots of wind from the southeast. The wind direction was good but force seven to eight took it above what would be comfortable

Under shortened sail and with our wind vane steering gear pointing us in the right direction, we got on with it. Three hours on watch and six off thanks to Jamie being on board - everything not tightly fitted into the lockers was rolling about to keep you awake.

Two days later we were approaching Cape Don, an area of very strong tides and a small boat like *Breakaway* cannot go against them. *Chinook II* is larger and faster and they were able to catch a flood tide to carry them to Darwin. We had to rethink our strategy, as the winds were not showing any signs of abating.

The north coast of Australia is known as Arnhem Land and

the chart just has 'Aboriginal land' printed across it. The Government of the Northern Territory gave this area back to the Aboriginal people to control and in theory you are not allowed to land without permission. I don't suppose anyone would have been too annoyed if we had stopped to seek shelter but we have no Pilot book of this coast and a gale was not the conditions to explore a strange shore for a safe haven.

One place we did have some information on was Port Essington, an area developed in the early 19th century by the British Colonial Office. At that time they had no port in the north, so in 1838 five ships arrived under sail to set up an outpost here. They had reasonable success as the Aboriginal tribe was peaceful. With a good water supply a township grew up as traders started to arrive.

HMS *Beagle* based itself here to do survey work on the north coast – a famous name because it was on board this vessel that Darwin came up with his theory of evolution. Then the age of steam arrived and Port Essington was no longer required as a strategic port as the modern ships could go against wind and weather, reaching lonely outposts in days rather than weeks. We were glad of the early explorers and their work for here was a place to ride out the gale, well surveyed and with good holding. Ashore there is a small trading post open from four to six every afternoon during the week. A National Park Ranger keeps a general eye on things.

There are four Aboriginal tribes or clans with a strong spiritual link to the sea. Their ancestors came from the creation era (Dreamtime) and created the land with all that it contains. Ashore you can see the tracks of kangaroo, snakes, and crocodiles in the sand. Water buffaloes also wander about. Things have not changed much over the years. Last night I got up to check the anchor and there was not a light to be seen - a lonely coast. I wonder how they got on at the market last Saturday.

Darwin, Northern Territories

In 1974 Darwin was hit by a cyclone and very little of it was left standing. The yacht club displays photos of boats of all shapes and sizes washed ashore, lying on their sides, stove in and wrecked, battered to death by the giant seas.

Now there are marinas into which you 'lock in' so the level of water inside is always constant. The theory is good. When the strong winds strike they let most of the water out, allowing the yachts to sink down below the level of the surrounding water and shelter from the storm. This also prevents tidal surge, which is the main cause of damage to moored craft. I am only telling you the principles. We shall not be here in cyclone season to confirm any of these theories.

The new system has caused problems because the marinas controlled the flow of water and the basins became home to the black striped mussel. This shellfish came in on the hull of an overseas yacht and fell in love with the environment, breeding in profusion. So all foreign vessels are now treated with suspicion, as the cost of eradicating the pest was $2.2 million.

As you arrive in Darwin you can anchor off the yacht club which is fine. The club offers associated membership free and the use of all its facilities. The down side is a dinghy ride of three-quarters of a mile to get ashore. With the boat at anchor it is difficult to do major work so the marina situation was the only answer for *Breakaway*. But of course the black striped mussel had to be dealt with. The approach to the problem was basic.

The yacht is lifted out of the water at great expense to the Northern Territory Fishery Department. It is then examined by an expert for infestation. Meanwhile the wise Yachtie is cleaning her down and checking for underwater defects at no expense to himself.

Back in the water for the next stage. All seacocks are turned off and any through hull fitting filled with a strong detergent left in the system for 14 hours. A procedure claiming to kill all underwater life lurking in the nooks and crannies. It certainly leaves you with a very clean boat. The boat inspector kindly donated a gallon of detergent to *Breakaway* for future use. Mixed with water at a ratio of 50-1 we now have a year's supply of good strong boat cleaner.

So *Breakaway* is now safely tied up in Tipperary Waters, a small but very up-market marina at the head of a river. You come in through locks to an area surrounded by fairly fancy housing overlooking the spotlessly clean overseas boats. Tomorrow night the management and residents have invited us to a sausage sizzle. They are going to supply the beer and the cardboard Chardonnay. We just have to supply ourselves. They seem to like the idea of boats from around the world in their front garden. Who are we to deny them?

The Custom's official arrived at the marina as arranged to give *Breakaway* and ourselves official sanction to depart Australia. She was a Chinese lady originally from Hong Kong. As forms were stamped, she complained bitterly about the influx of immigrants into the country from the Middle East. I just nodded in agreement.

We were to leave with another yacht and Peter, the Lockmaster, tied *Joy* up in the tiny lock first and *Breakaway* followed her in and then the gate was closed behind us. The water started to drop, lowering the boats down to the level of the river outside. Negotiating the river caused no problems as the falling tide swept us through Darwin Harbour and into the Timor Sea. Next stop Kupang, West Timor.

Breakaway has spent a long time cruising the coast of Australia making many friends but with the Aussies this was not hard. From our first arrival where we tied up in Aquatic Paradise, with each house having its own boat dock as well as a garage, we have been shown kindness.

The people of Townsville who lent us cars and invited the two crews to their homes for family Christmas, a welcome break from working on *Chinook II*. The men of the bush at the farmers shows, the lovely anchorages in the Great Barrier Reef and the excitement of the Escape River with crocodiles on the banks. Surfers Paradise with the bronzed bodies of the young and the sun damaged bodies of the old. The lovely coast of Arnhem Land, home of the Aboriginal. Torres Strait, hidden reefs and strong currents and some of the best sailing we have ever enjoyed. The windblown graves of the early Irish settlers, buried where they worked in the godforsaken gold fields of Queensland, people with no return ticket.

Fare ye well Australia – farewell, we have enjoyed it all.

Christine

I have been reading up on the customs and traditions of the areas ahead. The information is all in the Pilot Book of South East Asia, paying particular attention to Indonesia, Malaysia and Thailand. Some we already know but there were new ones.

Don't sit with your toes pointing towards anyone. Don't sit with legs crossed or stand with hands on hips, it is considered disrespectful. Don't point with your index finger. Always use your right hand in any personal contact – (not that one again). As yachts are a source of interest you can be overwhelmed with the entire village coming out to visit you at anchor.

A useful tip on how to encourage your guests to leave, "We have to pray now," sends them on their way with no offence taken.

Indonesia, the Timor Sea

I write this becalmed in the Timor Sea, next port of call the island of Rote. *Breakaway* is back in the Doldrums, the Horse Latitudes or as the Americans have named them - the Inter Tropical Convergence Zone (such romance).

Yesterday the morning's first light came with a blood red sun appearing in the East. Once it tipped the horizon it came up very quickly. Then the dolphins appeared, their dorsal fins breaking the flat pink sea - *Breakaway* a new toy to play with - the day started off well. The few clouds were reflected on the ocean as our early morning companions dived under the boat, each one trying to outdo the other. Suddenly they were gone and all was quiet again.

The surface of the ocean is covered in sand blown from somewhere but there are no waves to scatter it. Then it was time for the main act. The humpbacks were going to entertain us. With a crash one came out of the water half a mile away. Coming out of the depths to balance on a massive tail like a ballet dancer on her toes – awesome strength to lift a body weight of tons out of the ocean, rearing higher than our mast. Then he would crash back into the sea, mighty tail flukes breaking the surface again before disappearing into the depths to gather himself for his next charge to the surface.

We watched in awe at what must be one of the greatest shows on earth. There have been tales told on our voyage so far of yachts destroyed by the mighty whale and we have often seen them from afar but watching this display, fear was not part of our feelings. The mighty male was putting on a show for his lady friend, strutting his stuff as part of the courtship ritual. If she was as impressed as us, there were going to be a couple of happy whales that night.

The wind picked up four days out just on the edge of daylight. *Joy* appeared as dawn broke and we shouted our hellos across the water. Indonesia was only 150 miles away. Too far for a day - too short for two. We stayed together and slowed the boats up, planning for an early arrival at the island of Rote. Ten miles offshore we hove too - a sailor's way of going into neutral, stopping to rest but still controlling the boat. Another dawn but this time we could smell land. The scent of greenery, the smells of man, the smells of pollution. We worked the boat down the north shore of the bay, this let us see the reef with the new sun over our shoulder highlighting the dangers –

'into deep water and head for the corrugated iron tin roofs, anchor in a suitable depth,' says the Pilot book.

As the anchor hit the bottom, the cooking fires in the village were putting smoke across the bay. A dugout canoe passed, they waved, we waved back - they came alongside, handed me a rope, said, "Hello mister", and climbed on board. Christine made a cup of tea, Jamie handed out the barley sugar sweets. I sat back and enjoyed.

It is good to be Up Island again.

PS We did not go to Kupang, West Timor.

Christine
It took us six days to do 450 miles. A slow trip even for Breakaway but from the crew no complaints - Jamie on board makes all the

difference. The sea state was flat and the whole journey was very enjoyable - a good shake down sail to get us back into the way of things. Chinook II is still in Darwin and will be leaving in a few days. We look forward to meeting up with them along the way.

Rote, Indonesia 10.35S 123.22E

It takes a village like Pepela, Rote, Indonesia to bring us back down to earth.

Australia is a western culture separated by a small sea from South East Asia, which is a mixture of many people and many religions, but Indonesia is a land of unrest at the moment.

Indonesia is the oldest of all the one time European colonies, disputed and fought over for hundreds of years. The Dutch, the Portuguese, the British all struggled to control the spice trade of the East Indies.

Fishing boats off the Island of Rote

Tonight, as we lie behind the reef in the secure anchorage of Teluk Pepela, the sound of the faithful being called to prayer echoes across the bay. The congregation put down their prayer mats and kneel - pointing towards Mecca in the East.

Ashore the village is poor but these are a kindly people with no wealth, people struggling to live by the soil or sea. There are a few shops to supply their needs but not shops as we know them - small buildings with an open front displaying their wares. There are perhaps half a dozen tins of beans, small bags of rice, some withered potatoes, and powdered milk in abundance. The 'tick' book sits on a wooden stool with the names of those owing money written down – each rupiah marked off and accounted for. A rupiah is worth a tenth of one penny.

We wanted to explore the island so, as in the past, *R Phurst* the American catamaran took on the task of investigating the possibilities of a tour. Tomorrow two local buses will collect us at 7.30 in the morning for a day's circuit of the island. Each mini bus can carry 10 passengers. The cost including petrol, driver and bus is £15. That is not each, that is the bus and driver for the whole day and the driver probably thinks he is overcharging. It seems quite reasonable. We are all looking forward to it.

When school gets out, all hell breaks loose. The dugout canoes are launched and the children come out to *Breakaway.* "Hello Madam," they shout to me, as they paddle their hollowed out logs the single handers bail by kicking the water out. Those with crew have the paddler sitting at the stern, the bow high and the rest of them all bailing furiously with coconut shells.

They come alongside and peer over the side at you just awaiting the nod. Somebody always nods or smiles and the boarding party takes over. Curious children exploring another world, a fantasy world which up to now was only seen on video. The video shop is the second on the left just past the village well where the ladies draw water in buckets. The children arrive to look, to observe, to crawl all over.

Breakaway now carries small gifts, and why not. Barley sugar and brandy-balls are the favourites. Convincing the wee ones to take the paper off the sweets takes time. Baseball hats make you friends for life and a cheap disposable lighter will seal a pact only broken by death.

A little girl climbed on board today. As she got out of the canoe she was clutching a schoolbook on how to speak English. She was determined to practice with us.

"Have you a cat? What is your name?"

We quickly ran out of conversation. Christine broke out the sweets. Our young friend propped herself up at the mast and popped a sweet in her mouth - paper and all. I diplomatically unwrapped mine and sucked it. She turned her back to take the paper off, realising her mistake. We both went for a second helping of brandy balls. The formalities out of the way, our visitor jumped in the dugout and headed towards home and homework.

She will be back tomorrow we hope. Well, after all, we have a lot to talk about over two or three brandy balls. I may go to the school and present myself to the teacher for an exchange of views.

As the youngsters climb all over the boat, they peer through the hatches and are amazed at our cassette player. It brings back memories of Short Fingers, Joseph and Winston on the island of Dominica in the Caribbean. Why do they put paper on sweeties, do we need this stress.

Now the Harbour Master is a different kettle of fish. This is a man not to be messed with. His son-in-law paddles the canoe for him and on his arrival there is a price to be paid, so while the chauffeur awaits in the canoe, the Master comes on board. Christine, as always, is aware of local customs. I said,

"Do you think yer man would like a drink?"

"This is a Muslim village – even the brandy balls are a bit risky."

So whilst he examined the paperwork and sucked a sweetie, I sucked one in sympathy. As he got off *Breakaway* he asked,

"Is your wife a Christian?"

"Yes," I said.

He looked at me as if that explained everything.

"The American boat over there?" he pointed.

"I don't think they are very religious and I am afraid they might offer you a drink."

"Okay, I go and check them."

I went along to help translate. Well you can understand the situation I was in. Columbus was trying to get to this part of the world when he discovered the continent of America. Marco Polo was the first European to arrive, followed by the Portuguese, in search of the Spice Islands. Then the Dutch turned up and for 300 years controlled what was known as the Dutch East Indies. The Japanese invaded during the war in the Pacific.

Indonesia is the fifth most populated country in the world and in the past it has not been that easy for a yacht to gain access. But now things are changing. Each year more and more yachts will arrive but for now we are a novelty. The people are small in stature - son Jamie is six foot. He is easily spotted among the crowds that surround us everywhere we go as he juggles to entertain the children.

Christine
We had our trip around the island – the highlight being the town of Ba'a. All us females wore tops with sleeves and long skirts, making sure there was very little skin showing so as not to offend. It takes a bit of getting used to - being stared at - but when you catch an eye everyone smiles.
Until we arrived, the town had not seen a tourist but I managed to find lovely batik sarongs in brilliant colours with the traditional design of a fan on them - everyday wear for men and women alike in these parts.

Labuan Bajo, the Island of Flores

Many years ago I watched *The World About Us* - or a programme very similar – on the BBC on Sunday night at 7pm. All that could be seen of David Attenborough was his head as he peered through a bush and whispered in hushed tones of his search for the mythical dragon. Well...we know where it is...and *Breakaway*'s crew is going for a look tomorrow.

The dragons inhabit the islands of Komodo and Rinca just to the West of Flores, Indonesia. Komodo and Rinca Islands are national parks and we will have to work hard on the tide tables to make sure the timing is right in the narrow straits between Flores and the islands.

Tonight *Breakaway* is anchored in one of the main towns in Flores, Labuan Bajo, a busy harbour and a low-key tourist jumping off spot for the area's major attraction, the Komodo dragon. There is a constant 'to-ing' and 'fro-ing' of tourist and fishing boats of all shapes and sizes, none of them ugly.

Indonesian boat builders construct the prettiest boats I have seen in a long while, all done by eye, not a line drawing in sight. The larger fishing boats have outriggers stretching far out over each side of the hull. The means of propulsion is a single cylinder diesel engine with no gear box so to stop, an anchor is hurled over the side.

To watch the fishermen manoeuvre in tight situations is a spectator sport all of its own. Of course all the other craft are crewed by experts who offer their advice freely and loudly. A 30 foot boat with outriggers spreading across 40 feet is unwieldy to say the least. They always seem to come to a stop in time – just on the edge of disaster.

Then there are the sailors, the men who work the wind. Moving the boat from where they are to where they want to go, easing ropes, shaping sails, making the wind their servant, using the currents and tide without the help of a combustion engine to drive the boat.

Sails are made of plastic; multi-hued they are made from the same stuff that we in our world use for the construction of shopping bags. You know the type. I mean the big ones that fit into a supermarket trolley with a weave running though.

Fishermen travel up to 250 miles offshore, cooking meals on an open fire in a cut down oil drum fixed on the stern. The local boats are not only used for work but are homes as well. During the day normal life goes on – each little boat going about the usual domestic duties. Just before darkness the anchors are lifted and off they go again, out to sea to harvest the fish. All around the anchorage the oil lamps bob up and down, the voices carried across the water. At daybreak in they come again and the boat becomes a house for the day.

Breakaway's fibreglass hull is viewed with amazement. Plastic is all right for making sails but not boats. If God had wanted fibreglass boats he would have grown fibreglass trees, seems to be the general opinion. Tomorrow we will hoist the Terylene sails on our plastic boat. Beyond here there be dragons.

Christine
Bob was 59 today. The anchorage held a party for him.
We have met up with son-in-law Andy and daughter Kirstie again. It was great coming round the corner into the bay and seeing their boat sitting there. Chinook II was to be the venue for the birthday bash and it was a pot luck. Meat was in short supply but ingenuity was not. The menu started with Japanese style sushi, complete with its seaweed wrapping and then a variety of main course dishes and of course birthday cake.
Breakaway's contribution was vegetarian and meat pies, the latter out of a tin but it seemed to go down well – also cassava chips. Cassava is called dasheen in the Caribbean and that is where I learned to peel and then cut the root up thinly, deep frying the slices until crisp. They make good nibbles.
Happy Birthday was sung in Indonesian and Bob received some unusual presents. A carved wooden Komodo dragon, four massage sessions, a navigation seat cover, Indonesian ground coffee presented in a clam shell, a bottle of duty free whiskey and hiking boots ordered in Darwin and delivered by Chinook II.
I think he was quite overwhelmed by everyone's generosity. Jamie painted a picture of an Indonesian village, snorkelled under

Breakaway and cleaned her prop, and I promised to scrub the topsides. Not too hard a task when you can break off and have a cooling swim.

The Island of Rinca

Breakaway and *Chinook II* were together again and what a wonderful place to meet up. Rinca had good holding and the bay gently shelved. Close to the shore were the underwater gardens of coral and the snorkelling was magic. On the beach in front of us was the mythical dragon.

Further along the beach a small deer was eating at the edge of the forest – the dragon watched with interest. They can move fast but the deer knew it wasn't that fast. The dragon normally ambushes its prey and all it has to do is inflict a bite. There is so much nasty bacteria in its mouth that the bite becomes infected and the dragon follows along and then takes the stricken victim at its leisure.

After a couple of days we faced some of the strongest tides in the world to make our way across to Komodo – the island called after the dragons. It is now a national park with the sole purpose in life of introducing the tourist to the dragon.

For a small fee the Park Ranger gave us the whole works. Now don't misunderstand me, he was good. But out the back of the staff canteen the dragons were rooting about in the garbage, obviously highly evolved from their Rinca cousins.

Christine
Bob did not take the guided tour deep into Komodo country but the rest of the family did. Our guide had a strong stick for protection, so we kept close. They used to tie a goat up to attract the dragons for the tourists but this practice is no longer allowed, thank goodness. Walking along, our man showed us unique features - sticky tamarind fruit, bark that provides quinine - and pointed out the baby dragons over our heads. As soon as they are born, the babies take to the trees before mum and dad eat them. They come back down when big enough to hold their own.

In a clearing we met the fully grown dragons and they are impressive with massive heads and shoulders. As our tour came back down to the beach where the dinghies were, a camera team was trying to create a scene of dragons chasing people along the beach. Out of sight, the locals were poking the giant monitor lizards with sticks to get a reaction. Partially tame or not, we were keeping well out of the way. It was all right though – they seemed to be heading in Bob's direction.

Bali International Marina S 08.44 E 115.12

Most of the long distance cruising boats are a husband and wife affair. We are slightly different at the moment as son Jamie is also on board.

Tied up beside us is *Chinook II* with son-in-law Andy and our daughter as neighbours. People now refer to us as the Irish cruising family. For *Breakaway* to have the third one on board makes a vast difference on the oceans - someone to help with the sailing and share the chores but mainly to allow more sleep. Although at times Jamie is loaned to *Chinook II* so they can have it easy for a while.

A small boat with modern self-steering gear can look after itself but the watch keeper is still required to keep a weather eye open for danger. Those long night hours pass slowly. With Christine and me it was four on and four off, but those four hours could drag. With Jamie on board we work three on and six off – talk about easy!

During the day we are flexible - Christine crochets, Jamie practices guitar and I doze. The night hours are different. No one wants to spend one minute more on deck than required. The minute hand moves slowly. At a quarter to the hour before the change of watch, the watch keeper puts on the kettle.

Breakaway is quiet with only the sound of the sea and the creak of the ropes adding to the silence. The boat moves along on its own accord, the Southern Cross is in the heavens, the ripples of the wake create phosphorescence. You just want to go to your bunk to avoid the loneliness. The kettle starts to boil - no whistle - just a sense of something different in the boat, a strange rattle on the cooker, the smell of steam. Still in the dark you pull out two cups and the tea, coffee or hot chocolate, the spoon lives in the sink to save you opening the cutlery drawer and making a noise – no lights to destroy night vision. Now it is time to shake the next on watch.

"The kettle's boiled, there's no hurry. Do you want tea, coffee or hot chocolate Jamie?"

"Can I have an Oxo?"

You can't win can you? Lockers are opened up, lights are put on in the search for the elusive stock cube. By this time Christine is peering over the side of the lee cloth (this is a bit of canvas like the side of a cot to hold you in your bunk).

"What's wrong?" she asks.

"Nothing is wrong."

"If anything was wrong you would tell me, wouldn't you."

"Go back to sleep."

"All right," says Jamie.

It's just not worth going through it all again. Anyhow I had slept all day.

Now not all the yachts are so lucky and they have to pick up crew where they can get them. There are certain rules to the game. First off, you have to find out where they intend to go to with you and what their time scale is. Is it flexible? Have they their plane fare home? Some skippers ask for a bond which is refundable, equal in money to the above mentioned plane fare.

When someone arrives in a country on board a yacht the skipper is responsible for that person and the crew cannot leave without an air fare. If this has not been sorted out beforehand the skipper/owner can be out of pocket as he must pay for the crew's deportation.

One South African yacht arrived in Bali without a cruising permit or visas - the skipper and two female American crew. On arrival the yacht was boarded and searched by customs. The boat was pulled apart as the sniffer dogs went to work, the ramp at the top of the marina being patrolled by armed police. A few months earlier the same yacht came under suspicion in Vanuatu where the Australian authorities had been called in to assist the local officials.

On this occasion the yacht had been tracked off the coast of the Northern Territory and the Indonesians were then informed of its arrival in their waters by the Aussie Coast Watch, the Customs Officials co-operating with each other. Once again the yacht was clean. Just as well, as in many Asian countries the penalty for drug smuggling is death.

One of the crew – Sandra – wanted to leave the yacht to join another. The authorities refused permission. The vessel's next stop was to be the coast of Africa and this was not part of Sandra's travel plans. She had joined the yacht after the earlier search and was unaware of its history but she now carried the same reputation. Sandra explained that she was an American hoping this would help, but mentioning Bill Clinton's name did not even work. Poor Sandra is now in the middle of an ocean going to a country she did not want to go to with people she no longer trusts, on a boat whose reputation goes before it. So both parties to the agreement have to be careful.

20 September 2000

Stan from the U.S. of A, our Cherokee Indian friend, had hired a car. The soul of kindness he invited the whole Irish sailing family out for the day to enjoy and share his pleasures. Things went well until the first set of traffic lights enhanced by a zebra crossing. Zebra crossings are plentiful but rarely used and if attempted offer no protection at all to the pedestrian. Anyhow Stanley stopped, as the lights were red, whereupon a policeman appeared from nowhere ordering him to drive across the road and park the vehicle. The rest of us sat very quietly, denying Stan any support in the face of Indonesian authority.

The outcome of the whole affair was simple, a fine had to be paid in whichever foreign currency was available, otherwise face the wrath of the courts. The negotiations were concluded as the rest of the travelling public ducked and dodged each other as usual, ignoring traffic lights, pelican crossings, white lines and all other motorists.

To be fair to the Police Officer he advised Stanley that if over the course of the day he felt the worst for wear due to the demon drink, he should call a policeman. This public servant on request would stop the traffic, allowing us to join the flow easily, thus preventing accidents. We continued, Stan clutching the wheel like a man possessed as we headed into the hinterland of Bali. Like every other place Bali has its tourist highlights and we were not about to be denied.

Jamie and Andy were wearing their sarongs proudly as it is the proper attire for entering a temple. I had mine under my arm, not quite ready to face the public dressed in a skirt. A sarong looks like a bit of curtain material you wrap around your waist but - life is not that simple. As in all things there is a certain etiquette. The female version is tied at the side with a simple tuck in, much as you would pull a towel around yourself after a shower. The males tie it with a knot in front and then make a couple of rolls at the waist, shortening the whole affair to just below the knee.

One other thing - nothing is worn below the sarong. I think not, you never know when you could have an accident

We travelled on. Each village has a craft – take woodcarving as an example – so for half a mile each household and little shop would be out carving masks, ornate sculptures, walking sticks and statues of the Gods. This work is sold all over the world.

One street was specialising in didgeridoo for export to Australia. Others were making totem poles and tribal masks for the Native American. You want it? In Bali you can buy it, made to order in any style, for any country. The furniture makers, the silversmiths – I watched the jewellery makers at work. To work silver you add 7.5% copper to the sterling silver so the craftsmen can bend it to their will. I did not know that. Beautiful hall stands handmade and carved out of solid mahogany, not a power tool in sight. Mantles for your fireplaces with a patina shine, which would break your heart.

'Antique furniture made to order', one sign said.

The next village was the home of the weavers and dyers, creating batik work famous throughout the world – materials with a unique design and beauty. Then there were the workers of bamboo, more furniture but for a different taste.

A wage in Indonesia is between 250,000 and 400,000 rupiahs a month. That is £25 to £40 in our money for the finest craftsmen we have so far encountered on our travels. Every time you stop the car the street people appear, the hawkers, the sellers of tee shirts. Nothing is easy bought. Everything has to be bargained for but after our first brush with the law Stanley was understandably nervous. The second time we stopped he got a parking ticket which was non-negotiable. Stan was not coping, only tourists were getting parking tickets. I suppose Cherokees also look like tourists to an Indonesian.

Bartering? We are no match for the professionals

By the end of the day everyone was exhausted, what with one thing and another. We saw a Hindu wedding and two cremations, which we tried to avoid. Hot pools, volcanoes, religious ceremonies and heavy handed bureaucracy. But the fun of the street hawkers brought us all back to normal. Two funerals and a wedding – what a good day out.

Christine
As I was having a quiet moment overlooking the paddy fields out of the range of the street hawkers, Jamie came up to me,

"What do you think of these carvings, I can't believe it, only £1 each." They were indeed beautiful, a matching pair superbly

made. The deal had been struck; the statues wrapped and handed over. Stan had just received his third fine so we all bundled back into the car and sped off before anything else could happen. Back in the safety of the car Jamie examined his purchase. He had been a victim of much practiced sleight of hand. The statues in his possession were not the ones bargained for but a much poorer quality. Stan had also bought the same statues but was convinced his eyes had never left his purchase. The plastic bag was opened and – yes, you guessed it – he had been duped as well. Well, you have to admire their skill and flair. Another lesson learnt. Jamie is resolved to try again, this time hanging on to the carving like grim death. Perhaps it will be a case of third time lucky.

Lovina Beach, Bali

Although we had left the marina, the two boats were finding it hard to leave Bali itself and so anchored at the top end of the island at Lovina Beach.

It was Christine's 56th birthday and the family had booked a hotel room for us. Now I knew about it but for Christine it was a total surprise. At mid-day Kirstie, Andy and Jamie arrived to take us to a swimming pool. We got the togs together and off we went, the two dinghies going full steam ahead. Christine and I were left on the beach to regroup and the rest went off to organise things. They returned and off we went - over a bamboo bridge like something out of a willow pattern dinner service and past the ducks drifting about on the lily pond - through the small forest of frangipani and sweet coconut trees. A dog scratched and a monkey screeched abuse as we came to our chalet, Christine's present.

Now I have never stayed in a 4 star hotel with an outside toilet. The first thing to greet your eye was a veranda overlooking the beach 50 yards away with a view of *Breakaway* sheltering behind a coral reef. There was a tiled roof in the Chinese fashion, shaped like a temple, over the above mentioned porch with two chairs made out of bamboo, just right to enjoy the sunset with the bottle of expensive Australian Red *Chinook II* had saved for just this occasion. Inside, the bed was bigger than our yacht with a large ceiling fan making us feel instantly cooler. Turned up full you felt as if you were in a gale, turned down it wafted gentle breezes in the tropical heat. A gecko climbed up the wall defending us from mozzies.

But – back to the outside bathroom. This had to be used to be enjoyed and it was private, for our use only. The back wall was high for privacy and dry stone built, enclosing a small area of tropical rain forest in miniature with examples of exotic flowers grown for our pleasure. The other three walls were woven out of rattan and the bath had hot water.

Can you imagine it? Birds singing in the trees, the palm fronds as a ceiling. A ceiling that swayed to expose the waxing moon, the tropical heat of the night caressing your body as you bathe. There was more water in the tub than we have to survive on for two months. Then there was the swimming pool.

Surrounded by banana trees heavy with fruit, there was a little bar in the corner of the pool with seats in the water so we could sip a cool drink and still stay submerged, the beverage served by a beautiful dainty Indonesian girl in traditional dress, treating everything as if it was normal. The whole thing was a lovely experience with breakfast served by the gentlest of people. Banana, mango, pineapple with a touch of lime for starters, all blended into a drink of paradise, a hard act to follow.

Then a cat rubs your ankles, a hungry cat, a cat that eats dry toast. You want to rescue the cat but it is not possible.

Everything in Bali seems to leave its mark on you. The poverty, the kindness, the beauty, the sadness. A religion with no ill will, gentle people with soft words.

The seamen of Indonesia are another superstitious bunch and a bad night's fishing can only be caused by evil spirits aboard the vessel. They have a simple way of overcoming this. They charge straight at *Breakaway* in the darkness, no lights showing. Suddenly you are aware of them heading towards you at full speed. The first few encounters can be nerve wracking with thoughts of piracy on the high seas foremost in your mind. At the last minute they swerve to avoid you and come to a sudden stop, catching the spirits unprepared, as it is a well-known fact that they cannot alter direction quickly. So as the boat does its handbrake turn, the ghouls and ghosties keep on going ending up on the decks of *Breakaway*. By the end of a night passage we are coming down with bad spirits but as we do not fish, it doesn't matter.

Another Indonesian trick concerns a stuck anchor. If the water is shallow and the anchor is jammed you can usually dive down to free it. Otherwise you go backwards and forwards, hauling, heaving, sweating and swearing until you release the offending bit of hardware. Not the locals. They pour some fresh water down the chain and the seabed releases its prisoner immediately. Some of the western Yachties swear this works. So far we have not had to prove the theory.

Christine, Andy, Kirstie and I are all suffering from a cold at the minute. Jamie has avoided it so far. Because of the bugs we are staying put for the next few days before taking off for Borneo to catch up with the Wild Man.

Christine
The Bali cold has us in its grip but for Bob and Andy it has gone to their chests. There is a little village ashore but no chemist and when we asked a local shop for assistance he did not disappoint us. Off he went on his moped to return a few minutes later with a special elixir. Nothing else would do - he would administer the medicine himself, so the boys were sat down on the shop step and duly received a large spoonful of syrup followed by a spoonful of water. He guaranteed instant relief and it is looking like he could be right.

Yacht crews gather to discuss passage planning

Kumai River, Borneo

It had taken all day for *Chinook II* and *Breakaway* to make their way up the Kumai River to the town of Kumai, a waterfront settlement 30 miles inland.

Bruce of *R Phurst* our American pal was already anchored and had permits arranged plus transport organised for us all to go further inland - what a star.

Three speedboats were to pick up 11 of us the following morning at 06:00 hours - synchronise watches. The plan was to go to the game reserve at Tanjung Puting National Park and visit the Orangutans. Orang in Indonesian means 'man', hutan means 'forest' - the man of the forest - or the fabled Wild Man of Borneo.

We were not to be disappointed as the day was pure Hollywood. A touch of 'James Bond', 'Tarzan of the Apes' with 'Jungle Book' thrown in for good measure.

At that hour of the morning the greetings were cursory as we climbed into our boats laden down with water, food, toilet paper and insect spray, dressed in long sleeve shirts, trousers and broad brimmed hats. The boatman hit the throttle and not a lot happened, there was too much weight aft.

The four of us moved forward under the driver's instruction. The engine stopped labouring and started to roar. We were up on the plane and going places fast holding second position, leaving the main river, sliding sideways across the water at 30 miles an hour, taking off into the air across the wake of the lead boat.

The jungle encroached down to the banks, with startled crocodiles sliding into the water as we roared by. Multi-coloured parrots flew from their roosts and monkeys squealed in protest.

As the river narrowed the sense of speed increased. The human inhabitants waved us on our way, men fishing, women doing the washing, the police men in their stations on guard against illegal logging, they also waved. The illegal loggers with their rafts of trees seemed to block our way but the throttle was never eased back.

More waves, cheering each boat on its way. The gaps through the bushes were almost non-existent. The lead boat hesitated and we were through to jeers from the passengers and cheers from us. People ask us if we have insurance. I was hoping the man in the dugout canoe had some form of third party cover.

We clambered ashore at the first camp to visit our cousins. It was home to the orphans who had been in human captivity and were being re-introduced back into the wild again. The young apes stay with their mother until about eight years of age.

As they make desirable pets in Asia, the poachers have to kill the mother to trap the baby. As I was straightening myself out, a gibbon monkey took my hand and swung up onto my shoulder. From this vantage point he surveyed the rest of the party whose grins were just getting wider and wider.

The young orangutans are set free to roam and gather their own food but each morning a few gallons of milk and dozens of hands of bananas are put out at the feeding station. We sat and waited in the humid forest, then above us we heard a noise and leaves falling as the first of the juveniles appeared.

There were more to follow, their bright orange hair a sharp contrast under the green canopy, making their way through the tree tops, vine to vine, branch to branch. Then they were among us. Young adults, big and strong were trying to steal our bags - putting their hands in ours, rolling over for a tickle and in general making you wonder who was watching whom - gentle creatures with the strength to kill. While all this was going on my chum the monkey was drinking the milk and pigging out on bananas.

Jamie and Kirstie with one of the juveniles

We moved up river to the next camp, home territory of the adults - a harem of females led by a dominant male ape that wandered this part of the forest. We were advised to hire a guide as an encounter with the king of the jungle in his domain could prove traumatic. The guide showed us the flora and fauna as we wandered the jungle paths, then he stopped,

"Jalan, Jalan."

I think this means keep walking.

"Jalan, Jalan, more faster."

I think this means run.

The trail was blocked by the big fella who had just come down from the trees to protect his patch. He was enormous. This was not Clive from *Every Which Way But Loose*, whom we think may have been a female by the way. This was the biggest ape I had ever seen. Even with his knuckles trailing the ground he stood tall. A head about two feet in diameter with shoulders the width of a house. We retreated.

Two females dropped in to join him. This took his mind off us. The retreat slowed and the tourist mentality took over. We crept back to take a photo.

Peering from behind a bush we watched His Lordship cavorting with the female of his choice while the other one pretended she was not interested in the first place. After a lot of roaring and rollicking they started to beget. Obviously he had lost interest in us. The guide was stunned. It seems that what we were observing is not a common occurrence. It had been 15 years from the last sighting of a begetting.

The guide whispered in awe, "They are mating."

Christine said, "I thought that was what they were up to."

She looks totally bored.

Later that day at the feeding station the king appeared looking a bit weary but content. What a great day out. The whole escapade took us through various emotions from fear to happiness and there was still the boat trip back to *Breakaway* to look forward to. I will remember the 'wild man of Borneo' for a long time.

The Big Feller

Christine
There was one last camp to visit as we headed back to Breakaway.
It was to see the baby orang-utans recently orphaned. A sign said,
       'DO NOT INITIATE CONTACT'
It was almost impossible. They wanted to be held so much. But it
was not allowed. As we tore ourselves away it brought the whole
thing home to us. Humans had taken them from their natural
habitat and it was up to humans to put them back where they
belonged. Up the Kumai River in Borneo a team of people were
doing their best to right the wrongs and make a difference and it is
working.

South China Sea, North of the Equator 01.11N 104.05E

From the Kumai River in Borneo, *Breakaway* and *Chinook II* were
heading north for Nongsa Point, the last port of call in Indonesia, 600
miles away across the South China Sea. That night the charts were
looked at and courses laid for the Northern Hemisphere and Bintan
in the Singapore Straits. Next morning the anchor was lifted and the
two boats motored down the river. The South East Monsoons were
gone and we were now late in the season.

Two days later our mistake of not moving with the seasons was
brought home to us. We sailed into the South China Sea and the
compass swung north, the first signs of lightning were seen on the

horizon. As the storms raged over Sumatra, the night sky would light up the bottom of the clouds like daylight. As they moved closer the humidity dropped and the wind freshened - no great strength in it. But the wind of change was blowing.

Local fishing boats leaving the Kumai River

The breeze suddenly changed direction as a black wall of rain charged at us. The first time we were caught unawares as the squall knocked *Breakaway* sideways. Too much sail up and the boat was uncontrollable. Gusts up to 50 knots (55 miles an hour), strong in anybody's language. Sails in disarray, just trying to weather it out, the air so full of salt spray you could not see. North Atlantic conditions, one degree south of the Equator. Okay, so the spray was warm.

Time to prepare the yacht for the next onslaught. The wall of wind and water would hit again but now we were prepared. *Breakaway* was rigged for storm.

We crossed the Equator at 10 o'clock in the morning and Jamie poured the rum. One for each of us and one for Neptune, the water was going down the plughole anticlockwise again and the storms were approaching from the north-east instead of the north-west. The respite was short lived.

Anyhow it is all history. We are tied up 10 miles from Singapore at Nongsa Point Marina. Hot showers and a swimming pool, all for £3 a night. Next we head up the Malacca Straits. I am told that is where the pirates are.

South East Asia, Singapore 01.17N 103.45E

Once upon a time, long, long ago, I came to Singapore. I had just crossed the Nullarbor Plain in Australia, 700 miles to the nearest waterhole, and from outback Australia flown up to South East Asia to Singapore, the Jewel in the Crown of the British Empire.

The old Dakota quivered and shook as we crossed the air stream of the Doldrums, the passengers quivered a bit also. Then we landed at Changi Airport, an airport with a tin roof. A taxi driver chauffeured me to the hotel, a cheap doss house that had an Indian Sikh sleeping across the doorway, cradling a 303 Lee Enfield rifle to guard against intruders or perhaps to stop the guests escaping without paying.

That night I was a nervous young man. The next day Kennedy was assassinated and the Beetles sang 'Love, Love Me Do', the world was changing. I now have a few more scars and a few more lines. Unfortunately Singapore has changed for the better. To get here we hugged the coast of Indonesia until the seaways of Singapore were close.

Breakaway now had to cross the second busiest shipping lane in the world to enter the most congested harbour in the world. One ship enters or leaves every three minutes, not including *Breakaway*. So now we are taking our lives in our hands to regroup with my past.

Breakaway tucked in behind a tug with a barge full of crude oil on tow, then slipped in front of a tanker moving east and now the west bound traffic passing the island of Singapore had to be faced.

Ducking and weaving, I was chasing dreams. Christine was navigating with Jamie on the tiller and we were heading back to the sixties.

"Now how do we get past that one in three minutes?"

A town of open sewers, 70 miles north of the Equator, a town of rickshaws and three wheeled bicycles, constructed to hold a box in front selling food. Noise 24 hours a day, squalor, dirt and pure excitement. To walk down the street was an adventure. Alien sounds and strange smells, learning to eat with chop sticks, slurping your soup out of a bowl, not even considering what was in that bowl. The smell of incense as ladies of the night approached you during the day. And of course Raffles Hotel. In those days I could not afford to go into it. That is the only thing that has not changed. We still can't and what is more we can't find it,

It is still there and so is the city, but all has changed much to my disappointment but to the betterment of the residents. Now they have McDonald's, KFC, The Tie Rack. A town of malls and worldwide franchisees, a civilised town with a structure to be proud of. A town like Brisbane, New York, Tokyo, Belfast, Paris, with a different accent but girls in the same clothes.

Where is the mysterious East? It is not on an underground urban railway better than London's. It is now a multi-cultured society run as a democracy. The terrible thing is, it works. Ninety percent of the population live in high rise, subsidised accommodation - no poor, no hungry, no crime, well not much, and no litter. There is a train service that runs on time and buses with air conditioning, which you can board as long as you have the right change.

Still, where *Breakaway* is tied up in the Republic of Singapore Yacht Club I have no complaints. There is a golf buggy to run us from the boat to the club - about 200 yards. The shower block is something to behold; a leather covered armchair outside each shower, a vanity area with underarm spray, not to mention sanitised combs and of course, free towels. The swimming pool is the best we have encountered and the morning paper is delivered to your boat.

But then you see you can't please some of us. A taxi driver with a meter is not the same as the rickshaw man who was exhausted going about his job. Sometimes when I felt sorry for the poor man I would run and pull whilst he sat back in splendour. Then I paid him.

This is the country where you can be fined and caned for dropping litter, smoking in public places, spitting in the street, carrying a cigarette lighter on the trains, allowing stagnant water to collect (encouraging mosquitoes). Chewing gum carries a severe punishment and there is a death penalty for drugs. I have seen no dogs or cats, though they are probably about somewhere, no long hair and colourful clothes, no vandalism or graffiti. Singapore is a small island that has captured most of the world's shipping, moving from East to West and vice versa, a society of wealth where all must earn money to live.

I miss the Singapore of Conrad's *Lord Jim*, the Singapore of Leslie Thomas's *The Virgin Soldiers*, the Singapore of black and white movies featuring Sidney Greenstreet and Peter Laurie, the Singapore of dreams, the first 'foreign' landfall of my youth. The town I knew so well.

Please Note. None of the facts above should be used in a pub quiz, as they are all questionable.

Christine
After Indonesia I am enjoying the order and reliability of Singapore. There is a standard price for the bus, for food, for anything you want to buy and I have to say it is a relief not having to argue over the amount for every transaction. The visit to the supermarket and the surrounding shops and stores was great fun, as were meals out

among the local people who watched with amusement at my ineptitude with chopsticks and cheered when a fork was produced. Breakaway's lockers are filled up again with a larger variety of foods than we have seen for a while and tomorrow we leave for Malaysia, along with Chinook II. Other yachts are leaving as well. It will be good to have company up the Malacca Strait.

Malaysia, The Malacca Strait 02.27.219N 101.50.246E

Breakaway left the Republic of Singapore Yacht Club at first light bound for Malaysia but before we reached the Malacca Straits the anchored ships of all nationalities had to be negotiated, plus the moving ones.

Tugs towing barges, small work boats supplying the needs of the ships at anchor, ferries transporting crews back from their shore leave, police launches, Pilot boats, oil rigs and dredgers. Then of course the ships themselves. Enough traffic to concentrate your energies.

'One long blast, I am altering to starboard.'

The ship astern was indicating his intentions. In other words, 'Move out of the way *Breakaway* – I am coming through'.

We moved. The VHF radio was never silent. English is the international language of this particular airway but the accents vary. The Chinese cook relaxing with a cigarette on the stern as well as the captain on the bridge deck waves us on our way.

Thirty-three feet of ocean going splendour with 'Belfast' on the stern, heading for bandit country. *Stormvolgen* of Sweden, *R Phurst* from the USA were close behind us with *Chinook II* in sight half a mile ahead. We were forming a convoy.

The Malacca Straits are infamous for the piracy attacks on shipping and we were working on the principle that there is safety in numbers. Some yachts, mainly American, carry guns for these situations but none of our little group was armed. The carrying of guns on board is a subject often discussed in the anchorages of the world but the majority of middle aged couples have no desire to get involved in a gun battle. If you have a gun you must be prepared to use it.

Most of the piracy acts in the Malacca Strait are from Indonesian shores and some reports are of official customs launches being used by the culprits so we were on the lookout for anything suspicious. In general the victims are the commercial ships, as they are known to carry large sums of cash.

The Malacca Strait has Malaysia on the east side and Sumatra, Indonesia on the west with the shipping lanes in the middle. Each side is shallow water so the ships are committed to a definite route. *Breakaway* does not have such restrictions because of her shallow draft - she just needs six and a half feet of water to float in.

So the plan was simple - hug the Malaysian shore during the hours of daylight finding an anchorage before darkness. No anchor lights to show our position, keeping a listening watch on a pre-chosen VHF channel in case one of the other boats was boarded. The pirates scan the radio frequencies for transmissions to obtain your position. This may all sound a bit dramatic but none the less necessary. Each night official Singapore or Malaysian radio stations would give out a pirate alert.

'All stations, all stations, please keep a pirate watch, suspicious vessels in sectors four and five - 20 or so armed and masked men.'

Anchored, tucked up behind an island in the hours of darkness, it all sounds quite alarming. In the distance the red and green navigation lights of the ships can be seen as they make their way regardless and they are more vulnerable than us yachts. While we were anchored at the Water Islands, a ship was boarded eight miles from us. The crew and officers were locked up down below while the raiders ransacked the vessel. Understandably all shipping in the area is concerned.

Breakaway is now tied up at Admirals Quay, Port Dickson, Malaysia. It has all the amenities of the Republic of Singapore Yacht Club plus a Jacuzzi and free film shows. The push is on to get north to Thailand as our eldest son Neill is joining us for Christmas in Phuket. Once there *Breakaway* can stop for a month and relax before heading towards Sri Lanka and the Indian Ocean.

Well, we deserve a break occasionally.

Christine

When the report came though of pirates in the area, I thought it might be wise to hide a couple of essential items. The hand-held GPS, an essential piece of navigational equipment, was an obvious one and I put it in our hidey-hole along with the hand held radio. The only trouble was that the bracket holding the GPS would have given us away so I put a little vase in it with dried flowers.

When I realised what I was doing it all seemed very funny and I could not stop laughing or perhaps I was just having a touch of hysteria.

It was infectious, however, and Jamie got into the act deciding what we would give the pirates and what we would try and hide away. The theory being if you make it worth their while they will not tear the place apart. Bob just shook his head in disbelief.

Klang River, Port Klang 03.00N 101.23E

Breakaway is now lying to a mooring outside the Royal Solangar Yacht Club in a tributary of the Klang River.

There is a little boat that works as a water taxi coming around once an hour to run us ashore if required. Each hour, on the hour, he sets off around the moorings, more as a security check than a ferry mind you, as this is not the place for cruising yachts.

Breakaway did not come here by choice but as usual circumstances have dictated our actions. The high-pressure fuel injection pump on the engine has decided to stop working. Now normally I can manage to sort out most of *Breakaway*'s mechanical problems but this one was beyond me. A real expert was required. So I hailed the 'jingo' (water taxi) and headed for the yacht club for local advice. The yard manager, an Indian from the great sub-continent, listened to me intently and then with a sharp intake of breath offered his opinion,

"It seems to me, dear sir, that you have a problem of insurmountable proportions" – sigh – "but help, I believe, is at hand. Unfortunately Ramadan is upon us and our engineer is not in a mood of severe happiness."

A good start to the day. The engineer was Muslim and Ramadan is a period of fasting from dawn to dusk for a month. Not inclined to put the faithful in a mood of severe happiness.

Still, the engineer turned up on time, refusing the offer of a jam sandwich and a cup of tea, and set too with a will. The engine is in bits and some of the bits left with the engineer. He assures me, however, that we will be back in business early next week.

Now the Royal Solangar Yacht Club is something else. The Sultan of one of the Malaysian states is the Commodore and everything is to a very high standard. Staff float about looking after your every desire. The lifeguard told me he had never saved anyone in his life as no member used the swimming pool. But he was there if the need arose. The Club dining room overlooks the river, which has to be the most polluted backwater in the world. The view is of tumble down houses on stilts with rubbish in the waterway you could walk across.

From far inland the locals dump everything in the passing streams. At one time that did not matter but now we live in the world of packaging and plastic and the less wealthy people of the world also deserve to use the supermarkets but unfortunately it appears, without the services of the bin man. So everything that man discards, floats past in the current. A WD40 can, a shuttle cock, video tapes, polystyrene hamburger holders, polystyrene hamburgers, coke cans, a sofa with matching armchair, an oil drum, a table, a palm tree with coconuts still attached, a dead chicken.

The list is endless - light bulbs, beer bottles - all the stuff we use to survive and then the tide turns and it all comes back again. In the middle of it all, collecting some of the rubbish round her like a skirt, lies poor old *Breakaway* disabled, no means of escape. Except sails of course – but the north east monsoons have not set in yet so there is no wind, although it rains heavily every day. Still I have faith in our follower of Allah. He is trying to put his youngest son through university and needs the money.

The chaos of the Klang River

Jamie and I set off for Kuala Lumpur today, the country's capital. The means of transport was the local train. The rail system is spotless and the cost is minimal. Thirty seven years ago I lost a camera in this very city. Today we were going to view the tallest twin buildings I have ever seen. Eighty four floors, all constructed in steel, towering toward the heavens – an awesome sight. Behind the buildings is a parkland for people to enjoy the view of the twin towers. More stainless steel in the form of a whale and dolphins erupting from the depths of a man-made lake.

As the tourist cameras clicked, three pretty young girls, nearly five foot tall, asked would I take a photo of them with Jamie. The child was the tallest thing they had seen all day, apart from the buildings. Then a passing Japanese tourist was roped in by the girls to take a picture of all of us together. Much bowing and smiling, cameras being handed back and forth. The end result was a good day out.

But the old Kuala Lumpur is still there - the houses of its colonial past along with the back alleys where the tourists don't go - the vendors with their carts - menus written in an indecipherable language and the chef of the day calling you in for your custom, competing with his neighbour - the dishes being cleaned with a hose pipe and the waste water running into an open drain at the side of the street. Chopsticks to eat with, constant noise, shouting and music along with tastes that will draw you back even if you sometimes don't know what you are eating.

The train ride home brought us back past the wooden huts with thatched roofs or sometimes rusted corrugated tin. Jamie and I had a good day out. By the way the camera never turned up.

Christine

In our present state of disarray the most sensible thing for me to do was get offside. After taking the jingo ashore, it was only a short walk to the town of Klang. The town serves the Port of Klang and although small, you can find most of the things you need in a recognisable form and some that throw you completely. There are strange fruit and vegetables on stalls which I would buy if I knew what to do with them. But the most interesting shop was the Chinese Medical Hall where everything was in polished wooden drawers along each wall and at the back of the shop in a red and gold traditional gown sat the doctor in front of an ornate shrine, surrounded by beautifully carved furniture - very impressive if a little daunting. I was tempted to go in and see if he could do anything about my wee bit of a head cold but I just did not have the nerve.

Phuket, Thailand 7.48N 98.22E

Well, at the moment we want to be tourists in Thailand. But as you know the pressure is on to get to Phuket to pick up our eldest son Neill who is joining us for a two week holiday.

After leaving Langkawi in Malaysia with *Chinook II* standing by *Breakaway*, there were four days left to make 120 miles. The only outstanding problem on *Breakaway* was the failed alternator, so we were using the alternative system for power - the towing generator.

The full moon dipped below the horizon and the sun came up as we approached the main anchorage on the south coast of the island of Phuket with one day up our sleeve. Just enough time to check out the lay of the land. You can hire a car here for between £6 and £8 a day but one of the main health risks to tourists in Thailand is traffic accidents so we decided to go chauffeur driven on the airport run. Now this is not quite as grand as it sounds, but a lot more fun.

The means of transport is the local bus or Tuk Tuk. We commandeered one for about £70 for the day. A Tuk Tuk is really a pickup truck with the back opened up and a long seat down each side. The roof is a bit of tin welded on to provide shelter from the sun and the sides are roll down plastic on the off chance of rain. Our driver Nin, was a font of knowledge so I explained my requirements – a new alternator.

Nin knew the very place - 'Huats', an emporium of the old school run by a diminutive Chinese lady. The long narrow shop with its mahogany counter was like Aladdin's Cave, full of treasures for the travelling yachtsman. Every inch of wall space was taken up with the most obscure bits and pieces - lamp wicks, nuts and bolts, jubilee clips, bicycle pedals, hurricane lamps. From the ceiling hung fan belts, necklaces of ball bearings on bits of string, along with other unrecognisable mechanical devices and engine gaskets. Stocktaking must be a nightmare.

The boss herself sat at a desk in the gloom at the back peering over a pile of paper, doing her accounts on an abacus, the beads rattling across the wire, her fingers a blur - no calculators for this lady.

I spoke to one of the assistants, explaining the type of alternator required to fit *Breakaway*. Without moving her head, the boss pointed and he disappeared behind a pile of rat traps stacked up in the corner, reappearing covered in dust but clutching an alternator. It wouldn't fit, I could tell just looking at it.

Mrs Huat climbed down from behind her desk to take over. The only option left was to order one from Bangkok, but this would require a 50% deposit on my part. I handed over the money, which was passed to three very pretty Thai girls who had giggled during the previous proceedings. Number one girl wrote out a receipt, number two girl examined it carefully before passing it to number three who handed it to me. As I left clutching my bit of paper, minus an alternator and £70, the three beauties were rolling about in hysterics.

The boss was behind her desk as the assistant dusted himself off before solemnly shaking my hand. Our driver was waiting, so having had enough excitement for one day we headed back to the anchorage. Everyone waved at the white people in the back of a bus. It is hard to be depressed when everyone smiles at you.

At our anchorage in Ao Chalong, a local lass has set up shop to cater for the yachts. This is the meeting place for sailors from all over the globe. Here you can have your laundry done, your cooking gas bottles refilled, a free shower, enjoy a reasonably priced meal and drink cold beer.

There is no shortage of advice from the other Yachties, everyone is an electronic genius when it comes to boat electrics. I agreed with them all, comfortable in the knowledge that Mrs Huat had everything in hand.

Thailand gives a month's visa to the yachtsman. When the 28 days are up, the trick is to sail to Malaysia and stock up on duty free and then sail back for another month. Some do not even bother to do this. For a small sum your passport can be taken to Burma to obtain the necessary stamps and the Thai visa is then renewed without the yachtsman leaving the comforts of the bar.

Jamie with Thai family living on the edge of a rubber plantation

A lot of yachts make Thailand their final destination, which is understandable. It is one of the most beautiful places in the world, with cheap and easy living an extra bonus. Some lone male sailors who choose to stay usually buy themselves a cheap moped – find a Thai girl and then regale the rest of us with their past adventures. With receding hairlines, ponytails, along with earrings and tattoos, Thailand accepts them. It seems to be that sort of place.

Next week we go to explore – to become tourists. Tomorrow we pile into a Tuk Tuk to collect Neill from the airport, Andy, Kirstie, Jamie, Christine and me, with the newly acquired alternator tucked under my arm. It's a long time since we were all together.

Christine
It has also been a long time since we had a swim in the sea – not since Indonesia in fact. But the offshore islands of Thailand were to put that right.
En route to Phuket we stopped at a small island group for a wee break. As we dropped anchor, to our delight, we could see the bottom. The water was wonderfully clear and the first thing on our minds was a refreshing dip. We were not disappointed, it was just perfect. Swimming among the small colourful fish, which surrounded Breakaway in abundance, after miles of murky water, this was a long awaited treat.
Then a call went out over the boat radios,
"Pot luck on the beach at four o'clock – everyone welcome."
A chance to meet other boat crews and swop yarns, charts and books – not to be missed. We took our food offering ashore – Chinook II rustled up a pasta dish with bar-b-queued chicken and I made a pot of chickpea curry. Well, the choice was becoming rather limited on Breakaway and did I mention Jamie had become vegetarian?
What a feast. One yacht had baked Italian bread - fish dishes were in abundance as it is the best fresh food supply you could have in our situation, and new friends were made.
Back to the boats for an overnight sail to make up for lost time, but the swim and the beach party more than compensated for the delay.

Christmas Eve, Phuket

Our eldest son Neill joined us for the Christmas festivities. His first night was a bit of a shock to the system arriving from an Irish winter to the tropical heat of the island of Phuket, Thailand. He climbed into the back of the Tuk Tuk hired to do taxi service and off we set for the anchorage. The streets were still busy with people as he tried to take it all in. What is normal for us is exotic to the visitor.

At the Yacht Club, an open fronted building on the beach, we dumped his gear in the dinghy and ordered a meal. It is always good to hear news from home. Of course he was also the postman for the two boats, delivering letters, Christmas presents and cards from family and friends.

We dinghied out to *Breakaway* stopping at *Chinook II* to let Neill see Andy and Kirstie's new home. The next couple of days were going to be spent relaxing and acclimatising before we took off for some gentle cruising. James Bond Island is on the list of places to visit.

Kirstie with young sea eagle in the area of Thailand often used by film makers

Island Hopping

The area between Phuket Island and mainland Thailand must rank high as one of the great sailing areas in the world, an area of outstanding beauty beloved of Hollywood.

It was here that they filmed *The Beach* and of course *The Man with the Golden Gun* starring Roger Moore as 'Bond.' Thailand was the backdrop to the adventures. So now we are sailing in places that we recognise from the silver screen. I am led to believe that there is a sequel coming out soon, 'Son of The Beach'.

Our first anchorage was to be in Phi Phi Don, recognised as the third most beautiful island in the world. Bora Bora takes first place but that was back in the Pacific French Polynesia, and not a great anchorage as it turned out. For us beauty goes hand in hand with a good night's sleep.

Which island comes second in the contest I am not sure, but Phi Phi was as good as we've seen. It has cliffs rearing up to the sky, deep clear water and good coral reefs, a shanty town ashore offering everything for the traveller, and sea eagles circling the sky with a beach of soft white sand to land on in the dinghy.

Neill was starting to get into the swing of things.

Now the shanty town was of special interest. The view from offshore of rusty tin roofs hint at poverty, but ashore it is quite different. As you pull your dinghy up to the beach all becomes clear. This is an island of entrepreneurs. The villagers are out in force to welcome the visitors.

Bringing the dinghy over the coral, you pull it up the sand to above high-water mark and tether it to a tree. Follow the narrow path past the little one room beach bungalows and then cross in front of the local boats pulled up on the sand, prayer flags fluttering from the bow, awaiting their first customer of the day. Continue on past the main jetty where the fast ferries discharge back-packers and tourists over from the mainland for the day. Stop at the local travel information centre - they have a water tap with a short hose - there you can wash your feet to remove the sand before putting on your sandals.

A five minutes' walk and you are already in town. The only traffic to contend with are the two Honda 50s with sidecars made out of reinforcing bar used to transport tourists to the island's main beach, a quarter of a mile away. The street is about nine feet wide. I know I should give measurements in metres, so it is two metres and 30 inches, give or take a millimetre. On each side of the thoroughfare the shutters are already up, waiting for today's new arrivals. Breakfast is a roti, very thin dough folded often and put on a griddle. You can try it with chocolate, cheese, pineapple, tuna, curry, strawberries, mango, or banana. My favourite way is with an egg on top, cut into slices and served on a banana leaf with a toothpick as cutlery. It is particularly good with a little sugar on the egg.

Neill was starting to move at our pace. We have enjoyed ourselves and enjoyed having the family together. It is Christmas Eve and at the minute Christine is taking all the football socks off the bottles. At sea we use socks to stop the bottles clinking, but tonight they will have another function.

Santa is reported somewhere over India on his way south.

Christine

Christmas dinner is going to be easy this year. A pot luck in the Yacht Club has been organised so the workload will be cut down drastically. There is no way a turkey will fit in the small ovens on board sailing boats and the heat generated from the cooking would not be welcome, so Chinook II plans to provide chicken from their Bar-B-Q on the stern. And I am doing salads and stuff. We have to turn up dressed in red, white and green and bring a small present each for a lucky dip. I know it won't be the same as a proper Christmas dinner. We will have that to look forward when we get home. Unfortunately Neill has to leave us soon but not before a visit to the tailors to be fitted for a maroon silk dinner jacket, black silk shirt and fine wool trousers – all very reasonably priced of course.

Merry Christmas 2000

Indian Ocean, Thailand to Sri Lanka

16 Jan 2001 – Day 1

Breakaway is now on passage to Galle Harbour, Sri Lanka having left Phuket six hours ago. Phuket to Galle is a distance of 1,200 miles, 300 in the Andaman Sea before passing through the Great Channel between the Nicobar Islands and Sumatra.

The Nicobars belong to India and visitors are not encouraged. It is said the reason for this is to maintain the unique culture of the indigenous people living on islands at the edge of the Indian Ocean.

The Russian military bases there of course do not have any bearing on the matter.

Sumatra is Indonesian but our cruising permit for this area unfortunately ran out a few months ago. So it is forever onwards.

Chinook II has laid a course further north with the hope of more wind. We have taken a chance on a rhumb line - a straight route from A to B. Sometimes the shortest distance between two points does not work on a sailing boat. A little while ago I spoke on the SSB radio to Andy. They have made it through the Nicobars and are now in the Indian Ocean with a fair wind. There were some problems with the track for the spinnaker pole but they have managed to drill the mast and re-tap, fitting new screws and the whole things seems to be holding together okay.

Behind us are two more yachts - *Mariah II* and *Karlmindi*. Noel and Jackie, who are on passage from Australia to England, own *Mariah II*. She is a lovely wooden boat and below decks is like a country cottage, all wood and oil lamps, right down to a solid fuel stove. *Karlmindi* is skippered by Karl, an Austrian who has lived in Australia for 30 years, and crewed by Mindi, his Philippine wife. They built the boat 15 years ago, cruising it extensively ever since. Four small boats spread over 30,000 square miles of ocean.

My main task today, with the help of Jamie, was making a wooden air filter for the engine - don't ask!

Day 3

Breakaway is now in the Indian Ocean, after a black squally night going through the Great Channel, no moon, with rain clouds obscuring the sky. The porthole over the chart table is dripping water. I have put the chart away to keep it dry. The visibility is half a mile, GPS and radar are coming into their own. On the deck the only thing visible is phosphorescence off the wave curling up the stern.

Breakaway lifts and settles again - the wave continues on. Conditions however have quietened down so, with a headsail set, we are rolling down the Trades, the miles slipping away under the keel. The sun is out now and the deck is covered with odds and ends drying. After last night the first flying fish casualties are on the deck.

Chinook II has a worldwide phone system on board and today they contacted us by radio to say Norman and Wendy, our friends from the boatyard in Carrickfergus, were just on the phone. They are joining us in the Maldives - great news. But first we have to get to Sri Lanka and the BBC World Service News is reporting heavy fighting in the north. *Breakaway* is going to the south.

Day 5

The four boats contact each other twice a day to exchange news and positions. From *Mariah II* Noel reported a bad night with lightning all around the boat. *Chinook II* had similar weather but, being a steel boat, is the safest of them all in those types of conditions, as all her systems are earthed directly to the ocean through the steel hull. *Karlmindi* is making good headway - fair wind and no problems. It gives us all a sense of security if others know where you are.

A yacht in distress in the English Channel called the Coast Guard for assistance. They requested his position. The Skipper said he was a retired doctor. A ship, *Pioneer Louise*, a LPG (liquid petroleum gas) tanker, has just passed half a mile to port. The mate called up to wish us Bon Voyage. Wasn't that nice?

Dinner is curry and rice. Jamie is cook today.

Day 6

A good sailing breeze coming in on the quarter. We are still further south than the rest of the little fleet but seem at the moment to be enjoying more favourable conditions. *Sediju* a Swiss yacht came up on the radio this morning with a mechanical problem. *Chinook II* answered their call. The bearings in their water pump had failed. They had passed Sri Lanka in favour of the northern atolls of the Maldives – the only spares were in Sri Lanka. Without the water pump there was no engine and therefore no electric. *Incandescent*, our old chum from the Pacific, was eavesdropping.

"This is Alan in Galle harbour, Andy. I will get the bits and deliver to *Sediju* – we will be there in a week, over."

The network of self-help was working again among the offshore cruisers. Peter and Heather of *Harmonie II* have joined in with our little morning and evening get-togethers on the radio. They hail from the West Coast of Canada, quite an international flotilla.

Day 7   06.004N   87.11E

One of the valve adjusting screws on the rocker arm is showing signs of wear with excessive tappet noises. We found a bolt with the same thread in the bosun's box and clamped it to the crash rail surrounding the cooker with a pair of vice grips. Jamie shaped it with a file to match the original. Then we heated it on the gas ring – once red-hot it was dipped in oil to cool and temper. Needs must, it worked. People ask don't you get bored at sea? Chance would be a fine thing.

Day 8

A quiet day without drama, little wind but enough to move us at a couple of knots towards the west. Some shipping to the south, bound for who knows where. We move forward in our own little world.

The North East Monsoons still have not set in. The season seems to be at least a month late. At this time of the year *Breakaway* should have steady trade wind sailing, day after day. On the radio this morning, Andy on *Chinook II*, who is 100 miles ahead, reported a sudden drop in his barometer. So far it has come to nothing.

The fresh food is now gone so it's pasta and rice. Christine made potato bread, which was fried with the last of the bacon.

This evening on the radio net I was modestly recounting for the third time how resourceful Jamie and I were at solving our valve problem when we were interrupted.

"Break, break, this is *Harmonie II*."

When someone breaks in, it's usually for a good reason.

"Go ahead Peter." (Canadian)

"I am alongside a Danish yacht called *No Frost*, the Skipper has been injured, hit by the boom. Above his left eye is badly cut. I have boarded and rendered First Aid. He appears to be paralysed in his right arm and leg. We may need outside assistance. Does anyone know how to get in touch with medical help? Over."

It transpired that another yacht, *Charingar*, was also alongside and they put their young crewman aboard *No Frost* to help steer.

"This is *Chinook II* (British), we have a satellite communication system on board. Do you want me to contact someone ashore? Over."

"This is *Star Cruiser* (USA), Mike of *Serenity* is a surgeon - I'll change frequency and try to raise him. Over."

The airways remained silent. Unless there was something constructive to say, the rest of us kept quiet and listened.

"*Harmonie II* this is *Serenity*. I believe you have a problem - may I help? Over."

Peter repeated the story.

"Okay, you are doing great. You have closed the wound using butterfly sutures, his pulse is steady, blood pressure you can't measure but when you shine a torch in the eyes his pupils dilate, is that correct? Over."

"That is an affirmative."

"Okay – you have to check his pulse every hour and if he falls asleep, waken him hourly. Also get him to squeeze your hand with his weak one and try to judge if there is any improvement. Make up a simple chart to record progress – *Chinook II* are you there? Over."

"We are here. Over."

"Okay – I am an orthopaedic surgeon. This is a bit out of my field. Here's a phone number of a colleague who is a neurosurgeon in Philadelphia. Give him a quick bell and explain the problem. Over."

Picture the scene. Yachts spread all over the Indian Ocean waiting for the opinion of a specialist in the States.

"*Serenity* this is *Chinook II*. I got through to your pal in America. He agrees with our treatment so far but suggests possible neck injury and the use of a surgical collar. Over."

"Okay - I hear what you say, I normally don't like the use of neck braces in my practice and only use them if an attorney insists. Get a towel - fold it, each fold about four inches, wrap it around the patient's neck for support."

"*Serenity* this is *Harmonie II* - the towel is now in position, what next? Over."

"Break, break - *Harmonie II* this is *Chinook II*, I have phoned

Air Sea Rescue in Australia and the Aussies have alerted the equivalent authorities in Colombo. They have my phone number and are standing by. Over."

"Okay - good, excellent, this is *Serenity*, everything seems to be under control, let's meet up on the radio every two hours to monitor the situation. Okay? *Chinook II* and *Harmonie*. Over."

For the rest of us listening in, this was better than *Dr Finlay's Casebook*, *The Flying Doctor* and every other medical soap ever invented for television. We were a captive audience huddled around the chart table with the radio tuned in, plotting the position of the boats running the emergency.

Soren, the Danish patient, continues to improve. Each morning an update is given over the radio. His leg has started to work again – outside help was not called in, except for a quick consultation from America.

Day 10
Chinook II made landfall in the early hours. When we last spoke to them they were waiting to be searched by the Sri Lankan Navy and to clear Customs - standard procedure.

Day 11
Serenity is about 50 miles behind us with *Harmonie II* another 70 behind them. *Mariah II* came alongside us at noon and we passed them 10 gallons of diesel. They were down to vapours in the tank and they responded with three cold cans of beer.

A fishing boat approached looking for cigarettes or whiskey. I threw over a pint of long life milk – much better for them. Unfortunately during manoeuvres they crashed into our side. I was not too well pleased. They disappeared over the Horizon rather smartly.

Sri Lanka is about 80 miles away. We should make landfall in the early hours of day 12.

Jamie throwing a line to *Mariah II* – sending over some fuel

Christine

It was while Jamie and Bob were putting a reef in the mainsail and I was looking after the cockpit end of things that I glanced over to see if there were any squalls forming on the horizon.

"What on earth is that?"

I pointed at an ominous cloud with a black column reaching the surface of the sea where water was being sucked up into the air to a great height. We all watched in horror as it moved towards us – Breakaway directly in its path. Instead of a reef, the mainsail was taken down as we frantically tried to take evading action. After a few nerve-wrecking minutes, it took itself off in another direction. Reading up in the Indian Ocean Guide, we found out it was a giant water spout. Let's hope it was our first and last one. Latest news on Soren is that he continues to improve and expert opinion is that it was the neck injury not the blow to the head causing a temporary paralysis, which was the lesser of the two evils.

Mike on Serenity is of course very eager for his patient to reach land and be examined in a hospital and all were grateful that an airlift was not required.

Galle Harbour, Sri Lanka

"Sir, my intentions are to give the full service of my capacity. If at any time you discover me as telling you an untruth you may hit me on the head."

Breakaway is now at Galle Harbour in Sri Lanka, once known as Ceylon, and our Tuk Tuk driver, Saweega, was setting down the ground rules. Now the Tuk Tuk is the local transport of Asia and they come in many forms - the canvas covered pickup truck of Thailand, the multi-coloured buses of Malaysia, the mini buses from hell of Indonesia.

In Sri Lanka they are more or less a motorised Italian rickshaw; a customised Vespa scooter, a covered-in, three-wheeled conveyance. The driver in front at the handlebars, and Christine and me pushed in the back seat, each of us looking over one of his shoulders. If it rains there are little canvas covers you can lower at the sides for added protection.

Indian Fishing Boat

The previous day had been spent sorting out the officialdom of the country. To achieve this an agent was hired who looked after most of the paperwork. Before going ashore we had first to be searched by the Navy. Three nice young men climbed on board and asked if we had a gun. I said no and they left. All very reasonable.

Then ashore to the agent - Dick Turpin in flip flops - but that's the way the system works. The last call was to Customs. In an old colonial building with louvered windows and doors, we awaited the arrival of the boss. He made his entrance to much forelock tugging from his staff. I solemnly shook his hand.

"Have you any strong alcohol or nicotine cigarettes on board your vessel?"

I looked shocked and told him I was a reformed smoker, which pleased him greatly. At this stage I could have done with one.

"Your *Breakaway* will have to submit itself to a search by my officer as soon as it is inconvenient for you."

We met the officer out on the yacht half an hour later. He sat himself down at the table and requested a beer. I apologised saying that we were right out. He compromised with an orange juice. I showed him the contents of the drinks' locker, which were sparse. Just bits and pieces of this and that along with a half bottle of Thai whiskey which cost 75 pence. I wrapped the Thai whiskey in a plastic bag, setting it beside him. He directed me to write 'nil' across the forms and he and the plastic bag left, wishing us a pleasant stay in his country. It is really all about how you treat people I suppose.

So back to the Tuk Tuk. Today we start to explore. Off we put-putted in our Tuk Tuk heading for the bank to use the hole in the wall, our trusty Visa card at the ready. First problem of the day, this ATM machine does not accept Visa and already I am in debt to Saweega our driver. I explained the problem.

"This, my kind sir, is not a problem - already I look upon you as my mother and father. We shall continue to tour. Someday you shall have money again to repay me."

I happened to mention to Christine that the pangs of hunger were setting in. Saweega obviously overheard. So with the debt mounting I agreed to let him treat us to lunch, but only if we could dine where he would normally eat.

"Do you mind eating with your hand?"

"Of course not. God invented fingers before we invented knives and forks."

So off we went to the local eating-house. Well it was great. Tamil food from Southern India at its very best. Egg roti, chapati, samosas, curried sauces, rice noodles and onion bhajis. But first we had to clean our hands as eating was communal, all reaching into the same dish. Water was poured over our digits and we wiped them on little squares of cut up newspaper.

The plates were stainless steel condiment dishes, like a tray with hollows in it - the indentations designed to take a different sauce and the main area for rice or bread. The plate was covered with cling film and you placed the food on the film. It saved on the dish washing. We ate our way through the lot, finishing with a cup of tea, beautifully served in china cups and saucers with 'Lipton' engraved on the saucers.

Saweega with Tuk Tuk

We had left the Tuk Tuk parked on a hill and I had jumped out to place a suitably sized stone under the back wheel. Now as Segeewa revved up the Vespa I removed the brick and smartly leapt into the back. Christine and I were getting into the swing of things. We visited museums and jewellery shops as Sri Lanka is famed for its gemstones. Unfortunately the pieces were not cheap, but to see the craftsmen work is a pleasure in itself. By this time we were toured out so went back to the boat. There was one more stop before the harbour. We were to meet the driver's family.

Mum, sister, baby son, cousins, aunts, uncles, babysitters. Television was showing an Indian film so we sat down on the plastic chairs to enjoy it with the rest of the family. The fact that it was in Hindu with Singalese sub-titles did not take away from the enjoyment. Mother has invited Christine to join her to learn how to use the spices necessary in preparing a curry. Mum cooks over a wood burning fire in clay pots. The kitchen is basic, but she was manufacturing aromas which would have graced the finest hotel kitchens.

Christine

On the way back into the harbour we produced our security passes
and were given access. Everyone seems a bit embarrassed by the
security measures but the north of the country is under terrorist
threat. We find it all quite normal although it seems to put the other
Yachties under stress. Still - one day into the country and we love it.
The people, the buildings, the smells, the colours, the sacred cows
on the streets, and the vegetable markets are second to none.
The rest of the family have gone off on a tour for a few days leaving
Bob and me in charge of Chinook II. Noel and Jackie of Mariah II
are with them also, so we have a boat each to keep our eyes on as
well as Breakaway. There is a strong naval presence in the
anchorage with a small vessel patrolling constantly so their boats will
be safe enough. While we sit in the cockpit of an evening our
protector glides quietly past earning it the nick name 'the grey
ghost'. All is well in Galle Harbour.

This week we have gone tuk-tukking again, hiring Saweega for a day
tour on his three-wheel motor scooter. The request was simple,

"Take us to see your country. Show us what you are proud of."

Now Sri Lankans have a habit of moving their head from side
to side and up and down, all at the one time, when they are happy,
or telling you a lie, which they hope you will believe. The bold
Saweega's head was wobbling about on his shoulders with the thought
of an adventure. He explained to us that we might move off the
beaten track where the sight of a white man could cause a degree of
excitement. Could we handle it? Of course we could. Go for it. But
now there were three of us squashed into the back seat - Jamie was
taking the grand tour as well and the 125cc engine was working hard.

We made our way through Galle, at one time under Dutch
rule, and the capital of Ceylon. Then the British did a deal with the
Dutch overlords and the jewel to the south of India became theirs.
The English decided Colombo should be the seat of administration
and so it was. But Galle still shows signs of its colonial past.

The old fort, with its walls 10 feet thick, surrounds a
community remote from the main town. The cricket pitch with men

in their whites clapping and congratulating each other. The English common in tropical heat - hints of a colonial past. Raleigh push bikes of the 'sit up and beg' variety, no gears, a fixed wheel with a comfortable saddle - the cyclists sitting with backs straight moving along at a regal pace, their sarong just missing the chain as it moves round and around in time with the pedals. Their bare feet are callused and the flip-flop sandals hang over the handlebars to prevent shoe repairs. Occasionally they ring their bell - road rage in the East.

A bullock cart moves to one side and the Tuk Tuk squeezes into the space causing the cyclist to wobble and we are off into the country. Now the drivers of Sri Lanka do not know fear. If there is a gap they head for it. Our driver probably has a different overall view but Christine, Jamie and myself from the rear seat felt fear. At times I would hold my breath and clench other things to try to make us narrower. It was time for a cup of tea.

"Another few minutes or maybe longer, sir, contain yourself please, if I may so request."

I shut up.

The scenery was great. Low lying paddy fields of rice - terraces of tea bushes on the high ground with coconut palms growing where they wanted. We were somewhere in between. More people were about, waving at us and then the hill village appeared. Cup of tea time. We found the roti shop. I love them. This particular roti shop was about 10 feet wide stretching back into the darkness.

We walked into an engagement party. The young bride to be and her loved one sitting at different tables, mother sitting erect to the one side and packets of potato crisps, for some reason best known to themselves, hanging from the ceiling. The cake was produced along with cups of tea sweetened with condensed milk. We slurped the tea, grabbed at the crisps and ate a slice of cake.

Photos were taken, an invitation to the wedding handed out. Unfortunately we had to decline. In May it is the Mediterranean for us. Everyone looked relieved. We left to many handshakes and fond farewells.

The old town of Galle

Next on the agenda was a visit to the tea plantation which was closed, but they let us in for a look around while we were waiting. The girls were working in the terraces picking the top leaves of the bushes, backbreaking work, all very labour intensive. The machinery for drying and grading the leaves was closed so we are as wise now about the tea industry as we ever were. But it was interesting to see where that cuppa comes from.

We made our way back to the Tuk Tuk to continue the journey, stopping along the way to talk to workers drying the rice, school children making their way home and the women in their saris leaving the terraces of tea bushes to go home to the stove.

Passing through a village with the houses closing in on the road there were more people, more humanity, everyone living on top of each other, but that is Sri Lanka. Next stop the local church or Buddhist temple. So with shoes off we entered, aware of interfering in something we knew nothing about, conscious of maybe breaking rules, not wishing to offend.

Once, a long time ago in the high altitudes of the Himalayas, I experienced the power of Buddha. The Lord Buddha was a rich man, the son of a King and Queen. His ears had long lobes due to the heavy gold ornaments that stretched them in his youth. Married at 16, he gave up wealth and family to go on his pilgrimage, an odyssey, a search for truth. A journey to find peace, along with tranquillity in the human soul.

His image is everywhere, the 28th reincarnation of the first Buddha. The temple was charming with the monks in their saffron robes, the youngest only eight years of age. Like any other youngster, intrigued by aliens in his house, the blue-eyed, long-nosed, red-faced people. We wandered at will, the cells where the monks sleep, the dining room they use, everywhere we wandered we were made welcome. The monks live a life of discipline, only eating between the hours of six am and midday, the food they receive given to them by the villagers. The atmosphere was gentle with everyone courteous and kindly.

One of the monks chatted to us, a handsome man 30 years old who took up the cloth 16 years ago, still managing to visit his family once every couple of months. He was intrigued that Jamie was a vegetarian like himself and then gave us a blessing for our travels, to keep us safe. A bit of string was wrapped around our right wrists as he intoned the philosophy of his teaching. Each bit of string a 24 hour prayer giving us safe passage.

The three of us were moved by the experience and Saweega had done well. The finances were sorted out with our guide before *Breakaway* sailed, but more importantly we handed our man Saweega over to some very well-off Scandanavian Yachties who put him on the payroll straight away.

Christine
While on their tour inland the 'Chinooks' came across young orphaned elephants having their daily bath and the mahouts invited them to give a helping hand. They did not have to be asked twice.

The Maldives 04.07 N 3.26E

The archipelago of the Maldives runs across the Indian Ocean between Sri Lanka and Africa. 1,199 islands, of which 200 are inhabited. The whole group is divided into 19 atoll clusters. The word atoll is originally from the Maldivian language and has come to mean paradise for the cruising sailor.

Anyhow enough of the geography, *Edvina* and ourselves were boats on a mission, ably supported by *Chinook II*.

Edvina is owned by Gary, a Dublin man, his New Zealand wife Noreena and their two children. Him and her met in the Americas whilst studying to be chiropractors and what with one thing and another romance blossomed. So now they are on their way to Oman to set up a practice, but meanwhile a small diversion to the Maldives.

Our old chums Wendy and Norman had told us to be there as they had seen it on television and were coming to visit. Gary's mum Rose was catching the same flight by way of Dubai. So the boats had left Sri Lanka for Male, capital of the Maldives, for the gathering of the clans. The whole thing was to be a surprise for the grandchildren on *Edvina* who did not know Gran was visiting.

As we left the beautiful island of Sri Lanka at first light there wasn't much of a breeze. *Breakaway* averages 100 miles a day in the oceans, so we settled down to four days at sea, each day a 24-hour period, watch on watch off. Before too long *Edvina* and *Chinook II* passed us – bigger boats, shorter times, sprinters instead of joggers, they slipped over the horizon. Just before daybreak the following morning I carried the lonely watch, motoring in the still conditions. There was a light to port, something to be wary of in the oceans.

"Vessel to the south of me – this is *Breakaway*."

"This is *Edvina*, our gearbox has failed."

"It will be daylight in about an hour, I'll come and join you."

"This is *Chinook II*, can we give you a tow until the wind comes?"

"This is *Edvina* – it would be appreciated as I wouldn't want me mammy hanging about waiting on us."

So the three boats rendezvoused in the ocean to have a committee meeting. It seemed the problem was a lack of oil and a surplus of water in the gearbox. Andy and myself are never short of advice,

"Remove the water and put oil in."

It worked. *Edvina* slipped over the horizon again under her own steam saying they owed us one. I called them up,

"Did I tell you about my bad shoulder?"

Well - after all it's not every day you get the chance.

Chinook II, along with *Edvina*, arrived in Male safely and we turned up eventually to face Customs, Immigration, Health Authorities and the Marine Police. It seems we are not infested by rodents so were free to wander the atolls. But first *Edvina* had to pick up the mammy and we had to collect Wendy and Norman.

Breakaway is settled into the way of life of atolls where the only means of transport is the local boat. Male must be the only large airport in the world with no roads, no cars. The taxi is a boat, the traffic police man is on a boat. The means of access to the capital Male is by boat – a dhoni. So all these boats converge.

As the plane comes down towards the extended island runway, the sea is awash with the wake of countless vessels each and every one chasing a customer, with the conductor ready to take your money. Rose from Dublin was the first off the plane to scenes of great emotion from the crews of *Chinook II* and *Breakaway*. *Edvina*'s mob was too excited to get upset, seeing the granny for the first time in three years.

Then Norman and Wendy appeared, staggering under the weight of spare parts for the two boats *Chinook II* and *Breakaway*. What a great reunion, the couple who had done so much for us and *Breakaway*. Happy to see each other again in the heat, a 100 miles north of the Equator, we climbed into the water taxi.

The airport harbour was awash with the swirl of the dhonis' propellers, all making their way to the various resort islands. The police launch dashed about trying to create some form of control without much success. As we went over the reef into the lagoon of North Male atoll, the water changed from translucent green to dark blue – dolphins splashed away in the distance. A plane took off 250 yards away, running parallel to us on a runway level with the sea.

And then there were seven

Breakaway was anchored close to Club Med just a few miles away, as good a place as any to settle into island life after an Irish winter. Once on board our friends got into their tropical kit – shorts, T-shirts and wide brimmed sun hats. Christine and I sat at the saloon table which was covered in presents. Apart from the boat bits, there was mail from home, talking books in vast numbers from son Neill to help shorten the night hours, a new cockpit light, stock cubes and of course soda and potato bread for a taste of home. But best of all was the news and a good gossip, which we have missed. Norman also had brought a selection of newspapers that quickly made their way around the fleet.

Wendy said, "Can I go for a swim?"

"You can do whatever you like."

We haven't got her out of the water since. *Breakaway* is on her holidays.

Christine

The first thing I did for Norman and Wendy was hand them a sarong each. Multipurpose, it covered them at night, wrapped them up after a swim, kept them cool and comfortable and after a quick rinse through it was soon dry and ready for action again.

Bob and I have enjoyed the break from routine along with Wendy and Norman. It was just what we needed. Son Jamie went to stay on board Chinook II and the two boats sailed together from one atoll to

*the next, each with lookouts posted to spot the reefs and coral
heads. The snorkelling has been magnificent, the water crystal clear
and the fish life colourful and of an immense variety. We have had a
chance to relax in the company of good friends. Just what the
doctor, or should I say chiropractor, ordered.*

Male 04.13N 73.32E

Male, the capital of the Maldives, is an island about four square miles
in size. It might be slightly larger but not by a lot. The rest of the
country is spread over coral atolls, only a few large enough to support
life. The inhabited islands' economy is fishing, along with a few
coconut trees and tourism.

The island we are visiting at the moment is Thulusdhoo and can be
measured in square yards rather than square miles, but it supports
220 inhabitants. Here there is no unemployment. Along with Wendy
and Norman we got the grand tour of the Coca Cola factory, which
not only makes a full range of soft drinks but also manufactures the
bottles. From there, across the sandy streets, was a boat yard
employing 60 workers and building boats up to 80 feet long, as well
finished as you would find anywhere. There is also a drying plant
processing fish supplied by the other islands and as if that was not
enough, a clothing factory.

There is one vehicle on the island, a pickup truck which travels
100 yards from the factory to the jetty, loading the Coca Cola onto
boats which distribute the goods to the resort islands.

This small speck on the ocean also imports workers from Bangladesh and Sri Lanka. They work seven days a week for 11 months of the year, returning home rich men, to join their families for one month and then back to the atolls. The skilled of course are the best paid and they are on 200 US dollar a month – or about £140. A lot of these imported workers are employed on the resort islands spread about the area leased from the Maldivian government; each and every one a little kingdom in its own right, self-sufficient, with the sole purpose of catering to the whims of the holiday maker.

After our stop at Thulusdhoo, the centre of industry, we set forth with Wendy and Norman and *Chinook II* for the holiday resorts. First stop Club Med.

Our guests were going to treat us to a meal ashore. So, suitably attired for the occasion, we climbed in the dinghy and made our way ashore in the tropical dusk. Money is not used in Club Med so vouchers had to be purchased at reception, which was at the end of the wooden pier where we had tied up our transport. Receipts were handed over for the buffet meal and drink vouchers to be used at the bar. We set off to dispose of some vouchers. The bulk of the clientele was French, of mixed age groups, many of them families.

We seated ourselves close to the swimming pool and sat back to enjoy the ambience. The buffet was all you could imagine from T-bone steaks to pasta with a vast variety of desserts and a cheese board second to none. But the best thing of all was the fresh bread and butter. This is a treat we have not had for some time. The dining room was high roofed with open sides and ceiling fans working hard to circulate the warm air.

A night to remember. The evening finished with a cabaret, most of the artists performing were staff - much in the tradition of Billy Butlins Redcoats. We decided to get rid of the rest of the vouchers at the bar. French humour is not something to laugh at.

At some of the resorts, yachts are not made welcome and our cruising permit restricted us to the atolls of North and South Male. Only in one were we asked to leave the lagoon. We had to ignore their request. I felt it would have been dangerous to move *Breakaway* as it was late afternoon. Eyeball navigation is the method used for coral reefs and as the sun sinks the hazards cannot be identified.

Safe passage can only be made when the sun is behind you or high in the sky, so you must move between 10 in the morning and two in the afternoon. Before the sun drops too low in the sky, you work your way through a pass in the reef to anchor in sheltered waters. The locals negotiate these waters at night but for us to attempt it would have been asking for trouble.

On one of the Italian resorts we visited, the manager, a Sri Lankan called Patrick, took Norman and me on a tour behind the scenes. We visited the generation plant, the desalination system where sea water is turned into fresh water, and the rubbish tip. All the rubbish is sorted by hand for recycling. I asked Patrick if he spoke Italian. He said he didn't. He felt it was an advantage as the guests couldn't complain to him. The cold rooms held food for a week - separate ones for fish, vegetables, fresh meat and dried goods. An interesting day.

Norman and Wendy slowly began to tan, with Wendy snorkelling every day, exploring the reefs and their colourful inhabitants - fish and sea life of all colours, blues, purples, greens, reds, yellows - black spots and white stripes. Wendy had taken to wearing a floppy hat, a pair of white trousers, and a blue T-shirt over her purple swim suit to protect herself from the sun while in the water. What with yellow fins, a florescent pink mask and a snorkel with a bright orange top, the colours were hard on the eyes. The fish seemed to think she looked quite normal. Still, after the Lord Mayor's Show, comes the bin men and after our holiday in the Maldives we are now going to spend the next two weeks at sea on passage to Oman.

Christine
Norman and Wendy have had a great time. Sailors themselves they have really enjoyed listening to the radio and reports of other yachts and their movements. Before our friends left they helped us prepare Breakaway for sea again. The extra two pairs of hands were great. Everything we needed had to be bought and carted through the town to the water taxi and then onto Breakaway. We were loaded down with food stores, fuel containers, tins of soft drinks, bottles of

water, flour, bags of potatoes and gas canisters. Enough stores to keep us going until we can restock in Oman. At one stage I bought a hand of bananas and paid seven US dollars.

That couldn't be right – Wendy and I hurried back but the shop keeper, his stall and bananas had gone. Probably couldn't believe his luck. Wendy said, "I thought you would be better at the bargaining by now Christine."

Arabian Sea, Maldives to Oman

March 2001   14.17N 58.33E

The concern in this part of the world is piracy. There were many reports as *Breakaway* sailed up the Malacca Straits but the bandits concentrated their efforts on commercial shipping. In the Gulf of Aden and southern parts of the Red Sea, yachts are a definite target.

Two weeks ago *Ocean Swan* was towing another yacht that had engine problems, when a fishing boat appeared close by. One of the fishermen fired an automatic rifle in the air, ordering the yacht to stop. They were boarded and robbed. *Shady Lady*, the yacht under tow, was unmolested as was another sailboat in the vicinity, but they were powerless to help. The raiders disappeared towards the coast of Yemen, 15 miles to the north.

Our landfall is Oman and one of the reasons for going there is to allow us to refuel. Also it will give *Breakaway* a chance to join other yachts and form a convoy through the dangerous area. Boats group up according to size and speed, sticking together for 700 miles. The *Ocean Swan* incident shows that the convoy system is not foolproof but at least it lends some moral support.

Breakaway is 'tail end Charlie' at this stage as most of the other boats are now on passage for the Red Sea. *Chinook II* is about 200 miles in front of us, as are some Scandinavians, so they will wait for us in Salalah, Oman to allow *Breakaway* to rejoin the fleet. From there we take the lead as smallest boat, the others pacing themselves to our speed on the passage through the Gulf of Aden.

Ten days out of the Maldives and four days to Oman, all's well on *Breakaway*.

Christine
Some passages go quickly and others seem to drag on for ages. The Maldives to Oman run is proving to be one of the slow ones. The promised North East Trade Winds are not evident and we are doing a lot of motoring at low revs to conserve fuel. There is a consolation, however, light winds mean flat seas and it has been a very comfortable trip. We communicate regularly with Chinook II over the SSB radio and both boats have been very industrious making the most of the calm conditions. You won't believe what I have been up to. Under a blazing tropical sun I am knitting woolly hats! Well - it can get cold sailing up the Irish Sea.

The Middle East, Salalah Harbour, Oman 16.56N 54.00E

Mina Raysut, the harbour for Salalah, is about 10 miles from the town or a one day camel ride. We decided to hire a car.

The vintage was dictated by the amount in our pockets, so the choice was limited. The final selection was of Japanese manufacture but an unknown make as the badges had fallen off. Air conditioning, which was past its best, was blowing hot air and sand into the interior but still it opened up the desert to us.

In Oman they drive on the right hand side of the road which takes a bit of getting used to. The family was warned as we approached a crossroads or T-junction to keep reminding the driver. Andy did very well. In my defence it seems as you get older concentration can slip. At one stage as I slowed down to avoid a herd of camels, much as you encounter cattle on a country road at home, I had the first lapse of memory.

As I weaved through the ships of the desert, Christine hung out of the window taking photographs. The excitement over, I moved automatically to the left and continued the journey. Not one of the passengers noticed for a while. Daughter Kirstie was the first to realise that I wasn't lined up to pass port to port. I made the correction without incident.

The desert landscape was amazing. More camels wandered the barren landscape searching for food with the occasional Bedouin encampment nestled in gullies close to the road. Electricity poles disappeared into the distance with army posts looking like something left over from *Beau Geste*. Mirages made the road shimmer in the heat, then suddenly over the brow of a hill we were at the sea.

What a big beach. The shore was lined with funny little beach huts, each one taken over for the day by picnickers in their four-wheel drive vehicles. Lots of people were playing in the water, but all of them were covered from head to toe in flowing robes – no bikinis on this waterfront. Time was passing quickly and reluctantly we retreated to find a supermarket in Salalah.

Land in Oman is not in short supply so the town spreads itself out, making transport essential. Everything seems to be the one colour, the buildings the same as the desert, any paint faded in the sun. Even the local dress is not a fashion statement. White for the men, black for the women, with no varying shades in-between. Not that there are a lot of females about. They seem to be confined to the home in most cases. It appears to me to be a male dominated society.

All the shops have male assistants, even the ones selling female apparel, right down to bras and knickers. The restaurants and teahouses are meeting places for the lords and masters. Here they gather, sipping hot sweet tea, probably discussing another hard day in the cosmetic department.

On one evening excursion, Kirstie and Christine set off on a mission, leaving me to watch the world go by. A group of locals sitting under a tree at the side of the road were observing mother and daughter causing chaos as they made their colourful way – covered I might add from top to toe – through the crowds of men.

Now as I mentioned the men wear long white robes. They also wear a turban on their heads, adorned with ornate tassels and hold hands or clutch little fingers together as they stroll.

A few ladies can be seen from time to time in the supermarket. They are dressed in many layers of overall black material in a costume known locally as an abaya. The finishing touch to the ensemble is the burka or veil hiding the face leaving only their eyes exposed. Even this area is sometimes hidden behind gauze or in these more liberated times - a pair of Ray-Bans. Occasionally you make eye contact, the whole experience quite strange. A pair of eyes, smiling, frowning or just looking curious.

We did not linger too long, as the last of the yachts of the year to go up the Red Sea and transit the Suez Canal were having a meeting to discuss tactics. There were five boats left in the anchorage. *Trolldans* and *Impetus* from Norway. *Ashanti* from the UK, mum and dad, along with Joshua and Dominic, the two boys aged nine and eleven, both quite looking forward to meeting some pirates. Then *Chinook II* with *Breakaway* to make up the last of what the Mediterranean sailors call the Red Sea Mob.

The Red Sea Mob meets to discuss tactics

The purpose of the meeting was the pirate situation in the Gulf of Aden and how to avoid an attack. It has long been a problem for small craft off the Horn of Africa and the Somalia coast. Now the coast of Yemen is also a hot spot. So it was generally agreed the best protection was to tell no one of our destination and stick closely together, while maintaining radio silence.

Christine
Being suitably attired so as not to offend the community we are visiting, has been quite difficult. We all tend to wear light clothing to combat the heat and were having difficulty finding anything that would cover arms and legs, completely and yet be comfortable. Kirstie and I bought inexpensive, flimsy cotton wraps that covered up any part of exposed skin and, thus robed, I was happy to push my trolley around the supermarket, confident that I was offending nobody. I couldn't believe it as I searched the shelves. There were no packets of dates to be seen. Standing puzzled, Kirstie asked me what was wrong,
"No dates – I can't find dates."
Giving me the look daughters reserve for mothers who are being a bit dense, she pointed. There, in prime position at the top of the aisle, in splendid isolation, was a kiosk looking like a miniature Taj Mahal containing piles of glistening dates from the different Arab States. They were magnificent. Just the thing to sweeten the scones baked as soon as we got back to Breakaway.

The Gulf of Aden and the Red Sea, Oman to Eritrea

The Gulf of Aden is the danger zone for pirate attacks. The decision was made to go straight down the middle hoping the roughnecks from Somalia on the African side or the Yemen cut-throats from the Middle East would not venture that far offshore. Maintaining radio silence and showing a minimum of lights at night, the journey through 600 dangerous miles passed without incident. With the Port of Aden to the north we continued on for another day before turning right and pointing *Breakaway*'s bows into the Red Sea.

The Red Sea is where a lot of our history began, the lands of the Old Testament on either side of the 1000-mile waterway where Moses parted the seas. On the western shores Solomon travelled in search of the fabled land of Sheba and the Queen of renowned beauty who ruled there. The area of his search was either modern day Ethiopia or the Yemen.

Eritrea, and the harbour of Massawa, was our next port of call. The name Eritrea came from the ancient Greek name for the Red Sea (Erythra Thalassa), based on the adjective 'erythros', 'red'. But reading the history does not prepare you for Eritrea and Massawa Port. Here live the people who fought a 30-year war to gain independence from Ethiopia and succeeded in 1991.

Massawa Harbour, Eritrea, Africa

As you come through the pier heads, the wreckage of merchant ships litter the north shore with red buoys marking other debris hidden below the surface.

Massawa Harbour, Eritrea

Tying up to the wall I made my way to Immigration, housed in an old wooden building. As you climb the stairs to the second floor you realise the third floor no longer exists. What was the roof is now open to the sky. Once cleared in and the officials happy, we made our way to the anchorage to pump up the dinghy. Time to go into town to explore and after 10 days at sea we couldn't wait.

On each occasion when you leave or enter the port, passports have to be examined by the security guards on the gate. They don't seem to work shifts - the same people are there day and night, armed with an old Russian Kalashnikov rifle, the barrel stuffed with a wad of paper.

The footpath on the main street is covered in to provide shade, making the walkway a colonnade of archways. The roadway is littered with craters, bomb damage from attacks by air. Buildings are pockmarked with bullet holes – the local people with limbs missing. I did not realise that there were air raids on the town up to 1998.

Once off the main street the tarmac ends, leading to dusty alleyways with every other building a bar of sorts. The faces peer out at you and turn away if you catch their eyes. The only other white people in the country are United Nation forces and they are not in town. There is a thin coating of flour dust over everything, blown from the international aid trucks unloading on the quay. Painted white, they supply the hinterland with food. This is the Africa of the nine o'clock news, a land that had recently known war and famine. There are five yachts in the anchorage along with the aid ships, fishing boats from Saudi Arabia and wooden trading vessels out of India.

After 10 days at sea the five of us were going ashore for a meal in a restaurant half a mile away. We made our way through the darkened streets, oil lamps flickering in the bars as the inhabitants relaxed after sitting around in the shade all day. People waved and called a welcome, voices coming out of the night, inviting us to join them for a drink.

The eating house was furnished with Formica covered wooden tables and plastic garden chairs. A ceiling fan revolved intermittently. Locally brewed gin was the order of the day. The waiter told us the local custom was to order a bottle (cost £2) rather than buy a glass, explaining that it would save time for us and effort for him – when in Rome... The meal was freshly caught prawns fried in garlic, the gin was shared with diners at other tables. Hard to believe we were in a country recently torn apart by war. This had to be one of the shabbiest eating houses in existence but who cared. They sold relief from the real world.

We made our way back to the boat quietly, taking care not to wake up the security guard on the gate. You don't startle someone who is in charge of a rifle. But the future looks good for Eritrea. The docks are lined with modern cranes, forklift trucks and new tug boats. Let us hope international aid works. It was the war in this area that created Live Aid. I feel like Kate Adie reporting from a war zone. Did you ever notice that everywhere that woman goes, there is trouble?

Fresh water is scarce. All yachts paid for water.

Christine

The method of payment during our travels has been with credit cards, but Eritrea is not set up to provide this form of finance at the moment. Everything had to be cash and preferably US dollars. However it was just possible we might get our hands on some money in the capital, Asmara.

As things were a little frisky in the anchorage - a fresh breeze had dislodged two fishing boats and they had drifted through the assembled yachts causing chaos - Bob nobly offered to stay behind. So Jamie and I set off in a hired mini bus organised by Maria of Trolldans, along with Kirstie and Andy and the rest of the Red Sea Mob. Once business had been seen to, we were free to explore the city which had a strong Italian influence. One famous spot was the Medeber Market where cast off items are turned into something useful. A tin of corned beef becomes a rectangle cup complete with handle, and powdered milk containers become saucepans which you set on the top of a small oven fashioned out of a biscuit tin. Leftover war hardware is re-modelled and put to many practical uses in the home, quite fascinating.

I bought a copper bangle for Bob to help his aches and pains. He was pleased we had thought about him and put it on straight away. In the morning he showed me his present. The 'copper' had come off during the night and he was left with a piece of metal.

I wonder what it had been in a previous life.

Asmara, Eritrea

The Sudan

My father, just home from the War and a house in Dundee Street on the Shankhill Road, Belfast - not a kitchen house, let me add, but one with a parlour. Around the corner was a feast of shops and stores and a choice of entertainment as well. 'Wee Joes' and 'The Shank', two picture houses a couple of 100 yards apart, both in competition.

Every two days the programmes changed. Three adventures a week in each palace of the silver screen. That is if you had the money or knew Mary Lamb. Mary was the lady in charge of the torch - a person of great authority in the field of entertainment. Here I had an edge. Myself and her son Billy were playmates. Somewhere between Pathé News and the 'Big Picture' Mary would push up the horizontal bar on the side door to let Billy and me slip in.

Do you remember *The Four feathers*? The hero was branded a coward. Billy and I knew he wasn't of course. He was really a spy in the Sudan. It took an hour and a half to prove us right. In one scene the so-called coward crawled across a desert to warn the British,

"They're coming."

As the enemy appeared over a sand dune, Billy shrank behind the seat. I just closed my eyes. The warriors came down the hill, hurling spears and whirling like dervishes. As you can imagine it all turned out all right in the end. The spy returned home to a hero's welcome and Billy and me fought off the warring tribes of the desert again and again.

So, back to the real world. A few hours ago *Breakaway* ran into an anchorage just in front of a gale with a sandstorm starting to obscure visibility. We got the hook down and the chain out to weather the storm. The full brunt of the wind passed us to the east, somewhere off the coast of Saudi Arabia. But *Breakaway* was in the land of the Sudan - illegally I might add - an anchorage that transported me back to 'Wee Joes' and 'The Shank'. To tell you the truth my nerves were wrecked. I couldn't sleep. At any time we could be under attack. Christine said,

"Would you give my head peace and go to bed."

Easy for her to say.

The night passed. Next morning the wind had eased and across the reef a small fishing boat started to make its way towards us.

"Christine - down below."

"Why?"

"They're coming."

"Who?"

She was no fun - where was Billy Lamb when you needed him. The fishermen gave Andy and Kirstie a fish for a T-shirt and then it was our turn. We passed over four cigarettes, a packet of biscuits and some second hand engine oil for a bit of a chat. There is nothing nicer than to awake in the tropics before the heat of the day sets in, sit under the shade of our canvas cover and share the morning with a local.

It is very hard to explain our lifestyle. Like everyone else there are highs and lows. Our low at the minute is an engine that does not work. Our high is a boat called *Chinook II* that is towing us up the Red Sea. The low is a wind on the nose, the high is a calm. But then when the breeze fills in from the right direction, *Breakaway* makes passage and the world is at peace.

What a difference when sailing in a strong wind. Everything is taut, the sails reefed but still the wind presses *Breakaway*. The rigging on the leeward side sagging, an indication of the bend and strain on the mast. The next wave hits, green water crashes over the decks. The force of the water hitting stops us dead and then *Breakaway* gathers herself, moves on slowly again. We wear harnesses to attach us to the boat, fair weather or foul. At night you can sleep in your bunk safely, sound in the knowledge that the other shift is tied in. *Breakaway* trundles up the Red Sea day in, day out. It seems to be a long passage.

Christine
Because all the wedding guests knew that Kirstie and Andy were going to be living for a few years on board a boat, the presents for the newly married couple were most unusual to say the least. Charts instead of toasters, navigational books and all sorts of things that would prove useful at sea. One present the 'Breakaways' are very envious of, is a pair of binoculars. They have a tremendous range, with a built-in compass so you can work out the heading of an approaching ship. As we travel further up the Red Sea, traffic is starting to become congested as the shipping funnels in towards the Suez Canal. Although we have radar and GPS, there is still a place for a trusty pair of binoculars.

Egypt

April 2001
Breakaway pulled into Safaga, a port of entry for Egypt, to obtain a visa and restock for the last 200 miles of the Red Sea before the Suez Canal. Once through the ditch that made Africa an island we will be back in European waters for the first time in five years. From Safaga harbour, the land disappeared into the distance - sand - then mountains one after the other - seeming to go on forever.

Another yacht beside us was called *Ishtar*, the owner was Matthew, an American on his way to Greece to complete a circumnavigation of the world lasting 30 years. Our first boat was also called *Ishtar*, named after the Babylonian Princess of Love and War who sold herself into prostitution to save her country.

Now Matt suggested we team up with his crew and *Chinook II* to share the cost of a sightseeing tour for a couple of days. It seemed a good idea to become tourists for a while. Our new American friend was obviously a man of experience. What's more he looked a bit like Dick Van Dyke with an earring. I was suitably impressed.

The mini bus was on time at 06:00 the following morning and with a cheery greeting Mustafa, the driver, helped us pile our bags along with ourselves on board. Matt, as chief organiser, had the seat up front alongside Mustafa, where communication would be easier. Dawn was breaking as we set of towards the hills, the desert scenery stunning in its loneliness. Now the followers of Allah pray five times a day. Because the driver couldn't go to the Mosque on this occasion, due to his commitment to us, he had the appropriate religious ceremony on tape. So there we were in the desert with the Mullah calling the faithful to prayer, all part of the ethnic experience and a bit of prayer does not hurt any of us.

Matt reached across and ejected the tape replacing it with a Led Zeppelin of his choice. Mustafa bit his lip, I cringed and Matt gave an odd little lurch to the beat of the music. These two men were cultures apart.

As the day progressed communication between them would prove to be out of the question. Within half an hour of setting forth, our journey was interrupted by a one-mile queue of tourist coaches and mini buses. The surrounding sand hills had confused tourists standing about, not sure why they were there or what they were doing. We joined them. Heavily armed men dressed in black combat clothes, flak jackets and long, lace-up jumpboats, with the laces undone, examined each vehicle. Everyone was smiling and very pleasant.

To us coming from a land where peace breaks out on a regular basis, it all seemed reasonably normal. The other travellers were not just as casual about it, with Matt starting to show the first signs of tension with a nervous twitch below his eye, causing the earring to give strange little jerks.

The cause of the traffic jam was simple. We were forming a convoy as a security measure against terrorism. Because of our travels we are unaware of many events, not having access to English speaking newspapers and forgetting to listen to the BBC World Service most of the time. When we do manage to tune in, nothing changes. Hunger in Africa, floods in India, with re-occurring problems in the region of the Urals. So the fact that something like 80 tourists had been massacred in Egypt a few years ago had not reached our ears.

Now the road to Luxor and the Valley of the Kings is a one way system, starting at seven in the morning. The police check each vehicle through and then the charge begins, the road filled with air conditioned tourists being transported into the past, amid outriders armed fore and aft. At each village or town there is a curfew and the opposing traffic piles up, waiting for the passage of people released for a day from the resorts of the Red Sea.

The convoy was unstoppable, our little mini bus bouncing from side to side as Mustafa fought with the wheel. Our budget transport was not in the same league as the rest of the convoy. The first imposed stop was at an Egyptian motorway café set in the middle of the desert, a cup of tea five Egyptian pounds with another pound to use the toilet. A sand hill served my purpose. The wait was to allow the convoy to regroup and allow traffic going in the opposite direction to continue.

At a cross-roads, the traffic was held back as we roared past, the police talking into radios while locals in their cars and on their donkey carts and camels waited patiently for us to pass and for normality to return - at least that is until six o'clock that evening when the whole process is reversed. In one village a local man was knocked down by one of the buses. He lay on the road obviously dead from head injuries but even that did not stop the progress of the overseas visitors as we all roared past.

By this stage Matt was holding a conversation with Mustafa, trying to make himself understood by shouting at the poor man and repeating himself, to no avail. Eventually Luxor appeared and the pace slowed as we motored along the East Bank of the Nile in search of a hotel, with Mustafa asking directions from a camel driver. He deposited us safely at the St Mina. We sorted out rooms with bed and breakfast costing about £2.50 each.

The hotel had no roof, but then in Egypt there is a roof tax, so most of the houses have an unfinished appearance with reinforcing rods sticking up where the roof should be, in preparation for the next storey to be built in the unforeseeable future. On the roof that was not there you could drink a beer as the sun went down, overlooking the other roofless buildings and minarets of the Mosques.

The rising and setting of the sun held great significance to the people of ancient Egypt. As the sun rose, the Nile's East Bank was seen as the side that supported the living as new life started there every day. As the sun set over the West Bank it was viewed as the place of the dead. That of course is why we are here, to visit the Valley of the Kings and the last resting place of the Pharaohs.

I am sure the poor man who was killed today will have a more modest funeral. Not only that, we were told his family would be fined for him breaking the curfew.

Christine
Our visit to Luxor was the first time we have left Breakaway unattended overnight in a foreign land without a member of the family keeping an eye on her. She was tied up in a small Marina under construction, along with Chinook II. On a short acquaintance

with the local skippers of the dive boats for the Sheraton Hotel complex, we felt we could leave her, secure in the knowledge that she would be well looked after, and it proved to be the case. It had been our experience throughout our travels that communities involved with the sea gave support to other sailors.

Time to Set Sail for Suez

9 May 2001

Our grand tour over, down the dark unfinished road with the smell of the sea in our nostrils once again, safe from our journey to the Valley of Kings, we arrived back at *Breakaway* in the wee small hours. The boat moved gently to the soft south wind.

Captain Mohammed from the dive boat next door who had been looking after things in our absence called over, "Welcome back." The next morning we greeted each other.

"Captain Mohammed."

"Captain Bob."

We shook hands and clasped shoulders. The weather was good for moving North for the next two days, or so my new friend informed us. A tall man with beard and limp, he had worked boats in the Red Sea all his life. Among the dive boat skippers, he was the one the rest listened to. And so would I,

"Leave now for Suez, Captain Bob, the wind shall be kind to you - but - if you are still here this evening we will share a rum and look at the moon together, she forecasts the weather."

Suez N29.57 E32.34

I never did share that rum with him but took his advice and set sail for Suez. As *Breakaway* cleared the reef, Mohammed was there also and waved us farewell as his customers explored the underwater world. His advice was good - 200 miles with a bright full moon to light the night and help us avoid oil rigs and unlit oil wells, and no head winds. A traffic separation zone was in place for the big ships but there was plenty of water for *Breakaway* outside the routes of the commercial traffic.

Part of the sadness of our lifestyle is the people we leave behind. Mohammed is a man I could have shared some time with but the weather was dictating his timetable as well as mine. The other side of the coin is the friends who keep turning up. The other cruisers, last seen an ocean ago, all being squeezed into the bottleneck of the Suez Canal, our gateway to the Mediterranean and Europe. Then for us a new sea to explore with the cultures and customs of Europe as we make our way back into the Atlantic and home waters.

Twelve more weeks and twelve more stories to tell. What do we do next?

In two days a Suez Pilot joins us for the transit of the Canal. It will be a two day affair for a yacht as small as *Breakaway*. The first day takes us as far as the Bitter Lakes, the halfway point. There we anchor and the Pilot leaves to be taken back to Suez. Next morning a new Pilot joins for the completion of the journey to Port Said where *Breakaway* says farewell to Egypt, continuing our journey to Cyprus, about 200 miles to the north.

Unlike the Panama, the Suez has no locks, just a straight forward waterway separating the Med from the Gulf of Suez, opening up the sea route from Europe to the Far East and Australia, without the need to face the Cape of Good Hope, or what the sailors under square rig knew as the Cape of Storms.

There are two convoys of ships a day - one moving north and the other moving south. They pass in the Bitter Lakes where we have the one enforced stop. So on the morning of our transit, the Pilot will direct us to the back of the North going convoy.

Part of the system of payment to the Pilot is in the form of baksheesh, a compulsory gift or what could be charitably called a tip. Each Pilot asks for a present in the form of three packets of Marlboro cigarettes and 20 Egyptian pounds. Baksheesh is a way of life here and everyone expects it. In most cases the locals leave us disappointed, expressing themselves in the strongest of Anglo Saxon terms to describe my mean streak. I quite enjoy these little encounters.

Of course Egypt is not the only country that tries to get as much out of its visitors as it can. A lot of countries have different prices for different people. There is a local price, a tourist price and an American price. A good haggle can be fun for both parties and after a lot of practice I can usually arrive at a price somewhere between tourist and local. As for Jamie, he is nearly as good as the Egyptians themselves.

In Sri Lanka the price of admission for a tourist to one of the cultural sites can be up to 10 times more than that paid by a local. In Egypt it is at least double. There is no attempt to disguise this as the prices are openly displayed. Imagine the scene at a Cultural Centre back home, for example,

"Yes Sir, yourself, the wife and two children that will be £10 please - Next. From Pakistan, you say, on holiday, that will be £40, have a nice day. Egypt - really? Welcome, we don't get many Egyptians here. £60 and four packets of Embassy King Size, please."

Christine
I always did the paperwork for entering and leaving countries but it became more difficult after Breakaway left Australia.
It appeared to me that in general terms it was not seen as a woman's role to deal with such matters. I would go along with Bob, but would be totally ignored by the officials, which is quite off-putting until I realised that they just did not know how to interact with a female. Poor Carmen Miranda, a boat crewed by two females. They were struggling to find a Pilot willing to go on board for the Suez transit. But back to women's work – I could not think of how to cater for the two Pilots who would be joining us on board. I really can't expect

*them to sit down to our usual fare at mid-day which can be as little
as cheese and crackers. At moments like this the griddle comes out
and the potato bread goes on. It seems to be a favourite with the
uninitiated so I think I will give that a go. Served with egg, baked
beans, Egyptian sausages and fried tomatoes...that will do the trick.*

The Suez Canal

17 May 2001

The big day finally arrived, the Pilot launch turned up with 11 Pilots
- one for each boat. Chaos reigned as we jockeyed for position, each
vessel being forced to go at high speed by the Pilots. Our Pilot was
politely ignored in his requests for more knots - our engine had to be
treated gently if it was going to last the distance.

Chinook II was holding the lead as we approached the first
bend, closely followed by *Windfall, Miss Q* was tying for third, but we
were rank outsiders. Holding ninth place along with *Breakaway* was
the Russian crewed *Libra* pushing hard. *Carmen Miranda* in the
hands of Cindy and Faith from the good old U.S. of A was bringing
up the rear.

The first day's destination was Lake Timsah and the town of
Ismailia, an enforced stop for small craft that cannot maintain the
speed of eight knots. There were strong wind warnings forecast in the
Eastern Mediterranean so it would be no bad thing to be anchored
securely in inland Egypt for the night. After about two hours into the
trip we started to meet the South moving convoy along with tugs and

work barges. The sides of the canal are littered with debris from the six-day war so we cannot move outside the marked channel.

Our Pilot, Hamid, is a Muslim and today is Friday, the Holy Day for the followers of Mohammed. When he came on board he brought three loaves of bread. Christine had made stew for the occasion but he did not want to try it. So far he has sustained himself on one cup of tea.

In reality he is not actually a Pilot. We do not warrant a full professional. His day job is mate on a tugboat. So he steered quite happily nodding to the passing ships and waving at his mates. I have issued him with our handheld VHF so what with steering and shouting in Arabic into the radio, he seems quite happy. Long may it continue.

Hamid took a short respite in the form of prayers. Armed with a bucket of water to cleanse the body before starting on the soul, he got himself positioned on the foredeck facing the holy city of Mecca and sang the praises of Allah. When the man in charge starts to pray, it does not do much for your peace of mind and sense of security.

The following morning the Pilots for the next half of the transit were out in the anchorage early. *Chinook II* and *Breakaway* were ready to continue but the rest of the fleet decided to stay put because of a low-pressure system in the Med, much to the displeasure of the Pilots.

Breakaway's Pilot for the second leg was an older man who had been in charge only once before. As it is hard to get lost in a canal, I was not too concerned. After the lessons of the previous day, I handed over the VHF along with the tiller to give him his place, if you know what I mean. We started to zigzag across the lake as the Egyptian pushed the tiller from side to side, frantically trying to find out how it worked. I, with a degree of tact, suggested Jamie take over to allow him more freedom to give instructions and concentrate on the radio.

Like the first Pilot he had also brought some bread with him, which seems to be the local way and a nice way it is too. The man was not quite as devout as his predecessor, drinking tea in copious amounts and eating anything set in front of him.

Eventually we made it through the canal without too much drama, a Pilot Cutter came out to collect our man in the middle of Port Said harbour. I held station, the launch pulled alongside. We were left to our own devices to make our way out of the busy harbour and lay a course for Cyprus.

The wind was blowing from the direction we wanted to travel. Nothing strange in that, but the names on the chart were new. To the northeast lay Israel, Jerusalem, Damascus, Bethlehem and the Sea of Galilee, the birthplace of Christianity. Syria, Jordan and Libya curve around the Eastern Med towards Turkey and Greece, and somewhere in between them we were hit by a gale.

Breakaway staggered before putting her shoulder to the waves and then carrying on towards the island which is disputed over by both Greece and Turkey, the island of Mount Olympus, home of the Gods. It was here that the Greek goddess of Love, Aphrodite, arose from the sea. It is here that the people from Northern Europe fly to on package holidays to enjoy the sun.

After leaving Australia last August we were all wary of what was ahead. Indonesia, Singapore, Malaysia, Thailand, Sri Lanka, Maldives, Oman, Eritrea, Sudan and Egypt. It has been fascinating but there has been stress on occasions. It is nice to finally be somewhere where you can really relax and not worry about anything.

Christine
As we left Port Said and sailed out through the channel markers, there was a sense of relief on board that the Red Sea and the Suez transit were behind us. I could feel the stress lifting off my shoulders and did a little jig on the deck. The sense of euphoria stayed with us even when we heard a 'pan pan' call for help go out on the radio. Normally not something to treat lightly, on this occasion it was an emergency signal that had been activated by mistake, but the quick response by the authorities made us realise we were back in a world where help and support were only a radio call away.
The last time there was that feeling of security was in Australia, a lot of miles and a couple of oceans ago.
Oh, and I can wear T-shirts and shorts again.

The Mediterranean

Larnaca Marina, Cyprus 34,55N 33.38E

21 May 2001

As *Breakaway* pulled into the marina in Larnaca, Cyprus we were two days out of Suez and into a culture two centuries ahead of the one we had left.

Only 200 miles at sea and we had left Africa for Europe. It blew a bit on the way across, just enough to make it uncomfortable but not unsafe. The main concern was arriving too early. The whole passage had been planned to avoid the overtime hours of Customs and Immigration in Cyprus who close down their operation at 2.30 in the afternoon.

Ahead of us Kirstie and Andy on *Chinook II* were officially cleared into the country, and along with *Mariah II*, our old Aussie friends, were going ashore for their first meal in Europe. We had to remain at anchor with our yellow flag flying - aliens - at least until the police, Customs and Immigration turned up for work the following morning. To tide us over the shore party passed a bottle of wine across the water and a few beers to help us celebrate our arrival.

Next morning officialdom was easy, with everything cleared up in an hour. Christine back to doing the paperwork again, and not a bribe requested for the first time in a while. Off we went to explore – up through the marina complex, past the hard standing with yachts from around the world being worked on by their crews.

The yacht club had a bar/restaurant selling food of a style we had not seen since Australia - kebabs, salads, pitta bread and fresh fruit in profusion. The toilets were clean with a chain to pull, luxury of the highest order. For the last while the countries we have been travelling through offered a Muslim toilet, which is a hole in the floor to squat over with a tin of water to cleanse yourself.

It's quite nice to be back in Europe again. Five years - Australia, New Zealand, Polynesia, Asia, South America, Europe and Africa, not necessarily in that order. We can now slow up for a bit, but not for too long. Winter in the high latitudes soon sets in and there is no desire among *Breakaway*'s crew to sail the Bay of Biscay in an Equinox September gale.

A lot of the boats coming up from the Red Sea move on quickly towards the Rock of Gibraltar in preparation for the Atlantic. The weather this year has slowed things up, with the strong westerly winds impeding progress. Mind you it is no bad thing to be slowed up in Cyprus. This gives us time to meet the Mediterranean sailors preparing for their summer season in Turkey and other places - a lifestyle in the sun, which they organise for themselves. Pub quizzes, book swaps, barbecues with the occasional knees-up thrown in are all part of the set up. Dreamers one and all who have found their particular paradise - us still the square peg in the round hole, still looking towards the horizon.

A couple of ex-pats living the good life in Larnaca are Norman and Edna Childs from Co Down, Northern Ireland. They sailed away three years ago, taking five weeks to cruise their boat *Leander* down to Cyprus, no mean feat, and bought a house, leading a lifestyle to be envied. Each summer for three months they slip the lines on *Leander* and head for the coast of Turkey. From there they move along slowly towards the Greek mainland and the islands of the Aegean Sea. Not a bad way to enjoy your retirement, an active lifestyle with the sun on your back.

Each and every anchorage is full of couples of all nationalities leading this lifestyle, a floating community finding somewhere to shelter for the winter and prepare boats for the coming season. They come from all backgrounds and all walks of life but the social standing of the past does not concern most people, the professional and the artisan enjoying the experience together. Sometimes the old skills of a previous existence are produced to help someone out with a problem. Silver does not cross the palm, it could be you needing help the following week. Last week Bruce of *Dreamcatcher* spotted me hobbling along the quay.

"What's up Bob, you starting to show your age?"

I had jumped off *Breakaway* in Egypt without shoes on and cut my foot badly. Even though Christine had kept it clean there was no sign of it healing. Bruce, a prostrate specialist from the States, told me to sit down on the dock while he went for the tools of his trade.

So I sat in the sun with my foot propped up and the physician settled himself on a milk crate, a cup of vodka beside him. The forceps, pliers and tweezers were popped into the alcohol to sterilise them and Bruce set to with a will. He managed to remove something embedded in my foot. The vodka was tipped out, the tools put away for the next time and I continued on my now sprightly, way.

Christine
Bob, eldest son Neill who has joined us for a short holiday, and Jamie, took off for the day leaving me to have a good tidy up on Breakaway. I had just finished when there was a knock on the hull. Norman and Edna, our newfound friends, had arrived to take me shopping, along with their granddaughter Lea. How very thoughtful of them. Being sailors themselves, they know how difficult it was to get supplies on board. Two trolley loads were required for the job. Their local knowledge was a bonus and Lea, who is bilingual, was able to help me decipher the Greek packaging. I was back in the land of plenty. My favourite brands were on the shelves, there was a vast display of veggies and anything else your heart desired. Cooking dinner tonight is going to be a pleasure.

Parting of the Ways

29 May 2001
Tonight we are going to break bread with the crews of *Chinook II*, *Mariah II* and *Leander* as tomorrow we all go our different ways.

Andy and Kirstie are taking *Chinook II* to Turkey for a few weeks before heading for Greece where Andy's brother and family will join them for a holiday. Noel and Jackie point *Mariah*'s nose towards France. They intend to enter the inland waterways of Europe travelling to Paris along the Canals. Norman and Edna on *Leander* are off on their annual pilgrimage to Turkey and three months of sunshine cruising. As for *Breakaway*, she is bound for Malta.

It has been a week of hellos and goodbyes. Neill our eldest son joined us for seven days in the sun. It was good to see him again, the last time was in Thailand, five months ago.

Youngest son Jamie has left the boat to take up his life in Northern Ireland again after more than a year on board. From the Great Barrier Reef of Australia to the Pyramids of Egypt, he has enjoyed the ups and suffered the downs along with us. There was a minor hiccup when a Cypriot cat nearly made off with his bit of Buddhist string, but he managed to retrieve it. The night watches will be longer without him sharing them and we will miss him very much, but *Breakaway* is now on the fast track home.

The rest of the Red Sea Mob climbed onto *Breakaway* for a 'goodbye to Jamie' party and old gales were fought again. The runs ashore were fondly remembered, but now it is back to the real world and the hunt for a job for most of the cruisers - far away from the beautiful sirens of Siam, the distraction of Bali, not to mention the orangutans of Borneo. All good memories shared together.

Running Repairs

"The Israelis are coming, the Israelis are coming", the marina was in an uproar. It was a long weekend in Israel and the Yachties were on their way to Cyprus. The marina was full to overflowing with most of the Red Sea Mob anchored stern to the wall in true Mediterranean fashion in the outer basin.

We had managed to find a berth in the marina proper so were well away from the main action. Now stern to berthing is a technique all of its own. You line yourself up to an empty piece of wall and then drop the anchor. As it is paid out, you reverse the boat towards the wall and when close enough you tie the stern to the shore and tighten the anchor chain.

The arrival of the Israelites coincided with a festival of the Greek Orthodox Church, the meaning of which is unclear to me. With much ceremony in the fishing harbours, the local churchman comes down and after prayers for those who go to sea, throws a cross into the harbour. This is supposed to calm the waters and give safe passage. The locals will tell you it has the opposite effect and that on that particular day every year the winds blow, the seas build until the evening when all becomes calm again. Why nobody has ever mentioned this to the priest I don't know but the outcome of the whole affair was the arrival of the Israeli fleet in half a gale.

The freshening wind was blowing sideways across the harbour as they dropped anchor and tried to back in. It was not working, being a berthing method for calm conditions. Anchors hooked onto other boats' chains, lifting them, causing the yachts already there to drift. Tempers were lost, voices in many tongues hurled abuse at the new arrivals who ignored it all. Two days later they left and peace was restored to Larnaca once again. Meanwhile *Breakaway* was having an exhaust pipe problem. One of the welds on the stainless steel had developed a hole and as it is water cooled, water was leaking into the boat along with exhaust fumes making the whole affair unsafe. A few enquires on the dock and it was obvious that the man to solve the problem was Louie the Greek who operated out of his garage, not too far from the harbour.

Now when I turned up, Louie was whistling away to himself happy at his work. I showed him the offending part. With a sharp intake of breath he said,

"Why does everyone bring me the difficult jobs?"

He handed over a bit of worn sandpaper telling me to clean the exhaust so he could examine it. A youngster of about five years old arrived pushing his bike, complete with stabilisers, for Louie to examine. Our expert diagnosed the problem, put some air in the tyres and tightened a couple of nuts. Louie bent down, the child gave him a hug for his trouble before cycling off. Next was a woman who needed the handle put on a brush. Louie set to with a will, a quick kiss on each cheek and she was gone. And so it continued - odd jobs being undertaken for no payment other than thanks.

Then it was my turn. Louie with a welding torch was as expert as I have seen. Soon the exhaust was as good as new. He refused my offer of payment. I shook his hand in thanks, feeling I did not really know him well enough for a hug or kiss. What a lovely man.

We may change our minds now and think of heading for Crete instead of Malta. The Greek people are so nice. But wherever we go 'the whole of our crew is reduced down to two' as the song goes.

Christine
As Chinook II was lifted out of the water for an anti-fouling job, I watched her hanging from the travel hoist and thought of all the times she had been there for us. Always ready to help in times of need and acting as towboat when Breakaway's engine went through a series of mechanical problems. Although most of the yachting fraternity will lend a helping hand, it is special to have your family alongside to pull you out of a sticky patch. Thank you Chinook II and see you back in the UK.

Ayios Nikolaos, Crete 35.11N 25.43E

The weather forecast turned out to be bad. I had gained this knowledge over the radio from John of *Athena*. Now we first met

John and Carol from the Mull of Galloway when in Australia. I had talked to them on the SSB radio as they closed the Great Barrier Reef looking for an anchorage. It was a fine Australian evening with the sun dying over the Pacific and a full moon to ease their landfall as they closed the islands of the Percys. It seems a long time ago.

So, anyway, back to the bad forecast and John, now an old Greek hand.

"There are a few anchorages on the North coast of Crete Bob but I would head for Ayios Nikolaos – it's safe, it's easy, not a bad wee town at all."

The advice wasn't too far wrong. We were four days out of Cyprus with the wind on the nose and the engine working its heart out. A safe harbour was looking attractive. We are all stressed out at the moment. Four days here, five days there. Two weeks in the Indian Ocean, Oman to Eritrea, 14 days. The Red Sea – I can still see the wave that stopped us. So now we are in Crete listening to the good advice of John.

Everything you ask, the reply is 'Aye'. The Scots have a great way with words and John was as good as his. As we made our approach to the harbour, I had to react very quickly to avoid two topless young ladies in a peddlelow who were obviously unaware of the collision regulations. Instead of giving me credit for averting disaster, Christine told me to concentrate on what I was doing.

Ayios Nikolaos has all we require. It is a clearance port for Greece. We had not intended to come here but had planned to head straight for Malta. The water is drinkable, the marina has all the facilities and the showers are clean. But it has come as a bit of a shock to discover the cost of living in Europe. Fifty gallons of fuel cost £100. In Indonesia it was a fiver for the same amount.

The first job on arrival was to report to Port Authority. I am not quite sure what their role is but they are all dressed in white uniforms with gold epaulets and have cigarettes dangling out of the corner of their mouths. Forms were filled in, papers stamped with great flourishes, then we were directed to pay a visit to the Tourist Police.

We arrived at the same time as a prisoner who was being put into a holding cell. Surrounded by men with guns, the prisoner was either protesting his innocence or having a seizure. As the Greeks talk a lot with their hands it is sometimes hard to tell. We managed to avoid any confrontation, ducking round the action before finding the department of Tourist Police.

Everyone there seemed to be auditioning for a part in the 'Kojak' series. The man in charge of tourists squinted at me through a haze of smoke from the cigarette hanging out of the side of his mouth and shrugged to ease his shoulder holster. He turned out to be quite nice, advising us about the weather on the north coast of Crete and the best methods of obtaining forecasts.

More stamps and more forms. It is so much easier now with the European Community, borders that no longer exist and freedom of movement for all the members. But the place is great, with the marina situated right in the centre of town. There are beaches, cafes, bars, windsurfers, boat trips, wonderful shops and wall to wall tourists, mostly German at the moment, with everyone having fun.

At last I feel like we are on our holidays. As I write this I am sitting under a beach umbrella five minutes' walk from *Breakaway* resting myself as Christine goes to explore the local supermarket. People keep asking her directions, they think she is local.

A little stroll around the streets before nine in the morning is very pleasant. The holidaymakers have not got over the previous night's debauchery and the locals have the town to themselves. The pavement cafes are where the older men sit drinking strong coffee out of small cups - a straight caffeine kick - men with great flowing moustaches to be wiped, in between playing with worry beads. The older women, dressed in their best black, congregate on the steps of the church for a gossip.

Then the tourists start to stir and slowly the locals disappear until the next morning. For the rest of the day, streets designed for a donkey and cart are taken over by 4x4 vehicles, buses and motor bikes, with people coloured various shades of red. But then the industry here is tourism and the locals all look well fed because of it.

Anyhow, we have to content ourselves here for a few more days, as the weather is quite severe. It is not cold, in fact the wind is cooling things down to a reasonable temperature and there are worse places to be stuck.

Christine
I am enjoying the shops here. They are attractively laid out to catch the eye of the holidaymakers and they do that in fine style. Natural sponges are a popular feature along with local honeys, pickles, soaps and spices. It is wonderful to wander around and enjoy the goods on offer. There is one shop full off beautiful colourful woven carpets and I saw just the thing I was looking for - an oversized cushion which would be useful for storing a quilt and would fit in with the decor on board. The price quoted shocked me – £150 - and then I saw some flaws and a portion where the weaving had come loose.

"It's damaged," I said, hoping the bargaining would start.
"Yes," the assistant beamed, "It's a very old piece."
I was out of my league. I left the shop minus my cushion.

The Ionian Sea 35.33N 17.58E

After breakfast we went ashore to clear out of the island - destination Malta. The paperwork was quite straight forward so with fuel and water tanks topped up it was time to bid farewell.

We cast off the lines to the shore, heading *Breakaway* for the open waters of the Mediterranean, blue skies and gentle summer breezes. I think not. Though the sky was indeed blue, the wind pressed us harder and harder with progress down to a snail's pace.

Time to regroup. The only option available was a bay called Spinalonga. From Ayios Nikolaos we had watched the tourist craft plying their trade, the favourite destination - Spinalonga. As we eased, the sheets to come off, it became the obvious place to seek shelter. There on a small island at the entrance was a fort built by the Phoenicians, its solid walls standing up to centuries of erosion without too much sign of wear.

We sailed in through the quarter mile wide gap to the accompaniment of guides talking over the loudspeakers explaining the history of the place. Many centuries after it was used as a citadel of war it became the sanctuary for Lepers of the Eastern Med. So behind the fortifications were the remains of modern hospital buildings, now unused and in disrepair, the last of the patients having left in the mid-seventies.

We dropped anchor under its lee. With the mountains of Crete on one side and sheltered from the wind by the fort, we found ourselves secure in as nice an anchorage as you could wish for. A couple of other yachts had tucked in for shelter, one of them last seen in the Pacific Island of Tonga. Then Frans from Switzerland had a girlfriend but now he is single-handed, the crew back in the Alps with no desire to go to sea again. He joined us for dinner that evening. Also heading west, he had dived in for cover the same as we had.

The following morning I talked on the SSB radio to *Chinook II* bound for Turkey, *Mariah II* sheltering 100 miles north on the island of Thera, and *Impetus* from Norway bound for Malta. As each yacht reported conditions in their area, it was obvious that *Breakaway* would have to spend a few more days in shelter. The prevailing wind is from the west and so is Malta.

But the opportunity was not to be wasted, so armed with a paint scraper I went over the side the clean the bottom. *Breakaway* has not been out of the water since Australia. The last time she was dived on was in the Maldives where Wendy, who was with us on holiday, spent an hour a day in the water cleaning the hull. The water is a bit colder here.

At one time we had a hermit crab take up residence in the outlet to one of our seacocks, his neighbour was a small tropical fish squatting in the pipe next door. They had accompanied us from Indonesia to the Red Sea, abandoning *Breakaway* there for a tropical reef more to their liking. At least I like to think that is what happened. We had one attempt to leave Spinalonga, only to retreat once again.

The wind and weather, if not unsafe, was at least uncomfortable to life on board. I invited Frans over for breakfast and he arrived in his dinghy armed with three yoghurts, traditional fare in Greece, especially when served with a topping of honey. Christine had other ideas. Frans was introduced to the 'Ulster Fry'. As a single hander he was intrigued by the whole idea, enough food on a plate to last 24 hours and full of carbohydrates to boot - a supply of energy to keep you going all day. Our Swiss friend could see the advantages.

The weather had faired, the anchorage was calm except for the occasional blast down through the mountains. We stuck our nose out once again. This time it was a different sea, still in the wrong direction but a gentle swell we could motor against.

Five miles or so offshore the conditions started to ease and the bow of *Breakaway* pointed west towards Malta, 500 and something miles to go but a little step closer to home. The first night was kind to us with a waning moon late coming up but still giving good light, the evening stars reflecting on the still waters.

Safely hooked on for night watch

Crete, five miles to the south, was occasionally just visible mainly from the brightly-lit tourist resorts. The only other light was from a masthead north of us, our friend Frans also tracking west and still full of energy. There is not a great deal more to report, the forecast is fair for the next four days.

Unfortunately it will take us five days to the Grand Harbour of Valletta in Malta. With any luck we shall make it before the westerlies set in again. But once there we are in the safest harbour of the whole Mediterranean. I have been there before. It is nice to retrace your steps and be on familiar ground. Also I think Christine will enjoy it.

Christine

We are into the swing of things again. When Jamie was on board there was more time off watch for both of us but now we share the hours equally. For entertainment through the long periods on watch I listen to one of the many talking books our eldest son Neill brought out on his last visit to Breakaway. At the moment it is 'Around the World in Eighty Days'. With the earphones on I can still keep a good lookout while enjoying the yarn. At some stage soon we will be back in Spain so once a day I give myself Spanish lessons, again with the use of audio cassettes. I now know how to say 'hello', 'thank you' and 'how much'.

Valletta Harbour, Malta

The first time I arrived in Malta there was a strong wind blowing from the north, but then October was not the month to be cruising in the middle of the Mediterranean. The boat was *Hala II* belonging to a sheikh from somewhere. One hundred and twenty feet of ocean going splendour under the command of a captain from Whitehead, Co Antrim. Brian Kernaghan was the man in charge. I was there to keep watch while he slept.

The passage was uneventful, apart from the South East Asian cook who was a native of the Philippines throwing a wobbler at two o'clock in the morning. I had gone into his domain, the galley, to make a cup of coffee and he was not pleased. Now the Philippine was called Enrique and once tied up at Malta he settled down. Him and myself set off around the town to take in the things of historical interest, the cultural trail if you will. Museums, cathedrals, forts, all the monuments which trace the history of Malta throughout the ages.

Part of the history was the Royal Navy. From before the time of Nelson, Malta was a place of strategic importance. From here the fleet could set sail and intercept the other navies of the world as they moved East or West. The day's battle over, the home fleet would return to Malta to regroup while the enemy drifted in disarray waiting for the next onslaught. But the Navy being the Navy could not supply all that the men required, two tots of rum a day helped but did not solve the problem. The means of escaping the pain was to be found in a place called 'The Gut', the most famous street of prostitution in the world of the seafaring man. Here the sailors would go to receive love of the most temporary kind.

So back to the brave Enrique. The pair ōf us were walking down a street with a sharp incline, the steps leading us down between medieval houses were taking a bit of negotiation. I was lost but Enrique led on.

"Have you been here before Enrique?"

"Never, First Mate Bob."

We continued downwards. Unbeknown to me, into the infamous 'Gut', unintentionally you understand. The street narrowed and a window opened. A lady of the night called out,

"Hello Enrique."

Another stuck her head out.

"Is Enrique back? Hi Enrique."

They wore but smiles. Enrique cringed and I pretended nothing had happened although for two days afterwards the Philippine could not be found. When he eventually turned up I was allowed in his galley anytime. No more complaints. But back to the start and a landfall in Malta - not easy. There were a few clouds about, all moving to the east but one was steady. The stable cloud was marking Malta. The only hint you have, and then it materialises, just a small indication, a slight discoloration against the sky, reflections of light – land. Close to the shore, there is a sense of recent history.

The history of the Second World War, the war of my father. He was a DEMS, a Royal Navy gunner in charge of armaments on board a merchant ship. His job was sitting on the aft deck of the merchantman, aiming the gun and hoping for a run ashore in Malta, an island under siege. And so the war went on – men killed, sailors lost against German bombs and bullets.

The siege was eventually broken. An American tanker, the *Ohio*, broke through the blockade and Malta had its much needed supplies.

As we got close to the pier heads, it was with a certain amount of emotion, thinking of previous sailors and lives lost. Malta has a history of being under siege going back to the time of the Crusades. The Knights of Malta were under siege and down to the last three forts when the enemy gave up and went home. Meanwhile back on *Breakaway*, Valletta Harbour Control was issuing directions,

"Keep the breakwater to starboard and then turn right. There is a small wall, secure yourself and report to customs."

We did that but Customs was closed so we went for a walk, just to stretch the legs after five days at sea. What they had not mentioned was that you tied your shore line to a cannon buried in concrete. A cannon, yes, a cannon, in service to defend the island 150 years ago.

A piece of history now used to secure a yacht, memorabilia of Nelson.

Msida Marina, Malta 35.54N 14.30E

As you approach Malta the colour is bland, blending in with everything and no height to distinguish it. Closer in, the architecture starts to appear, the spire of St Paul's Cathedral, the fortifications and then you are there. The Grand Harbour to the south for the big stuff - cruise liners and cargo ships providing the small island with its needs. From the tourist, the dollar, from the ships, supplies, and to the north, Marsamxett Harbour for the rest of us.

Valletta has to be one of the best medieval cities we have seen. As you tread the streets you walk the past. The tourists congregate on the main thoroughfare where old buildings lead the eye straight and true to the Cathedral, the centre of the town. But nowadays the food, clothing and all the different retail chains mark the centre, where the new worshippers gather.

Step to one side, walk down the worn steps, cross a road where the path levels out and down again. Sit on the steps and look around. The doors are scarred with the wounds of the past painted over. Above your head from a veranda a voice calls out to its neighbour across the narrow street in the Maltese tongue.

In our travels around the world not a lot changes - still without stability where would we all be.

Christine
Next morning, after our arrival in Malta, I was putting out the washing and marvelling at the sights around me - the local fishing

boats and colourful craft, the walls of the forts, enjoying the whole
scene. A wee Maltese man caught my attention,

"I have fruit and vegetable, come with me."
I was off Breakaway like a shot, fresh food - great - and then as we
linked arms and he propelled me down the pontoon towards his
truck I suddenly remembered,

"I have no money, no local currency, sorry."

"Hey no problem pay me next time you see me."
What a good start to the day.

Mallorca

It is all coming near to an end. *Breakaway* is just seven degrees of
longitude short of a circumnavigation of the globe, though for us the
journey will not be complete until we sail into Carrickfergus, Belfast
Lough, our starting point five years ago. A lot of miles have passed
under the keel and if you add to that the fact that we are inclined to
divert a little, going off the beaten track, the distance and the time
have been stretched. The world should not be hurried.

Anyhow, what happened last week? Well before leaving Malta,
I changed the engine oil and filters. Then we moved out into the bay
to a very convenient fuel barge in order to top up the tanks along with
the countless jerry cans we now carry. You never know where the next
filling station is going to be.

As our lines were cast off and we bade farewell to our new
friends from Slovenia, I never told you about them, I am embarrassed
to say that I did not know where Slovenia was but they informed me
they were part of Yugoslavia, and when things started to go wrong
amidst great confusion and war Samo and Voyga bought a boat and
took off. I said to him that I thought that part of the world was
communist and he said it was, end of conversation. As Shaw once said,

"If you are not a Socialist before you are 21 you have no heart
and if you are a Socialist after 21 you have no head."

Samo and Voyga's philosophy lies somewhere between Shaw
and Stalin. They asked us about Ireland but I could not explain that
to them either, so we settled on talking about sailing round the world,

317

which is what they are hoping to do. Financially speaking their boat was worth about five *Breakaways*, a fine craft.

So we cleared Malta. It seemed to be one step forward and two back as we tried to move west. Wherever we pointed, that was where the wind came from. Progress was slow. Then we heard a forecast over the radio. Gales from the northwest. On went the engine as *Breakaway* moved north. If the wind was going to blow we wanted to be in the right place for it to move us in the right direction.

Breakaway was on a tour of the Med - Sardinia, Sicily, Italy France, Tunisia with Algiers to the south. We could end in any one of those places, but the evening found us off Cape Bon with shipping from all over the world converging. The night watch was long and arduous. To top it all, fog descended but with the radar switched on we could keep an eye on the movements of other vessels in our vicinity. After a close encounter with a fishing boat that suddenly appeared beside us, its lights barely showing through the mist, daylight came and visibility improved.

Sailing is like a game of chess - a game where you try to outwit the opponent - in our case the wind. But the wind lives under a law of its own. On this occasion we were now positioned to use the breeze and we had options - the Balearic Islands or straight on to Gibraltar. So we laid a course and ended up in Mallorca.

The marina at Puerto Portals said 'no room'. Six hundred miles - five days and nights getting there and we were told to leave. Tired after reaching our destination and finding it wasn't there, we set off again. Which meant another overnight to the next island, Ibiza. Then a few miles further on we spotted an anchorage that looked reasonable. Protected from all directions of wind except the east. For days we had wanted an easterly wind but hoped it would not arrive that night. The hook went down, a wine cask was opened, the last five or was it six days and nights behind us, forgotten.

Breakaway was in the world of package holidays. All around us little plastic boats with pedals crossed the bay. A speedboat with a big yellow inflatable banana trailing behind was filled with screaming men falling off in front of girls on floating bicycles; romance was in the air. Incredible blue seas with blue skies, the Mediterranean. A sea devoted to pleasure and supplying the demands of people from the cold north for two weeks a year in the sun - sunburnt bodies, the smell of Ambre Solaire, beach umbrellas, sun-beds, bronzed dive instructors. What a break from work, we watched with pleasure.

Then at six o'clock all became quiet, the sea was still again. No jet skis, no hired speedboats - I missed them. It is good to be among people enjoying themselves after lonely days at sea. Their happiness was contagious. But our rest proved to be short lived, the wind eased and moved into the east and we had to take advantage of it. *Breakaway* was out of there. The wind remained fair. Seventy miles short of Gibraltar the wind started to head us.

Breakaway was not making good progress so we diverted to Fuengirola, just beside Marbella and Torremolinos, where Spanish package holidays started. At one time a cluster of fishing villages, now a coast of tower blocks to house the holiday trade.

Fuengirola, Costa del Sol 36.32N 04.36W

Breakaway is now anchored off a playa or beach. Then there is the road, and the fish and chips, and the shops selling bottles of wine named after your favourite football team playing in the English league. Tattoo parlours and Prince William Hotels, the vindaloo and curry houses, the whole place geared to fun and full bellies, with pints of beer for less than £1 – well nearly.

So *Breakaway* is at anchor 40 miles from Gibraltar, the gateway to the Atlantic, parked among the young men posing and the young girls flirting. To tell you the truth I am holding my stomach in at the moment, after all everywhere is very busy with sunburnt bodies.

Gibraltar

The Straits of Gibraltar separate Europe from Africa by eight miles at the widest part. Through this narrow gap the current flows from the Atlantic into the Mediterranean and the prevailing winds are also from the same direction. But if you wait for the right time, the situation becomes reasonable. This was *Breakaway*'s plan.

So just before the moon was in the right quarter, with the breeze, known locally as the Levanter, setting in, when all was well for a passage north, I was struck down with gastric flu, known locally, or for those without medical expertise, as Spanish tummy. The doctor confined me to the toilet for four days.

The tide turned, the moon started to wax and the leaving of Gibraltar was put off, day after day. All the other sailing boats were eastbound into the Med but we were trying to get home and were stuck at the last hurdle.

Now Gibraltar is mainly English speaking so Christine was in her element, window-shopping with all the familiar brand names from home. BHS, Marks & Spencer, Wallis, Body Shop, Evans, and many more. I suffered in silence unable to leave the security of *Breakaway*, my only entertainment the radio tuned into the British Forces Overseas. Did you know that tonight there is a pub quiz in the NAAFI in Cyprus, a golf tournament in Germany and to top it all down at the Phoenix in Port Stanley the troops in the Falklands are being entertained to a film? Don't talk to me about hardships.

Back on *Breakaway* things are starting to come under some sort of control so we are now at anchor to await a change in the weather. The plan is to leave Gibraltar at 03:30 in the morning to start the last leg of the journey home. *Breakaway* seems to be stumbling over the last 1,200 miles. Perhaps the weather is not entirely to blame, perhaps we are just reluctant to give up our present lifestyle.

Today Christine started to clean out the lockers. Shorts, T-shirts and sandals are now moving closer to the deep storage section of the boat. Long trousers, body warmers, along with sweaters, hats, woolly socks and heavy oilskins are being put into readiness. My wellington boots were produced for the first time in five years. The legs or upper part, which covers the shins, were welded together by the tropical heat. As I tried to part them, they split. So I cut the top part off with a knife. Now I am the proud owner of a pair of wellington shoes. As a fashion statement I doubt if it will catch on.

Back to the plan, which is to clear Cape Trafalgar, Cape St Vincent, and for the first time in five years go into the Atlantic and harbours we previously visited on the coast of Portugal. But now we are reviewing the plan and may make the next leg straight to the south coast of Ireland. We are looking forward to going home.

Reminiscing - Trinidad, Antigua, St Lucia, San Blas, the Islands of the Pacific, Tonga, Fiji, Indonesia and Bali the Islands of the Gods. Everywhere *Breakaway* has dropped her anchor we have made friends.

New Zealand, Australia, the Cook Islands, the gentle Buddhists of Thailand - a day out with a Tuk Tuk driver in Sri Lanka where we met the nicest man of them all, a Buddhist priest who said a prayer and wished us well. He wrapped our wrists in string, whispering prayers to carry us safely home. Youngest son Jamie's string was stolen by a cat, recovered, and he is still wearing it. Mine rotted away after three months as we cleared Suez. Christine still has hers. What's left of mine is tucked up in the back of our log book. Well you never know.

Anyway, back to the Forces network and our Army friends with the latest weather forecast. The wind will move into the East in the early hours which means we will be on the road again, slipping past towns and villages in the darkness along a strange coast with no one knowing *Breakaway* is there; Cape Trafalgar where Nelson died,

Cape St Vincent and into the Atlantic, the ocean sea for the first time in five years. Grey skies and grey seas, everything against you – home waters as hard as they ever were.

Back in the Atlantic, Cascais, Lisbon, Portugal 38.41N 09.25W

Tonight *Breakaway* pulled into a marina in Cascais at the entrance to Lisbon, Portugal. Five years ago it was an anchorage free of charge. No longer - today it is a Marina costing £10 a night. The world is changing.

Last night we were in Sines, the birthplace of Vasco da Gama who was sent out by King Henry the Navigator to discover the Indies.

Vasco da Gama

Vasco did not have a professional crew or qualified mates, just the dregs of the jails who were given remission if they would sail with him. So to help his motley band to recognise the nautical terms starboard and larboard, as it was then known, on the port side he hung a potato and on the starboard a cabbage so when he wanted to change direction he would shout, "Hard to cabbage."

Many years ago, sailing as a mate on a sail training ship, the Ocean Youth Club boat *Lord Rank*, the crew joined as usual - 12 young people from all sections of the community. And as usual one of the mob shone. His real name I forget but we called him Vasco da Gama because of his in-built navigational skills. The rest of the crew, in true Ulster fashion, named him Vasco Dilemma. The brave young Vasco struck a chord in my heart. I wonder where he is now.

Breakaway is at the moment fighting the good fight against the Portuguese Trades. On the radio today daughter Kirstie and son-in-law Andy. *Chinook II* informed us they were one day out of Malta and 850 miles from Gibraltar trying to catch up with *Breakaway* for a party in home port Carrickfergus. Wouldn't that be nice?

Christine

For the last few years one of the problems with our lifestyle was how to keep cool and comfortable. In the last few days there has been a dramatic change. Instead of a night watch wearing shorts and T-shirt, we are now decked out in gear suitable for the colder climes. I even had to dig out a hot water bottle for Bob the other night as he complained that his feet were freezing. By midday the temperature is up again and we are enjoying beautiful sunny weather and still no sign of rain. Not a drop has fallen on Breakaway in over seven months. Are we in for a shock when we get home, or so all the sailors heading south towards the sunshine coasts tell us.

2 Aug 2001

At the moment *Breakaway* is back where it all began - or nearly - the Rias of Northern Spain, one of the best cruising grounds in the world in our opinion and on our door step.

We are just 600 and something miles from Tusker Rock, the light house marking the south east corner of Ireland and in home waters, the North Atlantic. Back to hearing accurate weather forecasts over the radio that are dictating our movements. Force nine North Finisterre, Bay of Biscay northerly force eight, not the type of forecast or the time for a small yacht to put to sea.

Breakaway is still the square peg in the round hole, the boat going against wind, weather and tide, homeward bound. All the other yachts seem to be moving south to adventure and enjoy the sun in the Mediterranean or cross the Atlantic to spend Christmas in the Caribbean. Fresh antifoul, new sails, polished fibreglass and varnished wood greet our eyes.

In comparison *Breakaway* looks a bit weary with faded sails, sun-bleached wood, dull fibreglass, her name almost obliterated by sandstorms in the Red Sea, still looking seaworthy but hard worked. Five years ago it had been our turn to head south so we know how it feels when we meet up with the people starting out to adventure, the majority like ourselves, the wrong side of middle age.

Now I must confess the thought of sailing in the Atlantic had me a bit edgy again but in general the oceans have been kind to us. There has been the odd gale with some lightning and fog thrown in and dreadful calms, but now *Breakaway* is back in the Northern latitudes and home waters.

From here, a sunny anchorage in Spain, our destination lies north and unfortunately that is the direction from which the wind is blowing. So this is the plan. Tomorrow morning *Breakaway* moves towards the west where eventually we hope to pick up the south westerlies. These should fill our sails and allow us to lay Ireland - perhaps Cork, Kinsale, Arklow, who knows where.

Then we intend to cruise gently up to Belfast Lough and the delights of Carrickfergus – home.

The Irish Sea

12 Aug 2001

Fresh plain bread, sausages and a cup of tea in your hand - that was the first real food after landfall in Wicklow just south of Dublin and as soon as we were able to manage it, proper fish and chips.

The previous couple of days had been stormy, big seas accompanied by strong winds, but around the world was now down to 150 sea miles. No more night shifts for either of us. We were looking forward to those last few miles. As *Breakaway* came through the pier heads at Wicklow to tie up, another yacht shouted,

"What's it like out there?"

"Fresh enough."

"Have you come far?"

Neither of us was sure how to answer. Eventually the truth had to come out. Around the world and other places.

People started to congratulate us. In Wicklow Sailing Club that evening a lady said to me,

"Sure if we had known you had just sailed round the world, we would have got some sandwiches together."

Next stop Howth where *Gentle Spirit* from Carrick was tied up. Another welcome and a sail in company up the shore to Ardglass the following day.

More Carrickfergus boats finishing their summer cruise were there, *Martingale* and the crew of *Wee Intombi* ready to celebrate with a party, and celebrate we did.

Carrickfergus 54.40N 05.40W

18 August 2001

The biggest party was still to come in our home port.

We entered Belfast Lough on a gentle day with little breeze and made for Bangor, the opposite side of the Lough from Carrickfergus, to be fresh and ready to see our family and friends next morning, and had a lovely surprise.

Daughter Kirstie and son-in-law Andy had finally made it to Ireland on board *Chinook II* after pushing hard to catch *Breakaway*, but not in time to sail up. They had driven from Cork by car and would sail with us next day for Carrickfergus.

Over 40 countries and 40-something thousand miles later I had mixed feelings about the end of our voyage. In my mind the landfalls of paradise were far away. I asked Christine how she felt. She smiled,

"I feel like a woman who has circumnavigated the globe."

That sort of summed it up.

Then the first boat appeared, a RIB handled by Rory Moore from The Boatyard transporting youngest son Jamie out to join us for the last few miles.

Old friend Norman Grant flashed past with eldest son Neill. Other boats of all shapes and sizes appeared, crewed by familiar faces, old friends out to bid us welcome back, jostling for position with camera crews.

Horns blew and bottles of bubbly were passed over and opened. *Cumbrae Isle* was in the middle of it all with a piper on the foredeck standing beside my mother who did not know whether to laugh or cry, but it was a day for laughter.

I felt the fleet was there not only to welcome us but also to see *Breakaway* journey safely for the last few miles. It was a far cry from the lonely oceans.

The line was crossed at Carrickfergus Sailing Club accompanied by a blast from the finishing gun, and it was all over. But in fact it had only started.

We were tied up by the local Sea Cadets - TS Warrior - under the lee of Carrickfergus Castle, stunned by the crowd who had come down to see us. The people of Ulster gave us a great welcome. From hamlets and villages all over the province they came to wish us well. The Mayor Alderman Billy Ashe made a speech and the homecoming went on into the wee hours.

The end of our journey around the world.

It was good to be home.

Afterword (2022)

It was difficult to settle down to normality after the freedom of the oceans. Sixty years of age, 20 of those self-employed, did not put me top of the list on the job market.

Christine and I continued to live on *Breakaway* in Carrickfergus Harbour - not quite the same as an anchorage behind that reef in Tahiti.

We found work - me as a temporary relief coxswain on the Pilot boats for Belfast Harbour and Christine in an actuary's office. Next job for me was driver of a bread van servicing the hotels of Ulster along with running night courses in navigation. We were starting to re-group.

We got a phone call requesting someone to move a yacht for a new owner. Off Christine and I went and the voyage was a success – the new owner was delighted. I was now a delivery skipper moving boats for owners who hadn't the time - Spain, Portugal, Denmark, Norway, around the UK and other places for bye.

Breakaway was not being used but she had been prepared for another adventure as she was too special not to let her have the freedom of the seas even if we had to stay put. As our old chum Norman said,

"If you two fell down a drain you would come up smelling of roses."

A little bit of truth in that as the perfect role came along for Christine - superintendent of the Charles Sheils Institute, listed buildings consisting of 25 individual houses, including Clock Tower House for our use. We had a roof over our heads once again and what a roof!

And *Breakaway*? Went off adventuring to foreign parts with her new owners. She will look after them, she knows the way. We couldn't watch her sail out of Belfast Lough, but it was for the best.

I continued with deliveries until the crash in 2008, which hit the world of luxury items, among them bright shiny new massively expensive sail and power boats - good fun while it lasted.

Twenty years and two precious grandchildren later, we are still at the Sheils Houses overlooking the sea and remembering those magical times on *Breakaway* when the world was our oyster...

Bob

Printed in Great Britain
by Amazon

87751971R00192